JOHN GOTTI TALKS:

"I curse people. Everybody does it. We're human. We're bums. We bums in the street."

"I want guys that done more than killing."

"This is gonna be a Cosa Nostra till I die. Be it an hour from now or be it tonight or a hundred years from now when I'm in jail. It's gonna be a Cosa Nostra."

"It's this 'thing of ours.' It's gotten to be a circus. I'm not gonna leave a circus when I go to jail. I don't wanna be a phony."

"One thing I ain't gonna be is two-faced. I'm gonna call 'em like I see 'em. That I gotta do till the day I die. . . . I'd like to kill all the lawyers."

"You wanna kill him for what he done, right? I mean, right or wrong, he's got to whack the kid down."

"All I want is a good sandwich. You see this sandwich here? This tuna sandwich? That's all I want —a good sandwich."

SAMMY THE BULL SPEAKS:

"He asked me whether I would kill if he asked me to. I told him yes. I pointed to my trigger finger. He pinched it. Blood came out. . . . He said honor the oath, that if I divulge any of the secrets of this organization that my soul should burn."

"We discussed who the shooters would be, what positions different people would take, and what time we would meet the following day, and that was about it."

"Sometimes I was a shooter; sometimes I was a backup shooter; sometimes I set the guy up; sometimes I just talked about it."

"When I was a kid I ran with gangs. I dropped out of school in the eighth grade. It didn't seem wrong. It was the environment. . . . The devil didn't make me do it. I did it on my own."

The Gotti Tapes

The Gotti Tapes

Including the Testimony of Salvatore (Sammy the Bull) Gravano

Foreword by
RALPH BLUMENTHAL

Afterword by
JOHN MILLER

Arrow Books Limited
20 Vauxhall Bridge Road, London SW1V 2SA

An imprint of the Random Century Group

London Melbourne Sydney Auckland Johannesburg
and agencies throughout the world

First published in Great Britain in 1992 by Arrow

1 3 5 7 9 10 8 6 4 2

Manufactured in the United States of America

ISBN 0 09 921281-1

Contents

Foreword

RALPH BLUMENTHAL

"THIS [IS] HOW we get in trouble—we talk," John Gotti says in one of the many extraordinarily revealing conversations that stand as a last testament of the flamboyant boss of the Gambino crime clan. Yet few talked as compulsively and incriminatingly to the government's secret bugs as the long-untouchable Godfather. In the end, it was not the FBI, his underworld rivals, or his turncoat underboss Salvatore (Sammy the Bull) Gravano who brought down John Gotti. It was John Gotti himself—by his own words. The longtime Teflon Don became the Velcro Don. Every government charge from racketeering to murder stuck, and barring a reversal on appeal, the fifty-one-year-old crime boss is likely to live out his days in prison.

Why did Gotti talk so damagingly? Because, as the tapes show, running a large family business like the Gambino mob takes a lot of discussion. Bosses simply have to talk sometime, someplace. And because he was John Gotti.

Here is an epic worthy of Shakespeare, or at least a daytime soap. In the long twilight of the Mob, an ambitious *capo* murders his way to the throne, only to find himself the victim, besieged by enemies without and within, suffocated by demands on his authority, and finally betrayed by his handpicked successor. (Gotti even says, like Dick the Butcher in Henry VI, "I'd like to kill all the lawyers.") Here is Gotti at the pinnacle of his power: "What am I doing here, Frankie? Where are we going here? . . . I'm sick, Frankie, and I ain't got no right to be sick." And also: "All I want is a good sandwich. You see this sandwich here? This tuna sandwich? That's all I want, a good sandwich." You know what they should do, he tells his acting underboss and later convicted codefendant Frank Locascio: "We gotta both buy chemotherapy with the money I got."

In his less-than-seven-year career at the top of the nation's most notorious Mafia family, Gotti seized the popular imagination as perhaps no gangster since Al Capone more than half a century before. In his trademark $2,300 double-breasted Brioni suits, hand-painted floral neckties, monogrammed sheer Gucci socks, and steel-gray "zipperhead" coif, Gotti stood out boldly from the "Fat Tony" look of his cohorts, with their stogies and short sleeves, baggy pants, porkpie hats, and beer bellies. He fed sound bites to the ravenous media beast and knew by name many of the reporters who covered him. He was even said to have a more-than-respectable IQ of 140. Would words like *sedate, parameters, hiatus, chastise,* and *fabricate* ever have escaped the lips of, say, Carlo Gambino? Gotti was a gangster boss who seemed made for Hollywood. The mutual attraction was there for all to see in the celebrities who filled the Gotti pews at the trial, actors Anthony Quinn and Mickey Rourke and pop singer Jay Black, among others, to the point where U.S. attorney Andrew J. Maloney threatened to bring in Clint Eastwood as Dirty Harry for his side.

Just as Gotti craved notoriety, the public seemed hooked on

him. Here, by God, was a gangster who looked like a gangster. The fancy threads. The swaggering walk. The great imperious face that appeared to have been carved from a single chunk of granite. The gambling addiction that supposedly lost him $90,000 in a single bad football weekend. In a nation starved for macho leadership and glamour, Gotti fit the bill. Diners gazed, awestruck, when he entered a restaurant and carefully chose a chair with a view of the door and his back to the wall. And if he was a stone killer, so much the better. He and his ilk only slaughtered each other, didn't they? Their own neighborhoods they kept safe. Besides, Americans had long found romance in such bandit kings as John Dillinger, Dutch Schultz, Legs Diamond, Al Capone, and Crazy Joey Gallo.

Yet it was precisely by courting celebrity that Gotti would sow the seeds of his own undoing. He forgot that criminals work best in the shadows. By flaunting his outlaw status, he set himself up as an irresistible target. After three acquittals, he was gaining a reputation as invincible. Lawmen could not permit it. He had committed the ultimate crime: he was making them look bad.

Old-timers had learned that lesson. They shunned publicity. Maybe Carlo Gambino didn't say *hiatus* or wear Brioni suits, but he didn't get caught on tape either. An astute observer of the Mafia scene, Douglas A. Le Vien, Jr., executive assistant to the Brooklyn district attorney, liked to contrast the styles of the tradition-bound old Sicilian Mafia and its flashier American offshoot this way: In America, the boss pulls up in a limo in the rain and a schnook immediately runs over holding an umbrella. In Sicily, the schnook holding the umbrella—he's the boss.

John Gotti may have had the laugh on the government, but the government had the last laugh. From a symbol of the invulnerability and arrogance of organized crime, he became, if not its epitaph, at least a big notch in the gun belt of the FBI's new

Untouchables. In the end, he was less the magisterial Marlon Brando of *The Godfather* than the squalid Robert DeNiro of *Goodfellas*.

"Nobody had it worse than I had it in life," Gotti tells Locascio in a reflective moment caught on tape. He came from a religious and loving but poverty-stricken home. His Neapolitan father, John Joseph, and his mother, Fannie, had sailed in steerage from southern Italy to New York in 1920 and settled in the South Bronx, where John Jr. was born on October 27, 1940, the fifth of what would be thirteen children, two of whom died in childhood. His father was a day laborer on construction jobs who struggled to keep the family alive on wages of $1.25 a day. "I wasn't born with four fucking cents," Gotti was later to recall.

When John was ten, his father landed a better job and moved the family into a tenement in Sheepshead Bay on the Brooklyn waterfront. After two years the family moved again, this time to the East New York-Brownsville section in the Italian and Jewish flatlands of interior Brooklyn. Here in the 1930s Albert Anastasia and Louis (Lepke) Buchalter had masterminded their contract-killing business called Murder Incorporated, and the psychopathic Anastasia was still king of Brooklyn nearly twenty years later, when young John Gotti began prowling the horse parlors and numbers joints. He was an uncontrollable teenager with a volcanic temper, often in trouble in school. He joined a youth gang called the Fulton-Rockaway Boys and dropped out of Franklin K. Lane High School at sixteen, managing nevertheless to set up a student betting ring. Dominating the *borgata* by his violent personality, he attracted a core of young thugs who were to follow him in years to come. They included Angelo Ruggiero, a talker even more compulsive than Gotti whose carelessness would set into motion a series of events that would end in the killing of Paul Castellano, and Anthony Rampino, who would later be one of the designated backup shooters in the 1985 assassination, a hit orchestrated by Gotti.

As a teen boss, Gotti came to the attention of neighborhood Mafia strongmen, including a Gambino *capo*, Carmine (Charley Wagons) Fatico, who had apprenticed with Gotti's idol, Albert Anastasia, and specialized in hijackings. Even then Gotti fancied himself a snappy dresser, but the purple outfit he had picked out for his audience with Fatico was a little extreme. "You look like a fucking guinea," Fatico said. But he soon took Gotti under his wing and introduced him to powerful mentors like the fearsome Aniello Dellacroce, later to be the Gambino underboss. One of Gotti's first assignments was to beat some respect into the operator of a Queens auto chop shop who had offended the Mob hierarchy. He and two other enforcers performed admirably, judging by the screams overheard by police, Gotti's first known encounter with his lifetime nemesis—a bug.

In 1960, not yet twenty, Gotti met the girl who would become his wife, Victoria DiGiorgio, a striking and strong-willed high school dropout of Italian and Russian-Jewish background. Her parents disapproved of the match but the couple, accounts say, wed after Victoria became pregnant with their first daughter, Angela. Four more children followed: Victoria, Peter, Frank, and John Jr. (Frank, a studious boy and Gotti's special joy, was riding a friend's motorbike near their home in 1980 when, at age twelve, he was accidentally struck and killed by a neighbor driving home from work. Several weeks after the funeral, the neighbor, John Favara, while leaving work, was pulled into a van and never seen again. The grieving Gottis were away in Florida at the time.)

Gotti ran cargo thefts and hijackings out of John F. Kennedy International Airport for Fatico's crew and in 1969 had a second encounter with electronic eavesdropping. Speaking from his Queens bar, the Crystal Lounge, he was trying to talk one of his men through a restarting of a hijacked truck that had stalled. But again the police were listening. Gotti ended up doing three years in the penitentiary at Lewisburg, Pennsylvania, where he made the acquaintance of jailed Bonanno boss Carmine Galante and other Mob kingpins.

Fatico, meanwhile, had relocated his base from Brooklyn ("The fucking spics and niggers are moving in") to a storefront headquarters on 101st Avenue in Ozone Park, Queens, that he named for no known reason the Bergin Hunt & Fish Social Club, Inc. Fatico's own legal troubles caught up with him, however, and when Gotti returned from Lewisburg in 1972, he found himself elevated to acting *capo* of the Bergin crew.

His first big assignment came the following year. A nephew of family boss Carlo Gambino had been kidnapped and murdered despite payment of a $100,000 ransom. The deed had been traced to a reckless stickupman, James McBratney, leader of a brutal Irish gang that would later come to be known as the Westies. Gotti was unleashed. Posing as cops, Gotti, Angelo Ruggiero, and an accomplice waylaid McBratney in a Staten Island bar, but instead of snatching him for appropriate torment, they ended up shooting him dead on the spot in a struggle. Somehow, however, the Staten Island district attorney was persuaded by the late Roy Cohn, a well-connected defense attorney retained by Gambino, to accept a plea to reduced charges, and Gotti and Ruggiero ended up with mere four-year maximum terms in the state pen.

In 1976, when Gotti got out, clutching a plaque from his fellow inmates ("To a Great Guy, John Gotti. From the Boys at Green Haven"), the landscape had immutably changed. Gambino had died peacefully in bed. But in a succession that sowed the seeds for later strife, he had designated as his successor not underboss Dellacroce but his brother-in-law, dour six-foot-two-inch Paul Castellano. To placate Dellacroce and his supporters, including Gotti, Castellano kept Dellacroce as underboss and made him the semi-autonomous chief of nearly half of the Family's twenty-three crews. Gotti was made a *capo*, in charge of the Bergin crew. But it was not sufficient.

The Mob was evolving. The wily and reticent Gambino, among others, had understood that the violent ways and traditional rackets of the old Mustache Petes were no longer the most promising roads to riches in an era of stepped-up law enforcement scrutiny. For close to a hundred years, muscle alone had worked. From its late-nineteenth-century rise in America on the docks of New Orleans, the Black Hand, among the Mafia's many guises, spread to the teeming immigrant quarters of Manhattan, "protecting" and victimizing poor Italians. In Sicily, the Mafia began centuries ago as a rural movement of strong-arm bands protecting the properties of absentee landlords from the peasantry. In America, it became an urban phenomenon during the bootlegging days of Prohibition. The foundations of the modern Mafia's control of the rackets, gambling, loan-sharking, and prostitution were laid by Salvatore Lucania, better known as Charles (Lucky) Luciano, along with Anastasia, Joe Adonis, Meyer Lansky, and Bugsy Siegel. Capone was left alone to run Chicago. The other prize, New York, was split among five gangs, or families, that came to take the names of their bosses, Gambino, Bonanno, Genovese, Lucchese, and Colombo. The leadership often consulted on important decisions, divisions of spoils, and top-level murder contracts. But the families could also be murderous rivals.

By the time John Gotti began to tighten his grip on the Gambino Family, some of the old ways were crumbling. Law enforcement was stripping away layer after layer of the veteran Mob hierarchy, exposing ever more junior and inexperienced successors to the prosecutorial onslaught. The Mafia was also confronting a generational crisis. The children of the bosses were no longer automatically going into the business (although Gotti's son John Jr. did). Instead, many went to college, studying law and accounting, business and medicine, seeking to forsake the ham-fisted ways of their fathers. Why rush to enter a dying industry? To some of the Mob's shrewder strategists, the future lay in the subversion of legitimate business, as best practiced perhaps by Gambino's son Thomas, whose trucking companies had long held a stranglehold on New York City's garment district, although he too would be finally brought down. In late February 1992, Thomas and his brother, Joseph, agreed to quit the garment trucking business and pay a $12 million fine in exchange for being spared prison sentences.

Castellano also favored a low profile and could actually discourse politely with FBI surveillance agents, a civility that drove Gotti wild. Although many bosses over the decades had issued edicts against drug dealing on the grounds that Mob members caught dealing junk faced such severe sentences that they were vulnerable to snitching and that the drug trade was somehow unmanly, in fact drug trafficking was endemic in all the families and widely winked at. Castellano, like his predecessors, had nevertheless reiterated the ban and Gotti, at some point, at least, feared he meant it.

As the Mob had grown more sophisticated, so had law enforcement. With significant exceptions like New York Police Lieutenant Joseph Petrosino, who in 1909 traveled to Sicily to investigate the roots of the Black Hand and fell as a martyr, the authorities had long failed to seriously pursue the Mafia. Indeed, J. Edgar Hoover, for one, never conceded the existence of a Mafia underworld. He was perhaps too busy looking for Communists under beds to notice the gangsters around the corner. It took the Senate's Kefauver committee in 1951 to turn a national spotlight on "a sinister criminal organization known as the Mafia operating throughout the country with ties in other nations." The abortive underworld summit that the New York State Police stumbled across in rural Apalachin in 1957 focused dramatic new attention on the Mafia, and a new round of Senate hearings in 1963 introduced an astounded nation to the revelations of Mafia turncoat Joseph Valachi and the secretive organization he said its members called "La Cosa Nostra"—our thing—the name by which the FBI still prefers to call the Mafia. (What the public didn't know—and wouldn't learn until many years later—was that Washington had occasionally found it expedient to enlist the services of organized crime. During World War II, for example, Lucky Luciano helped keep the labor peace on the East Coast docks. Later, the CIA would attempt to use the Mafia in its secret war to whack Fidel Castro.)

In 1968 Congress passed the Omnibus Crime and Safe Streets Act, empowering federal investigators, with court approval, to employ wiretaps and bugs for the first time outside national security cases. An even more revolutionary bill two years later, the Racketeer-Influenced and Corrupt Organizations Act, or RICO, created a vast new category of crime—operating or acquiring an enterprise, or conspiring to, through "a pattern of racketeering," defined as two or more proven racketeering charges committed within ten years of each other. All at once, prosecutors no longer had to prove narrow crimes against individuals. Befitting the broad scope of underworld conspiracies, the crimes now could be prosecuted just as broadly. Critics, however, questioned the constitutionality of so sweeping a law.

It took the authorities a few years to learn how to wield RICO but by the mid-1980s prosecutors were starting to roll up Mafia networks all over the country, in Philadelphia, Providence, Boston, Kansas City, and New York, where U.S. attorney Rudolph W. Giuliani successfully targeted nothing less than the entire ruling Commission of the Mafia itself, the heads of all five families operating as a national underworld junta. At the same time, Giuliani was prosecuting Paul Castellano, boss of the Gambino Family, for running a stolen car ring and conspiring to commit murder. And in the same courthouse he was trying Gaetano Badalamenti, the onetime boss of bosses of the Sicilian Mafia, and nearly two dozen of his henchmen for running a billion-dollar heroin pipeline, the so-called Pizza Connection, a landmark wiretap prosecution based on thousands of intercepted, coded conversations in Sicilian.

Meanwhile, in Queens, John Gotti was having his own legal troubles and laying the groundwork for others. On a September day in 1984, Romual Piecyk, a motorist blocked in by a double-parked car outside a Maspeth bar and gambling den controlled by Gotti leaned on his horn and got into a scuffle with one of Gotti's men, who snatched $325 from Piecyk's shirt pocket. They squared off, then Gotti came out and joined in. The police came, the bruised Piecyk pointed out Gotti as one of his attack ·rs and Gotti was arrested for assault and theft. But by the time the trial rolled around nearly a year and a half later, the hapless accuser had had a chance to acquaint himself with the identity and reputation of the defendant. Piecyk looked around the courtroom and said he could not identify Gotti. A *New York Post* headline captured the moment: "I FORGOTTI!"

For some time now, Gotti had been of interest to law enforcement authorities. In 1981, the Queens district attorney had briefly bugged the Bergin club and captured Gotti's tirade against an underling, Anthony Moscatiello, whom Gotti had had trouble reaching. "Listen," Gotti rages, "I called your fucking house five times yesterday; now if your wife thinks you are a fucking dunsky or if she's a fucking dunsky and you're going to disregard my fucking phone calls, I'll blow you and that fucking house up."

Not long afterward, Angelo Ruggiero's Long Island house was bugged, yielding tapes incriminating the loose-tongued Ruggiero and Gotti's brother Gene in narcotics trafficking, in defiance of Castellano's ban. Later when the court case revealed the existence of the tapes and Castellano demanded them from a balking Ruggiero, the stage was set for a showdown.

Meanwhile, a new prosecutorial assault on Gotti was slowly building. In the Brooklyn U.S. attorney's office, an energetic young assistant, Diane F. Giacalone, was investigating two 1980 armored car robberies, a trail that pointed her to Gotti, who, she learned, was also the target of a RICO case being put together in the same office. A bitter competition ensued, eventually embroiling the FBI, which complained that the prosecution was exposing its informants, including a close associate of Gotti's, Wilfred (Willie Boy) Johnson. (In 1988, Johnson, after refusing the prosecution's offer of protection, was murdered.) Boycotted by the FBI, Giacalone's case, with the RICO case now folded into it, proceeded and in early 1985, Gotti, Dellacroce (who was soon to die of cancer), and eight cohorts were indicted and arrested. Gotti was freed on bail, raising the curtain on a fateful drama.

Fearful that Castellano was plotting to whack him and Ruggiero for defying the drug ban, contemptuous of the big-nosed boss he derided as "Nasabeak," Gotti struck first. After clearing it with the heads of the other families, except for the unpredictable Vincent (The Chin) Gigante of the Genovese clan, Gotti had eight shooters ready when Castellano and his acting underboss Tommy Bilotti drove up for a prearranged dinner with associates at Sparks Steak House on East 46th Street in Manhattan on December 16, 1985. The hit went off as planned, overseen by Gotti and Gravano in a passing car, as Gravano later testified. In a meeting a few weeks later, Gotti was anointed as the new boss of the Gambino Family, long considered to be the richest, most powerful Mafia clan in America, with some 300 made members, 2,000 associates, and uncounted hundreds of millions of dollars of assets and illicit revenues.

Still, the Brooklyn RICO case against him was proceeding. It went to trial in August 1986 and lasted until March 1987, through 90 witnesses, many of them turncoat killers hoping to shave some time off their sentences. The verdict: not guilty. Gotti's aggressive lawyer, Bruce Cutler, had savaged many of the more unpalatable witnesses. But there may have been a more direct reason Gotti won: at least one juror had been reached by the Gambino Family and corrupted, according to charges later filed by the prosecutor.

Gotti would have one more courtroom victory. In 1989 he was charged with ordering the shooting of a union leader over the trashing of a Gambino-connected restaurant, the Bankers and Brokers in the new Battery Park City in lower Manhattan. John O'Connor of the Carpenter's Union, had been shot and wounded in the buttocks and legs in 1986. Shortly before, the Manhattan district attorney charged, a bug at the Bergin had recorded Gotti giving the order: "Bust him up! Put a rocket in his pocket!" Once again the witnesses against Gotti included some loathsome turncoats, this time from the murderous Westies gang. Again there was reason to believe that Gotti had tried to reach the jury. And again Gotti was acquitted.

The government's final and ultimately successful assault against Gotti began with U.S. attorney Maloney's burning desire for a rematch. Convinced that jury tampering had stolen a guilty verdict from him in 1987, the ruddy-faced ex–West Pointer had begun immediately assembling a new team for a new RICO case, this time with the cooperation of the FBI, and inclusion of the Castellano homicide, which Maloney, like almost everyone else, was convinced Gotti had masterminded. The Manhattan district attorney and Maloney's federal counterpart in Manhattan made a bid for the case—they too had been struggling to build an airtight new case against Gotti, and the Castellano killing, after all, had been in Manhattan—but the Justice Department, in a high-level sitdown in Washington, awarded it to Brooklyn.

In November 1989, as the investigation was well along—4,000 possible witnesses to the Castellano killing had been interviewed by the police alone—the FBI scored a remarkable coup. Under the direction of the tall and taciturn pipe-smoking supervisor of the Gambino Squad, Bruce Mouw, agents succeeded in bugging not only the leading Gambino Family hangout, the Ravenite Social Club at 247 Mulberry Street, and a hallway where members often lingered to chat, but also a private apartment above the club where intelligence indicated Gotti and his underlings sometimes huddled. The apartment belonged to the elderly widow of a former Gambino soldier who virtually never left the house. How a special operations team went unnoticed on a Little Italy street that is all eyes and ears and penetrated the clubhouse and an occupied apartment is a story that may never be fully told. What is known is that the widow did, at some point around November 1989, take a vacation. The FBI had pulled off a similar feat six years earlier when it bugged the "White House," the heavily guarded mansion of Paul Castellano on Staten Island, when the Castellanos went on vacation.

The harvest of revelation the government would reap from its electronic eavesdropping would yield a bounty beyond expectation. The Gotti tapes would open a vista into a sinister and darkly humorous world riven by greed and paranoia and ego run amok.

* * *

As the apartment tapes begin on November 30, 1989, Gotti, Gravano, and Locascio are badmouthing the dead Castellano, killed nearly four years before. Gotti calls him a "bum" and recalls the flap over the tape recordings that Castellano demanded of Ruggiero, evidence of drug-dealing that Gotti feared would do him in as well. With rich irony, they ridicule Castellano for being dumb enough to be bugged at home by the FBI. Then Gotti says of Castellano's murder: "I don't know who done it . . . . probably the cops done it to this fuckin' guy . . . probably the cops killed this Paul." The defense later seized on this as evidence of Gotti's innocence, but Gravano would insist, under oath, that Gotti, with a smirk, was just trying to cover his tracks.

Gotti turns reflective and melancholy, there are only a handful of guys they can trust, whom they can really count on: "It's us against the world." They lament a bygone era. Gravano says, "It's over." And Gotti agrees: "Not only it's over, where the fuck are we going here?"

Less than two weeks later, on December 12, Gotti makes a damaging admission. Talking to Locascio about a long-missing and presumed dead Gambino Family member, Robert DiBernardo, who handled the Family's pornography interests, he says: "I was in jail when I whacked him. I knew why it was being done. I done it anyway." A little later he says, "And every time we got a partner that don't agree with us, we kill him."

Later he talks about DiBernardo's murder again. "I took Sammy's word that he talked about me behind my back." And of the impending murder of another Family member, Louis DiBono, he remarks: "You know why he's dying? He's gonna die because he refused to come in when I called. He didn't do nothing else wrong."

Gotti turns self-pitying again. He feels the burdens of power.

He is called to mediate "beefs" around the clock—even on Sundays. Underlings are doing deals. Nobody tells him anything. Even Sammy keeps him in the dark. The world thinks he's a billionaire, but he's worrying about the Family and its future: "What happens when I go away or I'm gone? When I'm dead, Frankie?" Gotti doesn't worry about himself: "I don't give two fucks myself about going to jail. Don't I know they ain't gonna rest until they put me in jail? . . . But at least if I know you two guys are out here, we got a shot."

At times he seems overtaken by despair. He feels sick. He visits Sammy's son in the hospital. He gets caught in a traffic jam. He goes to a cemetery and a wake. "I'm not going partying . . . popping girls . . . I'm getting myself sick, Frank." Locascio, playing the shrink, is sympathetic. "Gotta get it out. You gotta get it out." At this point, Gotti sighs, he'd be satisfied with a good tuna sandwich: "That's all I want—a good sandwich."

He marvels at his celebrity, his tributes. Even in jail, he says, he was awarded ten percent of some million-dollar business. He remembers his roots: "Guy never had nothing in his life; a fuckin' jerk like me. Best I ever did was go on a few hijackings." But he wasn't greedy. "I would be a billionaire if I was looking to be a selfish boss. That's not me." But he alludes, incautiously, to under-the-table payments as opposed to what he's getting "on paper." He lives modestly, he assures Locascio, no mortgage, only a monthly car payment of under $400. Oh, and Blue Cross.

"Blue Cross?" Locascio asks. "You covered under Blue Cross?"

"Yeah."

"Extended coverage or something?" Locascio presses.

"Yeah," Gotti says, "special kind of coverage, you know." Who knew when he might be suddenly hospitalized?

On January 4, 1990, Gotti and Gravano are talking about "making" some new soldiers, or "hard-ons," as Gotti calls them elsewhere in an evocative phrase. But not just anyone, says Gotti: "I want guys that done more than killing." And looking ahead to his own possible imprisonment, he prepares his succession. "Soon as anything happens to me, I'm off the streets, Sammy is the Acting Boss," he says. But he was leaving it up to Sammy. What did he want to be called? Underboss? Acting Boss? Or did he want to stay *consigliere*? "How do you feel? What makes you feel better? Think about it."

But Gotti warns Gravano he is probably a target too: "If they ain't preparing a couple humdinger cases for you, I'll take it up my fucking ass, Sam." And Gotti knows why: "They're not stupid. I telegraph my voice. I couldn't help it." Locascio joins them and they talk about a government tape, apparently the one in the O'Connor shooting case. Gotti is happy to report it may be inaudible. He never said much anyway, he insists. "Like I just wouldn't say nothin' about poppin' people. I would say everything, but not that." The tapes are "a fuckin' heartbreak," Gotti complains later, "you know you feel like you're being raped with these fuckin' tapes." Gravano agrees: "I know. I hate it. I listened to a couple a tapes of mine. I was sick." But Gotti looks at the bright side. "Hey, motherfucker, what are we saying bad?"

On the business of "making" new members they run into an obstacle. As Gravano discovers, "I don't have their last names. I don't have the proper spelling." Gotti suggests that "Fat Dom" may be enough. They wonder if the last names could be added later but Locascio sees a problem: "If their last names are totally different handwriting, then it looks like we don't know what we're doing." Gravano agrees. Gotti has had it with Locascio: "He's like [a] fucking perfectionist, this guy." But Locascio sticks to his guns. "If you see a list and they say, 'Look . . .

one guy wrote this, one guy wrote that, one guy wrote the other thing.' "

It was left to Gotti to do a final job on the people most instrumental in keeping him out of jail—his lawyers. First he complains that he paid the lawyers $300,000 for the legal appeals of various Family members, cases he himself was not involved in. The prosecution would later argue successfully that this (and other statements by Gotti on the tapes) showed that some of the lawyers Gotti named were "house counsel" to the Gambino Family and should not be permitted to represent any of the defendants at Gotti's trial because, among other things, evidence of Gotti's payments to the lawyers on behalf of other Family members could help prove the government's claim that Gotti presided over a racketeering enterprise. Thus was Bruce Cutler, who had won Gotti his celebrated acquittals in the past, ruled out of the case. He and the other lawyers, however, were at pains to deny any allegation of improper or illegal conduct. Next, Gotti denounces lawyers Cutler and Gerald Shargel as "the Shargel, Cutler, and whattaya call it Crime Family," equating them to the Mob itself. "You know why they can't win, Sammy? They got no fuckin' cohesion. They got no unity. It's like us." And finally Gotti rails against his lawyers' escalating legal fees—fees that threaten "to leave my son destitute and my family destitute. What the fuck is it all about? Was it you that put me on this earth to rob and make you rich and me poor?"

On January 17, Gotti, Gravano, Locascio and some other members meet in the Ravenite apartment to prepare the induction of new members. They are nervous. Locascio talks about putting on a radio to muffle their conversation. Meanwhile, the new members are waiting downstairs to be inducted. Gotti and Locascio practice the key question to ask the inductees: "You know why you're here?" "Is there any reason why you shouldn't be here?" Gravano comes up with a funny line: "Yeah, I'm a fucking agent." Gotti is not amused. He takes this ceremony seriously: "It's not a toy. I'm not in the mood for the toys or games or kidding, no time . . . And this is gonna be a Cosa Nostra till I die. Be it an hour from now or be it tonight or a hundred years from now when I'm in jail. It's gonna be a Cosa Nostra."

Gotti tells them not to worry about traitors, boasting of his ability to smell them "the way a dog senses when a guy has got fear in him, you know what I mean."

Nothing suggests he suspects Gravano. In fact, Gotti's heir apparent will not "flip" until nearly a year after the final roundup of Gotti, Gravano, and Locascio at the Ravenite on December 11, 1990. Gravano will then have a chance to hear himself and Gotti on tape, consider his prospects, and make a call from jail. Only then will he decide to betray his boss.

Here, then, is the testament of John Gotti as given, unwittingly, to the FBI, words that would bring him down. Here, too, is the public testimony of Sammy the Bull Gravano, words that would complete the ruin of Gotti and his gangland monarchy.

The Gotti Tapes

A Note to the Reader

The conversations in this book were recorded surreptitiously by agents of the Federal Bureau of Investigation, acting under a federal statute that permits government agents to break and enter into homes and places of business or locations where there is probable cause to believe that criminal activity will occur. Transcribers working for the FBI compiled the transcripts that are here reprinted. No attempt has been made to alter the FBI's often idiosyncratic punctuation, or to correct John Gotti's often fractured syntax. Occasionally passages of incomprehensibility have been excised, and are so indicated by the use of four dots enclosed by brackets. Of the 600 hours of Gambino Family conversations taped by the FBI, the six hours recorded in the apartment above the Ravenite Social Club and entered into evidence during the 1992 trial of John Gotti and his codefendant, Frank Locascio, were decisive. Ninety percent of these crucial transcripts are included here. Prior to the start of the trial in January, Gotti's lawyers had sought, unsuccessfully, to suppress the tapes. Once introduced into evidence, however, little of their contents was disputed by the defense. Still, the defense insisted that some statements as they appeared in the transcripts were inaccurate. No challenge was made to the tapes themselves once the courtroom drama was underway. The accuracy of some of the government-supplied transcripts, however, were questioned. Judge I. Leo Glasser was at pains to remind the jury that they were to favor their ears over their eyes should they discern any inconsistency between the tapes and the transcripts. In the end, the jury believed the government.

A cast of characters is provided at the back of this book. Names are listed in alphabetical order and as they appear in the transcripts. Unless otherwise stated, biographical information corresponds to the time period referred to (or implied) by the transcripts. Not every name mentioned in these recorded conversations could be identified.

Not every person who is referred to in these transcripts is affiliated with organized crime or is in any other way associated with crime or criminals. One should not assume any guilt by reference or association.

NOVEMBER 30, 1989

FILE NUMBER:	183A-3507
PLACE:	Apartment above the Ravenite Social Club, located at 247 Mulberry Street in Little Italy, Manhattan
TIME:	8:15 P.M.
PARTICIPANTS:	JOHN GOTTI SALVATORE GRAVANO FRANK LOCASCIO

Government tapes are the bane of John Gotti's career; the FBI is his nemesis. Gotti's rise to power and the toppling of Paul Castellano as boss of the Gambino Family are partly rooted in a dispute over tapes, as this conversation reveals. In the early 1980s, Angelo Ruggiero, a member of Gotti's "crew," was arrested for dealing heroin, apparently a capital offense under Gambino Family rules. Castellano demanded that Ruggiero turn over incriminating FBI tapes—tapes the FBI had made from bugs in Ruggiero's home, and which were now in his lawyer's possession. Ruggiero refused—also a capital offense. Castellano asked his underboss, Neil Dellacroce, to lean on Gotti. Both men sought to placate Castellano while protecting Ruggiero from the boss's mounting wrath. A confrontation loomed, and fear deepened as Gotti and his men became convinced that Castellano intended to "hit" them all. It was not to be. On December 2, 1985, Dellacroce died of cancer. Two weeks later, Castellano and his bodyguard, Tommy Bilotti, were gunned down in front of Sparks Steak House in Manhattan. The assassins escaped. John Gotti became boss.

■ ■ ■

GOTTI: Now this fuckin' Neil was a man's man. He, he wouldn't, he wouldn't betray nothin'. When that fuckin' bum asked for the tapes, you were there, I'm best friends with Frankie.

GRAVANO: Yeah, absolutely!

GOTTI: Frankie said to me, he's crazy. "Hey, Frank, don't start." "Tell him not to give them fuckin' tapes." What was he, what was he gonna do, Sam? What was he gonna do if five of us got mad? *(Tap sound)* What the fuck was he gonna do?

GRAVANO: Nothin'!

GOTTI: Once he starts—

GRAVANO: Well, you know, that *(inaudible)*. He would've, he would've tried to make a move from outside, I think.

GOTTI: He couldn't succeed.

GRAVANO: It was evident to us.

GOTTI: He couldn't succeed.

GRAVANO: He, he already smelt it all.

GOTTI: He couldn't succeed because, Sam, he felt, and you know what we heard, "He felt he hadda hit me first." But, if he "hits" me first, he blows the guy who really led the ring, Angelo and them. Supposedly. That's the guys on the tapes.

GRAVANO: I think he would've "hit" Angelo and not you.

GOTTI: Nah! *(Tap sound)*

GRAVANO: No?

GOTTI: And what was he going to do with us?

GRAVANO: Because now—

GOTTI: He knows we were *(inaudible)*.

GRAVANO: Angelo *(inaudible)* he would'a done nothing.

GOTTI: "—Sally's." Nah! He knew we weren't "lay down Sally's." They knew we weren't "lay down Sally's."

GRAVANO: Well, not "lay down Sally's." He thought maybe, maybe would've conned you or explained it to you—*(Inaudible)* him. "Hit" Angelo.

GOTTI: Neil would have told him just like this: "Go fuck your mother." Listen to me, Sammy.

GRAVANO: Oh, I believe it!

GOTTI: *(Inaudible)*

GRAVANO: But I'm saying this guy was stark raving nuts.

GOTTI: And Neil was another one. Neil would've told him just like this, "What? What are we cops here?" Let's kill all the cocksuckers that *(inaudible)*, in the whole "Family." Every fuckin' Gambino; every fucking Castellano; Neil would've—. He, he wanted to—he didn't want no part of *(inaudible)* ya know, Neil, he wanted no part of the confrontation; which was a shame in itself. That's your "underboss." You gotta love him. You don't "break" him. Get rid of the cocksucker!

GRAVANO: I, I was privy to a lot of, you know, I was privy to a lot of his conver— I think he was stark raving fuckin' *(tap sound)* nuts.

GOTTI: Ah, he was a jerkoff!

GRAVANO: I thought he had—

GOTTI: Because he—

GRAVANO: He thought after a while he had a memory lapse.

GOTTI: *(Coughs)* Sammy—

GRAVANO: You know, like the President—

GOTTI: Sammy—

GRAVANO: —like Nixon, you don't think you could die no more; you didn't think nothing.

GOTTI: Nah, Sammy.

GRAVANO: John, what, what would it take just to—

GOTTI: What that, push the button, you go to the moon shit?

GRAVANO: *(Inaudible)* No, fuckin', button, the moon. *(Mumbles —inaudible)*

GOTTI: Yeah, because we were gonna send the people to the moon.

GRAVANO: Well, how, how could he have conversations with us? Me and Frankie, and Angelo. We were sitting there, says, "Yeah, I'm gonna go down Neil's—Christmas part—", ah, he looked at me like I had fuckin' five heads. Frankie was there. "You're on our side! Where you going?"

GOTTI: Our side.

GRAVANO: Our side. *Minchia!* That's when I "buzzed" Frankie. That's the first time I ever "buzzed" Frankie *(inaudible)*. I was with *(inaudible)* that's *(clap sound)* the first time I, I says, "Frankie, what happened? What's he have a problem? What do you mean on our side? What's he talking about?"

GOTTI: Ah, Sammy—

GRAVANO: The first time I ever, you know—

GOTTI: Sammy, let me tell you what *(inaudible)*.

GRAVANO: —recognized that, er—

GOTTI: When you see who done that—

GRAVANO: —I said, "What the fuck was that?"

GOTTI: You see who done that?

GRAVANO: But he said that open that time. I didn't like try to hide it or nothin'.

GOTTI: You see, yeah, but, Sammy, you see who done that? Pete, now he was a "rat" motherfucker. This fuckin' "rat" brother was, the brother-in-law was a "rat" motherfucker. A backdoor motherfucker. He wouldn't, he purposely wouldn't make him *consigliere*. He didn't wanna make him no "underboss." He wouldn't make nobody official. This fucking bastard. Because he was a "rat" motherfucker! He loved to fucking party. And this fucking "rat" motherfucker was no better. He divided the "Family." He was like the *(inaudible)* in like this.

GRAVANO: *(Inaudible)*

GOTTI: This is like you go home and telling your daughters, "Your mother is a big cunt. You don't know what I do with your mother. You don't know how many guys your mother blew."

GRAVANO: *(Clears throat)*

GOTTI: It, it's, it's the same thing. When you go—and you, if you don't like your fucking "underboss," "break" him! End of discussion! Then you'll fall in love with him. I mean, what are you kidding somebody or what? Youse are getting to be like—

GRAVANO: But he—

GOTTI: —brothers.

GRAVANO: You're absolutely right; Machiavellian-type a guy *(inaudible)*.

GOTTI: *(Coughs)*

GRAVANO: He won't break him because he won't look good.

GOTTI: Yeah, but Sam—

GRAVANO: You know, a whole con—

GOTTI: I don't know if you ever, ah, ah—

GRAVANO: *(Inaudible)*

GOTTI: —if you, how close you were with Neil. But he knows him as long as I know him. Did you ever hear Neil curse this guy or pan him?

LOCASCIO: I don't; never!

GOTTI: Never! Never! And even *(inaudible)* Carl I shouldn't see my kids alive. "I'll go see what the 'boss' wants." That's an "underboss." Ya fuckin'—

GRAVANO: Oh, he was great, John.

GOTTI: *(Inaudible)* That he should have "blew" the guy. But instead he was *gelosia* [jealous]! Because he wasn't half the man the guy is. If tomorrow I was to die and the, the "Family" voted, voted a new "boss," and they voted, ah—let's make a "wishy-washy" guy downstairs. Let's get a guy that's *(inaudible)* ah, Pete Castellano, our new "boss." He'd hate you two with a fucking passion!

GRAVANO: Absolutely.

GOTTI: Because he ain't a man! You a tough, hey, you a tough guy. He'd hate ya. Ah, ah, and any time he could knock you, he's gonna knock you.

GRAVANO: Yeah. He's jealous *(inaudible)*.

LOCASCIO: Hoping, hoping that something would happen to us.

GOTTI: That's right.

GRAVANO: Frank, he's not a man. Eh, ah—a guy—

GOTTI: He's not gonna be able to break ya.

GRAVANO: *(Inaudible)* right. He's not ballsy enough.

LOCASCIO: He's no man.

GOTTI: Yeah—

GRAVANO: So they gotta deal with deviousness—

GOTTI: But Neil wouldn't have—

GRAVANO: —scheming.

GOTTI: —Neil would've never fuckin'—he would've never tolerated Angelo with the tapes. He would've tolerated, put him on the shelf. And, what are you gonna do? You gotta understand.

GRAVANO: And it's part of life.

GOTTI: Using hindsight now, ourselves—he deserved to have his tongue cut out. If nothing else, his fucking tongue cut out. But I don't know where all our fuckin' so-called "friends" are. That they went to his fuckin' house. Where did they think they went, to clubhouse? You get a guy like Vic and "Gas." I wanna show you something. They're fuckin'—

GRAVANO: I tell, I tell you what I thought. I tell you what I thought. I wasn't there a lot of times, I only went there four times with—I'll tell you what I thought. I thought that this guy had tonnage. And I thought that this guy had the expertise. When you're a "boss," you gotta know you're hot. At that point. Maybe, ah, as a, as a "street" guy, or something, you think nobody is watching you. But, as a "boss," you gotta know you're taking the "heat." I figured that fucking house was impregnable. I thought he had that fuckin' house impregnable.

GOTTI: He didn't have one security thing there!

GRAVANO: No, he had security things there.

GOTTI: Fuck—

GRAVANO: His money.

LOCASCIO: You're talking about Angelo, and he's talking about—

GRAVANO: Well who, who you talking about?

GOTTI: Oh, you talking about Paul?

GRAVANO: Yeah, Paul.

GOTTI: I'm talking about Angelo.

GRAVANO: Oh! Oh, Angelo, I don't know.

GOTTI: Paul? *(Inaudible)*

GRAVANO: I thought that house was impregnable.

GOTTI: Sammy—

GRAVANO: I thought he had done—

GOTTI: —Paul, let me tell you about Paul, Sammy. He didn't —he was a fucking fish on the desert. He was a fish outta water! He don't know this life! *(inaudible).*

GRAVANO: *(Inaudible)* I know it. But I didn't know like that.

GOTTI: He, he goes to the door. He sees on the TV, O'Brien and the other guy *(coughs).* He goes there, "Hello, Joe." Tells, calls the [FBI] agent by the first name, "Come on in." Make Nina make coffee for you. You fucking "rat" motherfucker! My wife gotta make coffee for the fucking agents? "Hello, Joe." Come in my house? You gotta kick—

LOCASCIO: I tell 'em, "Get your fucking foot—

GOTTI: Yeah!

LOCASCIO: —out of the door!"

GOTTI: You gotta kick that fucking door down! Joe Gallo done the same thing.

LOCASCIO: "Wait, wait, wait, wait, wait!" Humph! *(Inaudible)*

GOTTI: Joe Gallo done the same thing *(inaudible)*.

LOCASCIO: —that fuckin' door.

GRAVANO: They got sharpshooters. They got a guy that can—

GOTTI: They fuckin' hard-ons! They not big shot; they're fuckin' punks.

GRAVANO: They'll tell you they think they are.

GOTTI: And he says, they turned around—Coffey came to him one night, told him, "These Irish guys are dragging you down!" He's not lying. He knew you a cocksucker. He's an FBI. He's, he's a cop, whatever the fuck he is. What does he do? What are you talking to this motherfucker? What are you a potential "rat" yourself? You fucking bum! When "Donny Shacks" and, and "Gerry Lang" came up, the two guys, from another "Family," two administration, a, a "underboss," and an acting fuckin', a *capodecina*—that's an acting, a guy helping him with the administration—come to your door with fuckin' jogging suits on. They came to your door with jogging suits on to show you they're "clean." They ring your bell. They know there's cameras. They know there's always four or five guys in the fuckin' house. And your wife gone. They didn't come to hurt you. He said, he said, "I looked at *(inaudible)* for about ten minutes through the fuckin' thing to make sure that they were clean." You fucking bum! You're a fucking "rat." You let a cop in, in a half a second, but two "friends" you won't let in. *(Tap sound)* You fuckin'— He was a piece of shit! "Rat," "rat" cocksucker. Yellow dog! Yellow dog, right? What *(inaudible),* Sammy? All this guy needed was a little whack in the fucking mouth.

[. . . .]

GOTTI: You know what got me sick?

GRAVANO: *(Laughs)*

GOTTI: I curse people. Everybody does it. We're human. We're bums. We bums in the street.

LOCASCIO: That's right. *(Radio in background)*

GOTTI: Every fucking time I went there on a Saturday or a Sunday, I hated it, Frank. I hated the fucking world. Because whoever was there before me, as soon as he left, he cursed out. "Scumbag," "asshole," "motherfucker." *Minchia!* I mean, ain't there nobody good here? Now you know when you leave that door, he's gonna say it about you. . . . I didn't wanna leave until the house is empty. *(Laughter)* . . . But, ya know, you know, your heart's breaking because you're saying, "I ain't got three cents in my pocket! I got nothing but heartaches. I gotta have this motherfucker—

GRAVANO: *(Laughs)*

GOTTI: —curse me again."

GRAVANO: [Remember] the meeting we had down *(tap sound)* in the basement? *(Laughs)* When we were talking, poor Frankie said something? *(Laughs)* Fucking Neil *(clap sound)* "jumped" on him! Remember? In the basement? When he called us all together. It was you, ah, Angelo, Neil, me, I remember Frankie, Paul, Joe Gallo *(tap sound)*. What we talked about?

GOTTI: I remember.

[. . . .]

GRAVANO: Know what I mean?

GOTTI: Yeah. But, no, I'm saying. Well, whoever done it, I don't know who done it. And I know youse two—

GRAVANO: Well, I knew he didn't have no balls!

GOTTI: That's right.

GRAVANO: I knew he didn't have no balls. Say, you were gonna do nothin'. *(Clap sound)*

GOTTI: Cocksucker.

GRAVANO: —to Nino. But, ah—

GOTTI: But, anyway—

GRAVANO: So, how come you never said nothin'?

GOTTI: But, anyway, here's a guy, whoever done it, probably the cops done it to this fuckin' guy. Whoever killed this cocksucker, probably the cops killed this Paul. But whoever killed him, the cocks—he deserved it. *(Snap sound)* He wasn't gonna do nothin' to nobody, anyway.

GRAVANO: That's right.

GOTTI: So why would we do it? We had nothin' to do with it; no reason to do it.

GRAVANO: That's right.

[. . . .]

GOTTI: I'm trying to think what's good for the overall picture, Sammy. First thing is this. With these fuckin' lawyers on all these cases like, even for a bail application, they gotta go in there, argue for your client, within certain parameters. Then after that, keep your fuckin' mouth shut. Like these guys, when Barry Slotnick got up on bail, on the bail hearing, "Your Honor, those charges don't pertain to my client." Sit the fuck down, or I'll knock you down, you cocksucker! "Let the record show that, that's Mr. Gotti they're talking about. Not Mr. Carneglia. Oh, that's Mr. Locascio you're talking about, not Mr. Gravano." Sit down, or I'll knock you down, you motherfucker! Talk within certain parameters, and we'll win, we'll win. We'll win, Sammy. We'll win these fuckin' cases. And we'll be out a year from now, somewhere, a year and a half from now, somewhere, laughing a little bit. Probably have new developments, but we will be laughing at the *(inaudible)*. *(Tap sound)* Believe me. Jimmy La Rossa, I already thought about that. But I'm gonna send him a feeler ahead of time. And I ask him—If he says "no," I'll kill him. *(Pause)* My pride *(inaudible)*.

GRAVANO: Don't ask.

GOTTI: —anything else.

GRAVANO: Don't ask. Let, let somebody put out a feeler. But don't even ask him.

GOTTI: Of course!

GRAVANO: *(Inaudible)* what I'm saying.

GOTTI: No, but see, I'm gonna say *(inaudible)* 'cause Eddie, Eddie Lino's nice like that. So, hopefully, he got time for a case—

GRAVANO: Yeah.

GOTTI: *(Inaudible)* This guy's nuts!

GRAVANO: Jimmy's crazy.

LOCASCIO: *(Inaudible)*

GOTTI: *(Coughs) (Inaudible)*

GRAVANO: *(Inaudible)* They gonna have, they gotta be so fuckin' dead, er, forget about it. Hey, I mean, they moved a case, but I don't think they got, ah, to have these guys. They, they beatin' the case.

GOTTI: They got a fuckin' tape that they played at Mike's case. Where they're arguing, this fat motherfucker turns around. There's five or six people in the room. I forget *(inaudible)*.

LOCASCIO: They remember this tape? They remember talking about this tape?

GOTTI: 'Cause I don't have the list *(inaudible)* ya know? I never spoke to "Fatso."

LOCASCIO: Ya know what I'm talking about?

GOTTI: Yeah.

LOCASCIO: Or that they may—

GOTTI: No, I know that.

LOCASCIO: *(Inaudible)*

GOTTI: I know what you're saying, Mike, ah—

LOCASCIO: I mean, Mike telling him—

GOTTI: —Mike doesn't know—Yeah, Mike isn't privy to *(lowers voice)* Eddie Lino's on that tape. Fat Angelo *(inaudible).* They gonna spring on them at trial. That's, that's their whole trial *(inaudible).* They got a fuckin' tape, this was on the *(inaudible)* whatever the fuck it was. Forget about it. This is that fat fuck! He ain't winning his point. They're talking about *(tap sound) (inaudible)* collecting monies from Sal.

GRAVANO: Angelo about the plane? *(Inaudible)*

GOTTI: AWACS—*(All talking)*

LOCASCIO: That's not, that plane legit *(inaudible).*

GRAVANO: This here—

GOTTI: Bringing in one they never heard!

GRAVANO: And fuckin' joking about it?

GOTTI: "It's two kilos! Yeah, but how, how do you know it's two hundred and fifty thou? There's two hundred and fifty thousand! Because it wasn't 'Charlie,' it was heroin! A hundred twenty-five thousand a kilo, my brother told me." He mentions everything word: heroin, "Charlie."

GRAVANO: *(Inaudible)* say anything, this conversation? *(Inaudible)*

GOTTI: Yeah! A code.

GRAVANO: *(Inaudible)*

GOTTI: *(Inaudible)*

GRAVANO: *(Inaudible)* with the plane—*(inaudible)*—

GOTTI: Ah—They can pick out one with, ah, "Gaspipe's" boat got caught in Howard Beach, or Freeport. Ah, fifty thousand bales, or fifty thousand pounds, fifty thousand tons. Did that happen one time?

GRAVANO: I really don't know. Ahh—

GOTTI: I mean, I'm not aware.

GRAVANO: *(Inaudible)* probably.

GOTTI: Ah, this is what I, I understand. They got one, a tape with that. Ahh—"See them fuckin' guys. That was half a ours—" Ah, "What do you mean half ours?" "Well, 'Gaspipe' called me up this morning; 'Gas' called me up this morning. It's half ours; half theirs; it's half the guy up the fuckin' block. Fifty thousand pounds, he partners this."

GRAVANO: Do they think there's even a conversation with Vic?

GOTTI: Oscar. Yeah. Vic was in there. He was one of the guys in that room. There's all these guys that they want a *baciuzzu* [kiss], or they need something *(inaudible)* got, people never see the real thing; they're all mopey motherfuckers! Hey, Sam, they gotta believe that they're doing dope. But these are all useless conversations. These guys would worry about where to put the furniture in the house before they bought the house. *(Pause)*

GRAVANO: Ah *(inaudible)*.

GOTTI: Let me tell you something, Sammy.

GRAVANO: *(Inaudible)*

GOTTI: If you think you could trust fifty fucking guys—

GRAVANO: Right.

GOTTI: —in a life-or-death situation, you're a hard-on.

GRAVANO: *(Inaudible)*

GOTTI: You're a hard-on. You're a dangerous motherfuckin' hard-on. Do you want me to tell you the guys, that they tellin' each other they're brothers, we're brothers, it's us against them; we're all in this together. That's probably when I heard them fuckin' three punks, "It's us against the world." You know I lie *(inaudible)* with that *(inaudible)* I don't do that *(inaudible) (background noise)*. That's their fucking talk! "It's us against the world!" Eddie Lino, Di B, Frankie DeCicco, Angelo, Vic, "Gas," Joe Messina, I'd go on for a fuckin' hour, Sam. How long you got to stay here? What the fuck are youse nuts? How many fuckin' brothers are youse? Vinnie, how many "brothers" are you? You wasn't stupid, Frank, or Sammy. You wasn't stupid. I ain't stupid. How many fuckin' "brothers" we got? *(Pause)* How long are we together? How long me and this guy together here, huh? Years ago. You don't talk about it.

GRAVANO: It's over.

GOTTI: Not only it's over, *(tap sound)* where the fuck are we going here?

GOTTI: —'Cause this is, he said, it can't *(inaudible)* ya gotta do it, and now. *(Tap sound)* You know what "Jo Jo" told me outside, in the car, today? We were standing about fifteen, twenty blocks from the other guy. He says to me, "You know, John," he says, "let me tell you," *(inaudible)* he says, "I never was so proud, so happy in my whole life," he says. "I knew," he said, "I was talking with a few 'Skippers' from another 'Family.' " He says, "Since youse are here, this is the first time that they could remember, in years, that the 'Families' ain't arguing." Nobody's arguing. *(Clap sound)*

GRAVANO: Right.

GOTTI: None of the "Families" are arguing with nobody.

GRAVANO: No.

GOTTI: Everybody sedate.

GRAVANO: That's true.

GOTTI: You know, think about it.

LOCASCIO: *(Inaudible)* about it.

GRAVANO: Yeah. No.

GOTTI: *(Coughs)*

GRAVANO: *(Inaudible)* or nothin'.

GOTTI: I was thinking about it. I says, "Ya know, he's right, the fuck."

GRAVANO: And if it wasn't for this guy. If it wasn't for him, I think this really would be so fuckin' united!

GOTTI: Greatest thing ever, yeah.

GRAVANO: It would be so united, we'd have somebody indicting the fuckin' agents and the fuckin' prosecutors—

GOTTI: And not only that.

GRAVANO: —fucking news guys.

GOTTI: Not only that.

GRAVANO: We'd be so close, forget about it.

GOTTI: Not only that. If there's a bad situation, hey, rules need a little changing or something . . .

GRAVANO: Five minutes. *(Bang sound)*

GOTTI: —send, send, send the five "underbosses" or the *consiglieres*. Together, boom. This is my way, *(tap sound)* my—thinking, because this "thing," in other words, the five "Families," put together *(tap sound)* bi, bah, bang! *(Clap sound)* That's the law!

DECEMBER 12, 1989

FILE NUMBER:	183A-3507
PLACE:	Apartment above the Ravenite Social Club, located at 247 Mulberry Street in Little Italy, Manhattan
TIME:	7:13 P.M.
PARTICIPANTS:	JOHN GOTTI FRANK LOCASCIO

Presiding over the Gambino Family is a thankless task. Ambition and uncontrollable avarice threaten at every turn. Mutual suspicion and possible betrayal lurk everywhere. In this conversation, John Gotti complains of the number of companies that his right-hand man, Salvatore (Sammy the Bull) Gravano, is creating or controlling. Gotti worries that Gravano's greed may divide the Family by "creating an army inside an army." His acting underboss (and later consigliere*), Frank Locascio, agrees that there is a danger of "creating another faction." Both men remember that it was Paul Castellano, the former boss of the Gambino Family, whose refusal to share his spoils with others in the Family prompted internal resentment. As Gotti puts it: "That's what made me hate Paul." At another point, Gotti remarks, "We got nothing but troubles," sighing that the whole business is making him sick. "You know what I want you to do, Frank?" he jokes. "We gotta both buy chemotherapy with the money I got."*

■ ■ ■

(Steps)

GOTTI: Today I go and have lunch. I mixed up about four lunches at once, you know? You know, Frankie, I, I, I don't like you—I love you. I don't like Sammy—I love him. As far as this life, no one knows it better than me. If a guy offends me, I'll break him—that's the fuckin' end of it. But not for me. It's this "thing of ours." It's gotten to be a circus. I'm not gonna leave a circus when I go to jail, Frankie. I don't wanna be a phony. I ain't gonna talk about a guy behind his back. Um, Louie was a fuckin' coffee boy. Know what a coffee boy was? A motherfuckin' coffee boy.

LOCASCIO: You told me once *(inaudible)*.

GOTTI: Never did nothin', I'm telling you again. Never did nothin'. He's a billionaire now. Billionaire, now! Owns buildings. Throws a half million into fuckin' factories, and, and bars. And all the rest of them. Yeah, yeah, make the faces. But, anyway, this is all well and good. I got guys around me aren't making five cents. This is my back! When "Di B" got "whacked," they told me a story. I was in jail when I "whacked" him. I knew why it was being done. I done it, anyway. I allowed it to be done, anyway. He got there. I saved that whole fucking industry. I got a piece of the company. For a year—an arrangement—a year! They haven't got a fucking job! One job! I got them a job. They got a runaround. I was sent for, you sent for my partners. To the *(inaudible)*. "Johnny Blowjob" sends for him. And they give him a runaround. Come down on the figures. Dupe this guy, dupe that. So, they, they told him taking him, they going to a party. *(Inaudible)* fuck them! Those Irish motherfuckers! Fuck them. They don't mean nothing to me. I send this "Joe Crotty" here, he's a good friend of ours. He's taken care of dozens of people is in the jail. He done nothing but good things for us. He's in the carpet business. Joe Gallo brought him to me about eight years ago. I put my vote here to get these jobs. "If my name could help you in any point in time, go ahead." He goes there, two months ago. He got thrown out! "Johnny Gotti wants Johnny G. to have it." Where's this guy come in the carpet business? They're in [the] rebar business. There's a conc, there's a builder up in the Bronx. A billionaire builder. The guy's with me, through ARC Plumbing. Sammy sends me word. You were there. Where they told me. Says, "I had the plans ahead of time. Everybody gets the plans when you build, when you bid for it." I sat with the fuckin' owner of the building today. They don't know who the fuck Sammy is. And they don't know who fuckin' Marathon is *(inaudible)*. They knew Marine and them way before that. They were told, this is where I wanted it to go. So it went to Marathon. "Who's Marathon?" he says today. "That's Sammy." Where are we going here? Where the fuck are we going here? Where are we going here? Every fucking time I turn around there's a new company popping up. Rebars, Building, Consulting, Concrete. And every time we got a partner that don't agree with us, we kill him. You go to the "boss," and your "boss" kills him. He kills 'em. He okays it. Say it's all right, good. Where are we going here, Frankie? Who the fuck are we? What do I get out of this here? Better not become a clown. Where am I going? What do I do with the rest of the *borgata?* You throw 'em in the fuckin' street? The rest of the *borgata.* What are we going to do with the rest of this *borgata?* Hah? Twenty-five *capodecinas,* we got twenty-two, twenty-five "beef" to me. What do I do here, Frankie? Sammy tells me you and him, took a walk, about a concrete plant in New Jersey? Somewhere? I told him when do youse decide to tell me about it?

LOCASCIO: There's nothing for sure. I just got the plans and I asked him. . . .

GOTTI: Yeah, but I told him, "Don't I have the right? Frankie's my 'acting underboss.' Supposed to tell me first, then I'll tell you if it's okay to go ahead or not. I told him, "Now, Sammy, Don't you people listen here?" I mean, where are we going here?

LOCASCIO: This was the plant *(inaudible).*

GOTTI: Frankie, I won't stop ya, Frankie. I would give ya, I'll go take it in the ass and give ya the money *(inaudible).*

LOCASCIO: There was nothin'. I just, he said he was gonna meet with, ah, Carl. I says, "Here, show him this. See if he knows this spot . . ."

GOTTI: Frank, I didn't say you did anything underhanded.

LOCASCIO: I would never do anything like that!

GOTTI: I didn't say that. I know you better than that, Frankie. Don't you understand? I want you to own five hundred plants, and I don't tell no one *(inaudible)* about a plant. But I wanna know about it, Frank. I got "beef," guys "beefin'" at me every fuckin' hour every day. Yesterday one of them fuckin' *capodecinas* sent, they sent for me for a glory fuckin' meeting. On Sunday. And the people think that this is my fuckin' green eyes.

LOCASCIO: *(Inaudible)*

GOTTI: Couple of our *capodecinas*. You think it's my green eyes. You think this is me doing this! This is not me, Frankie! What do I get outta this fuckin' shit?

LOCASCIO: Which building, er, is this?

GOTTI: It's a big building. I don't know where. Six, six million, twenty million, whatever it is. But what, what, where are we going here, Frankie? Frankie, where the hell did all these new companies come from? Where did five new companies come from? Ah, I mean, when, when Nasabeak died, you were nothing. Louie [Milito] had Gem Steel. You, you told me that the guy talked behind my back. Now you got Gem Steel. The other thing, you told me Di B cried behind my back. Now you got all that! And you got, uh, Bobby Sasso. *(Inaudible)* Hey, Frankie, you're not, are, are, are you gonna, are you in with me, Frank? I'll walk outta here, and we'll terminate our friendship. Is that the way this, is that what our "marriage" is? That's not the way it's gonna be, Frank. I give you my word, Frank. *(Pause)* I, I love you guys. I don't, I don't fabricate no part of it.

LOCASCIO: Why don't you pull him and—

GOTTI: And there—

LOCASCIO: —pull his coat.

GOTTI: —that's why I wanted to end tonight here. I wanted it to end tonight. I just *(inaudible)*.

LOCASCIO: *(Inaudible)* you want me to go and get him? I'll bring him.

GOTTI: No, no, no. No, no, no.

LOCASCIO: I'll go and get him.

GOTTI: This is bullshit! These people are being taken away from him. He's not a *capodecina*. He wants to be a *capodecina*, I'll take him down from *consigliere*, and I'll make him a *capodecina*. He can have all the fun he wants to have. Frankie, this shit ain't gonna take it.

LOCASCIO: I'll go and get him, for you and . . .

GOTTI: No, I'll send them. They're gonna do it. This is not the way this is gonna be, Frank. I'll see him tomorrow, and I'm gonna tell him tomorrow. I told him the other fuckin' day, Saturday. I see eight of our fuckin' kids, none of our kids supposed to be future prospects, like fuckin' bum "junkies," in the hall of the fuckin' house. Where are we going here, Frankie? Where are we going here? This is not my teaching. None of my teaching. *(Pause)*

LOCASCIO: Talking about a house for liars *(inaudible)*. He knows what he's doing.

GOTTI: He's not gone, he's home in bed. *(Inaudible)* He's home. He's home at his house. I'm on that, Frank. I'm on every fuckin' thing. *(Tap sound)* Selling half-million, four-

-thousand-dollar deal. You know, Frankie, you ove me, he loves me, I know he does. But Jesus ' Christ! This is not your candy store! You take a cocksucker like a fuckin' Johnny G., you make this guy rebel against his own cousin. You heard him just now downstairs, the cousin, *capodecina*. I never rehearsed this. I haven't spoken one word to this guy. Gets near you, he rebels against him? I think, he's in charge of, ah, two unions. You got him, Johnny G., working hand in hand with Joe Brewster, in Local 23. You convinced me that's good for me. You got Joe Francolino working hand in hand. Don't you see this or am I, am I talking to myself, Frank? Am I lying, am I out of order here? Correct me! You're my fuckin' "underboss." Correct me, Frankie.

LOCASCIO: I agree with ya.

GOTTI: Am I wrong, Frankie? If I'm wrong, correct me.

LOCASCIO: Fuck, ah, John, it's up to you to pull him up.

GOTTI: Yes, but am I wrong, I'm saying?

LOCASCIO: No, you're not wrong!

GOTTI: But Jesus motherfuckin' Christ, I'm with some people today. Ah, but I was Marine Construction. I said, "Maybe it's because—

LOCASCIO: Well—

GOTTI: —it's my company."

LOCASCIO: . . . you said it two weeks ago, with Marine Construction *(inaudible)*.

GOTTI: You, was he sitting there when I told him?

LOCASCIO: Yeah.

GOTTI: He got nothing! They got no job. If Angelo was sitting next to me, would they have a job? If Angelo was handling Bobby Sasso, would they have a job? You tell me. Right or wrong?

LOCASCIO: *(Inaudible)* they would get all the jobs.

GOTTI: Guaranteed! And I don't want that, Frank. You know me better than that, I don't want that. I said, "Give him one job." Now, I told him—

LOCASCIO: You get Bosco off your back, 'cause he keeps on breaking your fucking balls *(inaudible)*.

GOTTI: *(Inaudible)* Frankie, the guy gives Joe Watts nine thousand every two weeks. He takes a third, and I get two thirds. Don't I get two thousand a week? Don't I get two thousand a week pay? Who gives you two thousand a week? *(Inaudible)*

LOCASCIO: But he should, he shoulda done something.

GOTTI: Nothing! And, since March! That's too many months in a fuckin' year, Frank. And I'm not gonna go for this shit. And another thing, this shit about your "*decina*" is on welfare. And another fuckin' "*decina*" is on, on easy street. I purposely done that tonight with Jackie and this "Butterass." He gives me this Arpège, this fuckin' Jackie with this fuckin' guy. I purposely told "Butterass," "Bring the guy down, Tuesday." And I told Jackie, *(coughs)* "Can ya get the guy?"

LOCASCIO: When he comes, chase him.

GOTTI: No, I told Jackie, "Can you get the guy?" He says, "No, I can't reach him." "You can't reach him? Ain't he with you?" "Yeah," "And you can't reach him?" "No." So, I showed him. *(Low voice) (Inaudible)* You follow me, Frank? I mean, this guy's with you. Frankie, you'd think they'd know how to get him. Okay. Them two get "pinched." You follow what I'm trying to say, Frankie? Where are we going here, with this *(inaudible)*? This is the new game. You gotta *(inaudible)*. We got tough guy's tough guys with us. They look at me like I'm fuckin' nuts. And you think that I was, I'm reaping billions of dollars, Frankie. I, I, I don't want none! I don't want a fuckin' thing! And this guy, I mean, what's—I love you. Where are we going here? You know what's frightening to me, Frankie? I love him. I don't give a fuck, because I know I blast him a little bit and he'll slow it down. What happens when I go away, or I'm gone? When I'm dead, Frankie? Youse two guys are the fuckin' guys I, nothin'! Fuck me! The whole "Family" gotta go and find out. Is this what we gonna invite? This is probably what happen? I'll throw myself in front of a fuckin' . . . *(pause)* I'm sick, Frankie. I've been sick over the whole weekend. You know what I mean? I love the guy. I go up to the hospital, I see his kid. I find out he bought the fuckin' moped.

LOCASCIO: He did?

GOTTI: Yeah! No *(inaudible)*.

LOCASCIO: But did you tell him that he *(inaudible)*?

GOTTI: He's got them, he's gotta tell, if your kid done that, you would've, you would've—

LOCASCIO: Thank God that he's all right. You would've thought—

GOTTI: Good he's all right. But then you wanna kill him for what he done, right? I mean, right or wrong, he's got to whack the kid down.

LOCASCIO: You done good.

GOTTI: Yeah! So, I told him, "You didn't do a nice thing, son?" But then I kept my respect. I didn't, I didn't know what I said. I told him, "He didn't do a nice fuckin' thing. You're being buddies, that makes you happy? She's gotta cry? Make you happy he's gotta be sick. We gotta be sick? Dozens of your father's friends? That makes you happy?" I told him, "I had a son like you. Make a little tough for the guy. I go and visit him every Saturday, Sunday, eleven o'clock in the morning. That what you want your mom and dad to do? They'll do it. You'll have your fuckin' home in the cemetery." I mean where we going here? We're creating . . . *(inaudible)* these fuckin' kids. You know, Frankie? I'm not a jerkoff. If I see kids go, I should never *(inaudible)* I hate them, Frankie. I hate them. Nobody had it worse than I had it in life. And I didn't need that shit. You know what I mean. I didn't need that shit. Take a couple of Scotches and go fuck yourself, know what I mean?

LOCASCIO: Well, I wanna see what, what's happening. We got that tire disclaim coming up. 'Cause if . . .

GOTTI: *(Coughs)*

LOCASCIO: —I wanna see how he's gonna act during that. I'll fight it tooth and nail down the line, you know, because it's . . .

GOTTI: There's nothing to fight, Frankie. It's *(inaudible)* said.

LOCASCIO: It's my people against his people.

GOTTI: Yeah, but no, Frankie.

LOCASCIO: But you—

GOTTI: That's no good. I don't even want none, part of it.

LOCASCIO: *(Inaudible)*

GOTTI: I gotta be honest with ya. I don't want any part these kind of things here because I could see, we ain't got our, we ain't got the *borgata* in hock no more. Now we got ourselves gain *(inaudible)*. And that's not for me. That's not John Gotti. At least I hope that's not me. Maybe I see myself in the light that I'm not in, I don't know. But that's what I feel I am. But, but, but, he's gonna get it off me pretty good tomorrow. And I wanna know everything that every one of these guys are in. What businesses they're in. I wanna know when they got in them, and how they got in them! That fuckin' guy.

LOCASCIO: That's it, the key. That's the key . . .

GOTTI: I wanna know when and how they got in them. These are all businesses that nobody had a fuckin' year ago, Frank! On my back? I got a million *(inaudible)* good guys. My son didn't open no new companies up. My brothers didn't. My son-in-laws didn't. Nobody opened no new companies up. They took it upon themselves. "Joe Piney" and, and, and Sammy, he made my brother Pete get involved with that fuckin' asshole with the "Windows." Never made a dime. He's going to jail for it. Well, tell me something that one of my family got that they never had it before. I'll make ya fuck me in the ass. But that ain't what I'm getting at, Frankie. That's not the way this is run. And you should know better than that. You've been around long enough. This is not the way a fuckin' *borgata* is run. And I shouldn't break my fuckin' heart. When, when I hear you're *(inaudible)*.

LOCASCIO: In reality *(inaudible)*. In reality, you put everything on him.

GOTTI: Yes.

LOCASCIO: If it's anything to do with construction.

GOTTI: Why did I do that? *(Tap sound)* What, what did, what did I do that for, Frankie? What did I do that for, Frankie?

LOCASCIO: You might be able to, the way you said before—*(inaudible)*.

GOTTI: *(Inaudible)*

LOCASCIO: —fuckin' *(inaudible)*.

GOTTI: I did! But why did I do that for, Frankie? If I did that to you, that means you gotta make a ple—a pleasure thing out of it? *(Pause—radio in background)*

GOTTI: For Christsake, I love you more than I love myself, for fuckin' Christsake! I'm worried about you going to jail. I don't give two fucks about myself going to jail. Don't I know they ain't gonna rest until they put me in jail? So I fight it tooth and nail to the fuckin' end. But at least if I know you two guys are out here, we got a shot. Somebody got a shot, Frankie. Maybe our kids gotta, my kid's in trouble. Maybe some other jerkoff's kid's in trouble, they come to you. You guide them right, give them a little lecture. And maybe, we gotta think there's some proper resemblance of a "Family." Where else can you lead them? Don't you see it? With this Johnny told me on the phone, forget about it. Don't you see what I mean, Frankie? *(Inaudible)* the guy cried today to me on the fuckin' phone. He's in jail. Says to you *(inaudible)* he send his lawyer, his private investigator. You asked for help, I send you the help that you asked for, you listen? Did ya speak to the lawyer. *(Inaudible)* Yeah, he walked away. He says, "*Minchia,* he treated me like an equal." Johnny told him. And he got through with it. He said he sent word to that other guy, about what they should do with the other guy. He told him, "I don't know." *(Tap sound)* Pretty fuckin' *(inaudible)* but that's selfish people. We're not selfish, Frankie. And every time I sit down, every time you fuckin' talk with somebody, they have another business. What business you in? Where the fuck are you going here? Where the fuck are we going here? Ya know what I mean? Where the fuck you kidding somebody, or what? *(Pause)* Listen, Frankie, I coulda been like other cocksuckers. Put Sammy in. Who's gonna challenge me? Who's gonna defy me? What are you gonna do? Take a shot, *(inaudible)* sleeping, like I did to the other guy? No! *(Inaudible)* Frank, I welcome that, Frank. I'd welcome that. I'll kill their fuckin' mothers, their fathers. I, but I would welcome that, Frankie. But I'm saying, I'm not going for that. They don't belong here. You belong where you are! That's the way I feel in my heart. He belongs where he is. What tomorrow, I didn't give him no fuckin' gift, bring you no gift, Frankie. I didn't give you no gift, because you make good meatballs? You deserve to be here! But that don't mean you gotta fuckin' rob the "Family."

LOCASCIO: He's telling the truth. He belongs—

GOTTI: He does, he does belong.

LOCASCIO: He belongs there. More than anybody that I can think of.

GOTTI: He does. You're right.

LOCASCIO: They think they only control *(inaudible)* whichever way—

GOTTI: But you know that, Frankie, as well as I do.

LOCASCIO: But this has been going on for two years, John.

GOTTI: I know it, Frankie—

LOCASCIO: *(Inaudible)*

GOTTI: —but I'm trying to say . . .

LOCASCIO: You said it two years ago.

GOTTI: Yeah, but I'm trying, you know what happened? Joe Arcuri came to me one day, crying. He's a fucking pain-in-the-ass old-timer. He's one of us. He ain't a bad guy. He's one of us, Frankie. He's an old-time "captain." They thought they were in trouble when we first took over. They so comfortable now. They, they've seen, people see them. They make us stronger by people seeing them. *Minchia*, these guys didn't gobble up the old-timers. It's good for those guys. He says to me, "Jesus Christ." He says, "John. I'm there like I'm lying." I said, "That's my fault. Go ask Joe Arcuri." I said, "That's my fault. I picked on him." It wasn't my fault. I didn't pick on him. He, he uncovered a guy through this Johnny G., uncovered a guy through this Bob Levy. Where, where are we going here? What are you create snakes here? Monsters? *(Pause)* I mean, Frankie, I don't like you guys, I say it and I don't say it loosely, I love you guys. But, but I gotta be honest, I gotta be me, Frank. I can't, I can't just fuckin', ah, and, and if you tell me you put an extra fifty thousand in the envelope, I don't want it. If, if you're gonna fuckin' break everybody's heart, I don't want no extra fifty thousand. Keep it. I got no big fuckin' needs. I ain't [got] no big mansion needs, you know what I mean? And this is fuckin' insanity. The guy, the other guy comes, there's three in a row. Don't even know each other, the three lunches, Frankie, I was sick to my stomach. The last one I know better. We go by the Marlin where *(inaudible)* kill ourselves. They're crazy. I meet this Buddy Leahy. The guy's the nicest guy in the world. He's giving that fuckin' punk ten thousand a month. In jail with Jimmy, ah, Coonan. This kid's gettin' "shaken down" for like thirty thousand a month, Frankie. What the fuck? He's gotta live. Fuckin', I said to him, "What happened with that job down there?" He says, ah, ah, "Carbone, whatever the fuck his name, Mike Carbone called up and he hollered at me. I'm not to go, bid any jobs." "Who the fuck are you talking to? This guy's my partner! Who the fuck are you? You're a legitimate hard-on, and he's a legitimate hard-on. Youse two legitimate hard-ons. Where did you get this confidence from?" You follow what I'm trying to say, Frankie?

LOCASCIO: Confidence comes from Sam.

GOTTI: Yeah! So, where did you get this confidence from? *(Pause)* But you know, I even told him, "You know, Sammy, you, you see the fuckin' trust I put you, in faith. I told the whole 'Family.' " I told Joe Watts, "You see where I put *(inaudible)*." You tell me that you don't want nobody to see, "Jeez, 'boss' to protect you, I'd rather nobody sees Bobby Sasso but me." You think I'm fuckin' stupid? *(Pause)* I mean, I mean where am I going here? "Yeah, yeah *(inaudible)*." I got other people I'm responsible with, too. So, the guy told me, he said, "I just, I just fired ninety of my guys." Tell Joe Watts downstairs, if I, on my son's grave, I told him, I said, "Well, I don't know how you could salvage anything right now. Ya, you're not gonna get me, my nose all—Whatever Sammy done, he done on my orders. You could ask for, for this mama *(phonetic)*, Mamona *(phonetic)* cocksucker, didn't do it on my orders. His ass I'll fix! Sammy done it on my, I'm responsible, totally responsible *(inaudible)*." Joe Watts *(inaudible)*. I says, "And you can start by ending my salary. I don't need no salary. Whatever you gave Joe Watts for him and me, end it. We don't want it no more. So, that's a burden off your fuckin' back. You're right. Eleven months I never got you one job. I got you chased off three jobs. That job, that's, that's six, seven-million-dollar job. That job belongs lock, stock, and barrel! 'Cause I was with the boss, the owner, and the contractor today."

LOCASCIO: Who wound up—

GOTTI: They did. They did. Marathon, Sammy. Sammy and this guy, Joe Madonia, whatever the fuck his name is. He says, he said, "I waited for orders for a month." He said, "I sent word to who you'd want me to give it to!" He said, "This is what I was told." I don't care if I had to pick between Sammy and this Irish fuck. Sam's with me anyway. But this Irish fuck, I never woulda got two hundred thousand from. He had me in conversation. But I don't even care about that. But you don't need eight jobs, he don't get nothing. This guy's been in the business for fuckin' seven years. You just formed this fuckin' company. But, ya, ya, ya, I don't know if you follow me, Frankie. I mean, maybe I'm—

LOCASCIO: But I'm hearing it.

GOTTI: I mean this is not right here.

LOCASCIO: Of course not.

GOTTI: This—

LOCASCIO: It ain't, ain't right. It ain't right. Let's not argue. But I think you should pull him up and say this, er, this is '89. It ain't gonna happen in '90 because—

GOTTI: I'm gonna do it. I, I'm telling you. Listen—

LOCASCIO: Whatever happened, happened in the past. Let's forget about it.

GOTTI: But not only that. But there's no past with him and I, and you and I, Frankie. We're too close for that. We're too close. I, I, I coulda done this a stupid way. *(Inaudible)* and there's no future *(inaudible)*. This bothers me. And you shouldn't wanna bother me. Correct it. If I had an end coming, which is gonna hurt you there, keep my end. Do it right. Don't you understand make people love you? Doesn't he understand people gotta like you guys. I mean, don't you understand that, Frankie? You're, and don't have to [have] people fuck you in the ass for people to like ya. Ehh, believe me, Frankie, people are scared. I like it when people *(inaudible)*. Don't you realize people hate it? But you don't believe me. So, now, now, that's no good, because it breaks my fuckin' heart. Breaks my fuckin' heart. Who the fuck wants to be here? We got nothin' but troubles. I got cases coming up. I got nothing but fuckin' trouble. I don't feel good. I gotta fuckin' sit here. I gotta sit here with my closest two friends. Not even, even if I sit here with guys which are, a *capodecina* that's from New Jersey, you wanna pull his cover a little bit. Ya, ya, ya, you guys are, ah, youse are supposed to be pulling my covers, I, I gotta pull his fuckin' cover. And I tell him a million times, "Sammy, slow it down. Pull it in a fuckin' notch. Slow it down! Pull it in a notch! You, you, you come up with fifteen companies, for Christsake! You got rebars; you got concrete pouring; you got Italian floors now. You got construction; you got drywall; you got asbestos; you got rugs. What the fuck next?"

LOCASCIO: How the fuck did he get "Windows"?

GOTTI: Yeah, they goin' to jail!

LOCASCIO: We got, we got the word. But I shouldn't blame him.

GOTTI: Garbage! You told me—

LOCASCIO: *(Inaudible)*

GOTTI: Don't you think I, I told him the other day, when he said to me, "Jesus, the, the garbage club, ah, if Joe Francolino gets you a hundred thousand I don't want one hundred thousand. You take the hundred thousand. Give me the piece that you've got. *X* amount for a week for the rest of your life."

LOCASCIO: *(Inaudible)*

GOTTI: "But no, I'll give him the book." "I don't want it, Sammy. I want what's right here. You're torturing Jimmy Brown. The *capodecina* gotta come crying here. The fuckin' docks guy's gotta come crying. You got all the *capodecinas* coming crying." And you know I'm not gonna side with them, Frankie, I never did, and I never will. What do you think I told Jimmy Brown, Saturday? You go down and you ask Danny Marino, word for word. I told him, "That's my fault," I says, "Sammy got nothin' to do with Joe Francolino." I said, "I told him," but I didn't fuckin' tell him *(inaudible)*. I don't want them to not like Sammy. I don't want them to hate the guy. "It's my fault." I said, "Sammy had nothing to do with it. *(Inaudible)*" I can't keep going around and say it's my fault!

LOCASCIO: The way youse told him, "Construction you take care of. Anything with construction. When it comes to the garbage, Jimmy Brown's *(inaudible)*.

GOTTI: But that is Jimmy Brown's—

LOCASCIO: —Brown's decision."

GOTTI: Right.

LOCASCIO: Can't be—

GOTTI: That's right.

LOCASCIO: *(Inaudible)* okay.

GOTTI: And I just told him that.

LOCASCIO: The grudge *(inaudible).*

GOTTI: And I just told him, last night he was there, I grabbed Joe Francolino. I told Joe Francolino, "Listen, Joey, you're a nice fella. *(Coughs)* You're a 'friend of ours.' I made you a 'friend of ours,' through your cousin Eddie Lino, and that gang *(inaudible)* we knew good things about you, or because Sammy put a good word out for you. For no other reason. No other reason. Your cousin is a *capodecina* now. I'm supposed to put you with him. Johnny Gammarano's cousin, he was a *capodecina,* I should put him with him. I don't take all our money people and put them in a fuckin' *decina* and leave the *capodecinas* naked." That's not the way this goes and you know that, Frankie. How would you like it if you had nephews or cousins and they put them in different fuckin' *decinas*? That's not the way this goes here! All right? So, now I told Joe Francolino, I says, "Joey, you're making a decision? Tomorrow *(inaudible)* you're making the decision, without Jimmy Brown's knowledge, you *(inaudible).*" "No," he said, "I thought you wanted it that way." "Well, maybe I slipped and told Sammy that. Maybe I told Sammy." You know I never told him that. I never told nobody to override Jimmy Brown. I mean where are we going here, Frankie?

LOCASCIO: Anybody would ask ya, Jimmy Brown woulda asked ya. This we don't want.

GOTTI: Heh, but Christ almighty. Where the fuck are we going here? This is not, ah, yours for keeping. You're gonna die someday. Even, if God forbid, hopefully, it's when you're ninety-five, in your sleep, a heart attack. But, like Angelo, he's gone; you're dead! Gonna go to jail, or some fuckin' thing. Is this what we working for? To leave a fuckin' mess behind?

LOCASCIO: Messes we don't need.

GOTTI: For Christsake.

LOCASCIO: Just got over messes.

GOTTI: *Minchia!* And you know I tell you the fuckin' truth, Frankie, I, I don't believe I'm lying. And, more important, I don't believe in that fuckin' bulldozin'. That's what made me hate, really, fuckin' Paul. You, ya, you couldn't get a fuckin' ham sandwich. Everyone is right. He sold the *borgata* out for fuckin' construction company. And that's what we're doing. That's what we're doing right now. I don't know if you could see it, but that's what we're doing right now. Three, four guys will wind up with every fuckin' thing. And the rest of the *borgata* looks like fuckin' waste.

LOCASCIO: In defense, in defense *(inaudible)* what would happen to these businesses if he didn't put these people? *(Inaudible)*

GOTTI: *(Inaudible)*

LOCASCIO: Would, would there be other people involved?

GOTTI: Sure!

LOCASCIO: Except for Marine I'm talkin'.

GOTTI: Sure! Sure they'd be involved, what are you talking about?

LOCASCIO: In other words, the people that he's putting are taking away from *(inaudible),* from others.

GOTTI: Sure.

LOCASCIO: That ain't right. That ain't right! Eh, if there was nothing there, and he's creating something, that's different.

GOTTI: Yeah, but you're creating under this flag, Frankie!

LOCASCIO: It's not like *(inaudible).*

GOTTI: Where, where's my piece of these companies?

LOCASCIO: Right. That's another thing. But there's nothing wrong in creating new.

GOTTI: Yeah, but where, er, let me tell you, Frankie, there's creating and there's creating. Now look, Frankie. You wanna put your head with a fuckin' Sammy. You're too bright for that. *(Pause)* Di B, did he ever talk subversive to you?

LOCASCIO: Never.

GOTTI: Never talked it to Angelo, and he never talked to "Joe Piney." I took Sammy's word that he talked about me behind my back. Louie, did he ever talk to any of you guys?

LOCASCIO: No.

GOTTI: I took Sammy's word. Louie DiBono. And I sat with this guy. I saw the papers and everything. He didn't rob nothin'. You know why he's dying? He's gonna die because he refused to come in when I called. He didn't do nothing else wrong.

LOCASCIO: You have that meeting yet?

GOTTI: No. Gonna have it tomorrow.

LOCASCIO: Because at that meeting, I predict he's gonna bring you fifty.

GOTTI: But I wouldn't take nothing.

LOCASCIO: You don't think—

GOTTI: I wouldn't even take it, Frankie. I'm not a goon. I'm not a grease—

LOCASCIO: He's buying it, he's buying lunch.

GOTTI: Never take me, bring me to lunch, Frank. Frank, if it wouldn't be for the other guy I wouldn't take nothing. That I shouldn't see my kids alive. I will not take nothing. This guy can't bring me nothing. But I should take that and more, the cocksucker! I wouldn't take nothing from him. He's gonna get killed because he, he disobeyed coming. And we had no bad intentions when we first sent him his fuckin' *(inaudible)*. But where are we going? What am I doing here, Frankie? Where are we going here? Every fuckin' time we, we're parking a fuckin' company. Where's my end of these companies? These other people wanna open companies. Gonna give me a, a sixth. Gonna give me ten thousand a fuckin', every two weeks, a month, whatever the fuck it comes to. Where's my fuckin' end of these things there that my name is all over the fuckin' lot? A fuckin' hard-on like Johnny G. He's one of the reasons Genie's in jail. He's a fuckin' hard-on. *(Pause)* Go against your own cousin. Go against your own uncles. Fuck you, think you're kidding? Love nobody. Love nobody. Who do you think you're fuckin' kidding? *(Pause)* I, and I'm not gonna get myself sick,

Frankie. And he's, he's, he's creating enough *(inaudible)* these fuckin' situations. But one thing I ain't gonna be is two-faced. I'm gonna call 'em like I see 'em. That I gotta do till the day I die.

LOCASCIO: What was he telling ya? *(Inaudible)*

GOTTI: Yeah. I was gonna, I, I, I waited, a lot of people *(inaudible)* see even Johnny D'Amato knew it. You know I was gonna over it tonight. Today I would bet, I don't feel that fuckin' good *(inaudible)* it looked like it had the earmarks of a nice day and to, to get all this Christmas shit out of my system, and I go—

LOCASCIO: *(Inaudible)* names suggested.

GOTTI: Yeah, yeah. I don't know. Think, have a few names *(inaudible)* Frankie. But I don't know if I wanna do that either, no more. I don't know about this tokenism shit. What, what, where these, what did these guys ever do? Tomorrow they'll ask me to make them "captains." Ya know? What, where are we going, Frankie, here? Gotta prove whether we need them, and who deserves it. This here tokenism shit is over, Frank. I'm, I'm a *(clap sound)* I'm, I'm sick, Frankie, and I ain't got no right to be sick. I ain't got no right to be sick. I had twenty *capodecinas* with us Saturday. Ten or twelve were ours. Five or six from other "Families." I, I excused myself. I told them, "I gotta go meet a girl." I went to the hospital to see Sammy's son. I gotta get myself double sick. I came home I got caught in that fuckin' traffic. The next morning, triple sick, we're at the cemetery. Then go make other guys happy, at a *(inaudible)*. Then go to the fuckin' wake. I, I'm not going partying. I'm not going to race, popping girls. I'm not doing nothin' fuckin' selfish here, know what I mean? But I'm not gonna go every fuckin' block and hear a "beef." And I keep telling people it's my fault. "I told him to do that. I told the guy to do this. I told the guy to do that." What the fuck? Am I nuts here? If I go to jail they'd be happy! "*Minchia, (inaudible)* we finally got rid of him." Hah! They don't know, they got no new *cazzu*! [prick]. *(Pause)* I wasn't even gonna say nothing until he was here. Ya know, I wanted to have the two of youse together. But I'm, I'm getting myself sick, Frank.

LOCASCIO: Gotta get it out. You gotta get it out.

GOTTI: I, I don't—

LOCASCIO: You can't hold it.

GOTTI: —wanna get myself sick.

LOCASCIO: You can't hold it. So, tomorrow, I think it's the best thing for you—

GOTTI: These guys look, these guys look at me, these people look at me. But they, I don't even have to explain it. Anybody that don't see what's going on is a fuckin' lunatic. Is a fuckin' jerkoff. Hand job, and that's the end of it. I mean, you kidding? You wanna take these fuckin' guys that were welfare cases. People hanging around Frankie DeCicco. Welfare motherfuckin' cases! They end up *(inaudible)*. Nobody is gonna act that. Just by that. Frank—

LOCASCIO: If I could *(inaudible)* here comprehend that. I know, I know what you told me. But I can't comprehend that. Who *(inaudible)* fuck asked that he's this?

GOTTI: Oh, he's in good shape, you know that. Oh, you don't know he's in good shape? Whoever gave him the money, if Sammy gave him the money, or you gave him the money, the guy's in good shape, come on. The guy was a bum. He owed every fuckin' Tom, Dick, and Harry will you please? The guy was a bum! You, do you know the guy?

LOCASCIO: I don't know him. But you told me.

GOTTI: I know the guy intimately! For twenty years. What am I talking? Sixty-eight is what? Twenty years. I know the guy intimately twenty-one years. Do you know what "intimately" is? Used to bring the coffee to me and Frankie. *(Inaudible)* shot? That was this scumbag. So, you don't know the guy, that's what I'm saying, Frank. It's amazing how, I don't understand some people. I don't *(pause)* I got five hundred guys that *(inaudible)* none of 'em are like that.

LOCASCIO: Even me.

GOTTI: We got guys that have been hanging around, caught with *(inaudible)*. I could do that. Can't I do this here? Can I put guys in spots? Can't I fuckin' give guys, ah, these positions? And make guys rich? I never did that for one guy, and I'll never do it for one guy. This fuckin' cripple downstairs, "Jackie Nose," I give him, every week out of my pocket. Every week, Frankie. Every week he gets two thousand dollars. Where do ya think I get it? From a fuckin' mulberry bush? That "junk" business? I told him the other day, "When you, when, when are you gonna start providing for yourself?"

LOCASCIO: Start providing. Jump off with a, a reduction.

GOTTI: Do some fuckin' thing! *(Pause)* But I'm not, ah, again I'm not "beefing," Frankie. That's not the way things, and I told him, "What am I creatin' here?" Ya know, I don't create a cripple here. Ah, even these other guys, ya know, you gotta get a tongue-lashing, you'll get it. I gotta get one, I get it *(inaudible)*. Look at this fuckin' guy, too. Jesus Christ! You know what this guy told me today? This, ah, carpet guy? "*Minchia,*" he says, "ah—

LOCASCIO: *(Inaudible)*

GOTTI: —I thought I had the fuckin' contract. As soon as your name comes up, I get pushed out by our people! With, with the construction company, *(mumbles)* I, I, I, I was making all kinds of money," the guys says. "I was the biggest in the city. I made you a partner, I can't get a job!" He don't make—*Minchia*! My fuckin' nose is wide open! You fuckin' kiddin' somebody, or what? And I see it. I see it myself. I don't need him to tell me, I don't need nobody to tell me that. *(Pause)* Fuck, where ya going here? Where ya goin' here? *(Pause)*

LOCASCIO: Who's that builder Marano? Builds in the Bronx, ya says?

GOTTI: He might be, Frankie I, I, I, I lose. I know the guy, Jamie, that's aligned with us. The guy we meet today. I was waiting for you to meet him. *(Inaudible)* Who do I got prove this kind of shit. I don't, I don't know nothin' about building. I don't *(inaudible),* anything. All I want is a good sandwich. You see this sandwich here? This tuna sandwich? That's all I want—a good sandwich. *(Background noise)* I was thinking, Sammy gives me the shit. I send that fuckin' moron I got downstairs for a brother, he says, "I have the, the, the plans there." Yeah, you have the plans there. Don't you think I wasn't gonna inquire about that? Every fuckin' guy that bids the job gets the plans! How you gonna bid the job without plans? How could you bid a job without plans? Without no plans you bid a job? I didn't know that. 'Cause I told the guy. He's, he, he had the plans *(inaudible)*. He says, "John, we all got the plans. Every fuckin' company."

LOCASCIO: *(Inaudible)* company *(inaudible).*

GOTTI: What the fuck, you crazy or what?

LOCASCIO: You pay so much for the plans.

GOTTI: Yeah! You tellin', so you tellin' a *babbeo* [a dope] like me, I don't know that. How would I know about that shit, you know what I'm saying, Frankie? *(Pause)* I put him in charge of that, and even more, for the simple reason, Frankie, I think he's qualified and capable. And I love the guy. Then I don't wanna have to fuckin' watch a situation, so I put him there. If I put you there, I gotta watch you? You there to watch it for us. *(Pause)* Fuck! Make ninety billion dollars! You wanna make legitimate businesses? Make them! Give me a third of the illegitimate shit, keep the fuckin' *(inaudible).*

LOCASCIO: But ya see like *(inaudible)* you know Jimmy Brown is unique. He's unique *(inaudible)* 'cause Jimmy Brown is there. There's an older guy. And that's all he's doing.

GOTTI: That's right.

LOCASCIO: He ain't putting *(inaudible).*

GOTTI: Right, and they make a candy store out of it.

LOCASCIO: Jimmy's unique.

GOTTI: And ya make a candy store out of it.

LOCASCIO: Whatever he does, all right, comes in here.

GOTTI: And what *(inaudible).*

LOCASCIO: Should watch them. Jimmy's unique. And ya got to be nice *(inaudible).*

GOTTI: But, but, but, Frankie, you don't need *(inaudible)*. Once you got *(inaudible)* we're gonna be all right. We get rid of these fuckin' lawyers and fuckin' "rat" tapes, we're gonna be okay, Frank. We're all gonna be okay. And nobody seem to create.

LOCASCIO: Ah—

GOTTI: But you don't cripple people.

LOCASCIO: If, if I could suggest something. Why don't you try and get somebody that is qualified *(inaudible)* in construction. Make him just to handle the administrative things, you know?

GOTTI: Well, you know—

LOCASCIO: You know like ah, ah, ah—

GOTTI: —but you know what, Frankie—

LOCASCIO: —I think that would take the greed away from—

GOTTI: What happen, you know what, Frankie? That doesn't bother me. It doesn't even bother me if he had six, seven companies, companies himself. You know what I would tell him? You would be, I'll tell him, "Let me know when ya feel you're gonna choke. Keep that. *(inaudible)* you're gonna choke. But you're not doing that! You're creating a fuckin' army inside an army." You know what I'm saying, Frankie?

LOCASCIO: End up creating another faction.

GOTTI: That's right!

LOCASCIO: *(Inaudible)* you're, you're saying it mildly.

GOTTI: You know—

LOCASCIO: Another faction.

GOTTI: —what I'm saying. And you're not gonna do that! I'm not gonna allow that.

LOCASCIO: Shouldn't be.

GOTTI: He wants it, he could have fifty fucking businesses! I don't care, Frankie. If you, but I'm your brother, Frankie. You know when I hear something good about a guy, I'll probably be in jail, because I get caught on tape bragging about it. But, but, Frankie, how many times you tell me *(inaudible)*, Frankie, and Tommy Gambino we brag about his *(inaudible)*. *Minchia*! I'm proud for the guy. I don't, I don't wish the guy no bad. But, Jesus, we're, we're bragging about a guy with his money. *(Coughs) (Inaudible)* want his money? If I hear good about you, and we got no problems, I'm glad. *Minchia!* Ah, ah, I got one less Jackie to worry about, all right? But you ain't gonna create a fuckin' faction. No. That, that shit, I saw that shit here. I saw that shit and I don't need that shit.

LOCASCIO: No good. And that's what got him weak. That's what got him weak.

GOTTI: Sure. But you'll see—

LOCASCIO: The reason I don't want to lead to that.

GOTTI: You'll see that, Frankie. I mean—

LOCASCIO: "Let's get this and let's get that, and maybe we can sweeten this here, maybe we can get this here. How, how could we do? Well, we get rid of that." No good. That's no good.

GOTTI: We're making fuckin' laughingstock. We be back like other "Families." Laughingstock. *(Pause)* I called the shot. They already got that in the Colombo "crew." Now they're gettin' it in, ah, Vic and "Gas." For what? The troops can feel it.

LOCASCIO: *(Inaudible)*

GOTTI: Ya kiddin'? It's only natural, Frankie. But it shouldn't be here. It shouldn't be here. We see each other three or four times a week. It's not like the guy's in Boston, and we're in fuckin' Providence. We see each other three or four times a week. There should be nothin' that we can't fuckin' talk about quick! Over with, next problem! Ya know what I'm saying? The thing that I don't see you for three months. You got a problem up there, and I don't, I don't handle it for three or four months. *Minchia*! I'm a cocksucker. We see each other, only three days *(inaudible)*. Thursday morning, that's it. No big deal! And Sammy I meet four or five days a week. There's no, there's, there's no need for this fuckin' nonsense. And you know, there's nothing wrong with you. What are you giving these fuckin' kids? Every kid who comes on your corner are gettin' all our piece of the company jobs. These are not your fuckin' private toys. Every Teamster foreman, the guy comes from his neighborhood. Do you know that? I see that, I see that.

LOCASCIO: That's why Tuesday night is a big night.

GOTTI: Huh?

LOCASCIO: That's why Tuesday night is a big night.

GOTTI: Yeah! And that's not good, Frankie. Come on! Where are we going here? Don't you think other people see it? How many guys told me this? How many *capodecinas* tell me?

Don't I tell them? Because I don't want a fuckin'—I could even say it, that he's wrong. Will say I'm a jerkoff. So I say, "I want it that way. That's the way I do it." *(Pause)* You ask Joe Arcuri tomorrow, Thursday, if I didn't say that Sunday. "That's the way I want it. I don't wanna hear nothing." But I don't want it that way! What am I saying that's the way I want it. *(Pause)* You tell me, "I got a million irons in the fire, chief." What am I supposed to, love that? Money's—That's not me, Frankie. I never was that way, and I never will be that fuckin' way. I remember how I used to fight. I wanna hear, if we got fifty jobs, maybe three, if Frankie's got three cripples in the Bronx, give him three. Give this other guy a cripple, over there one. Give that guy two, take four! *(Coughs)* Ya got cripples to be here, *(inaudible)* to come over here on Saturday, payroll day? Who has it coming to them? *(Pause)* Ya know, I, I, I could never see that, even years ago. Any good leader stops these things. He won't let these things happen. Can't see that situation happen. Someone'll think you're a figurehead, some jerkoff *(inaudible)* and that I ain't, know what I mean, Frankie? You know, I didn't care, ah, Louie DiBono, opened up a business for him. He hates Louie, Louie hates him. Why did they go together, Frankie? *(Tapping sounds)* You know he hates, he wanted permission to shoot Louie DiBono. Louie DiBono wanted permission to get him shot. Why did they go partners, Frankie? After Nasabeak got sick. Well, if the two guys hate each other, why would you think they become partners? Greed! Both sides. I mean, ah, ah, ah, unless you can come up with a fuckin' magical word. To me it was greed on both sides. Him, he figured Louie, *(inaudible)* himself. Louie figured he's close to the top, hearing everything. Ya know, it was just a little greed. *(Mumbles)* But ya know, he was looking to fuck him, and he was gonna fuck him. *(Clap)* And just what happened now. Know what I mean? We got another fuckin' situation *(inaudible)* fuckin' *(inaudible)*. They sent me word in jail that you got ten percent. Guy never had nothin' in his life; a fuckin' jerk like me. Best I ever did was go on a few hijackings. Never had nothing in my life. Ya know *(inaudible)* they grab everything. *(Inaudible)* bucks. You're telling me, I got ten percent of a million-dollar business.

LOCASCIO: Million, million dollar's worth of business!

GOTTI: Yeah. *Minchia*!

LOCASCIO: *(Inaudible)*

GOTTI: You know what I want you to do, Frank? We gotta both buy chemotherapy with the money I got. You know, so this is what we get after two and a half fuckin' years. So, so why do you give me Arpège when you got a piece of *(inaudible)* a piece of what? A piece of what? And every time I see a kid that was a hobo, "Kid's a no-good cocksucker." You were telling me the story. He tells who with this Frankie Dap? He tells me, "This kid's a little cocksucker. I'm gonna split his head. I wish you would let me split his head." This [was] over three and a half years ago, four years ago. Frankie DeCicco [was] alive. Frankie dies, the kid hangs around with him a little bit. What a beautiful kid, the kid is. Got him the head Teamsters job. The kid drives a fuckin' Mercedes-Benz. He makes somebody to straighten him *(inaudible)* take it easy. Let's go back to your first opinion. Take it easy. You know, Frankie *(inaudible)* where are we going here? *(Pause—radio in background)* No, no, good, Frankie. No good. I know you know, and I know I know *(inaudible)* that, that, that he knows it, too. Sammy knows it.

LOCASCIO: You gotta pull him up—

GOTTI: Sammy—Frankie, if I thought different, believe me—Frank, *(inaudible)*, ya know I love the guy. Much as I love you, but I'm more—But I just gotta say what I feel, Frankie. He's my brother. And if I think he done some wrong, I'll slap him on the hand. He knows it. You know that. You know I'll pull him up a million times. But do you agree with me to, to, he's doing—

LOCASCIO: Definitely, it was wrong.

GOTTI: I mean—

LOCASCIO: There's creating, there's creating, and there's creating.

GOTTI: I'm gonna go to jail and leave him in charge! So obviously, I gotta love the guy! I gotta think he's capable. But not for things like this!

LOCASCIO: I, I think you should pull him up and I think you should take away—

GOTTI: *(Coughs)*

LOCASCIO: —*(inaudible)* business.

GOTTI: I'm gonna do that, Frankie.

LOCASCIO: Let him, let somebody else handle *(inaudible)*.

GOTTI: You know why?

LOCASCIO: —*(inaudible)* somebody else handle *(inaudible)*.

GOTTI: You know, you know what I'm gonna tell him? I swear on my mother.

LOCASCIO: I'm sure that you know somebody that, that's capable as him when it comes to business. That could handle.

GOTTI: Here's why—

LOCASCIO: Ya start thinking about it—

GOTTI: I could. Yeah, yeah, I could. You know why I didn't, Frankie? I put it all in his lap for one reason, Frankie. You know something, Frank? They used to bring me a pay *(inaudible)* times five weeks *(inaudible)* seventy-two hundred *(inaudible)*. *(Coughs)* But, Frankie, you're the underboss. You're my brother. Why I gotta see a paper, *(inaudible)* from you? *(Tap sound)* If you tell me there's two hundred thousand, there's two hundred thousand, Frankie. So, he used to bring me the paper. I told him, "I don't, er, Sam, don't bring me no paper. I don't wanna see no paper." "You know up there I hear?" "Yeah, but what happens if something happens to me? What if that happens to both of us? Look, I don't wanna see no paper." I haven't seen a paper in two years. 'Cause I didn't want to find this out. "Joe Piney" used to show me the paper. You know why I used to look at 'em? Frankie—and I love "Joe Piney." He's a fuckin' idiot. He used to go like this. This, he didn't know what the fuck he was talking about. I know that. But I figured—I didn't know what I'm talking about. He didn't know what he was talking about. So he won't know that I don't know what I'm talkin' about. *(Laughter)* Fuck this. I swear to God, Frankie, I still didn't show it. "What's this?" I used to go *(inaudible)*. "Huh, hah." *(Laughter)*

LOCASCIO: *(Inaudible)*

GOTTI: *(Coughs)*

LOCASCIO: "Hah, hah, hah, hah, all right?"

GOTTI: So like with Sam *(inaudible)* Sam, not you. "Whatever you say is there, that's what's there."

LOCASCIO: *(Inaudible)*

GOTTI: "Take what you gotta take. Sammy, if you were broke take twenty percent, if there's such a thing." There's six guys in the fuckin' city. Whether it's right or wrong, I *(inaudible)*. I would be a billionaire if I was looking to be a selfish boss. That's not me. You don't know the best part of it. A guy passed a remark just recently. I swear on my mother. "Chief, can I get ten thousand a week?" *(Inaudible)* I went up to see him. Fuckin' MCC [Metropolitan Correctional Center] third floor. "What do you think this [is] some fuckin' gang here? What do you think this is a park here? You a millionaire fifteen times over! What do you need *(inaudible)* bother ya? What are you kiddin' somebody?" Then he said, he said, "I was just kidding." "Yeah, but the guy you were kiddin' *(inaudible)* was a half a cop! I go to jail for that stuff. I don't need you to put me in jail." They don't say it, Frankie, but what I'm getting at is, I don't, I don't, I don't, if I was that other motherfucker! Everything goes on there and nothin' goes out. You know I'm taking care of the people. If you don't believe me, you take care of them! God, God fuckin' bless you! Gimme fifty percent, take the other fifty percent. Knock yourself out because I'll be getting way more than what I'm getting now. What? Bring in papers, we don't need no papers. We brothers, Frankie. We don't need none of these papers and shit—nothin' like that. We don't need none of that. We're too close for that shit. Know what I mean? But Jesus fuckin' Christ! Ya see I got that kind of fuckin' trust and put that *(inaudible)* "Cosa Nostra." We are where we belong. We're in the positions we belong in, Frankie, and, and nobody could change that. But this business thing. Ahh, it's brothers! Please. And if you robbing people on my behalf, stop. When I say "robbing," I don't mean robbing. You know, ya taking work out of other people's mouths. You wanna rob people on my behalf, stop on my behalf. You feel you gotta *(inaudible)* yours. Like you said, Frankie, guys gotta a right to be in businesses. *(Inaudible)*

LOCASCIO: As long as you're off the record. *(Inaudible)*

GOTTI: *(Inaudible)*

LOCASCIO: Not like you're gonna outsmart them.

GOTTI: *(Inaudible)* It's like you were put in charge of the gas and six months from now—

LOCASCIO: What, what, what happened?

GOTTI: Tellin' people I, I think he just told me he got thirteen or eleven thousand *(inaudible)* he's gonna come down. He wages a fuckin' battle and then he—Ya see today's paper? With that? Frank, you should read the column about the thing with that "Frankie the Bug." "Rat!" But look how he got in the paper. But, anyway, listen to me. *(Tap sound)* Ahhh, six months from now, nobody's gonna be in the gas business but you? You'll be in the gas business, Tory, ahh, Vinnie. Whoa! Wouldn't it be the same thing? Ya see how crazy that sounds? Listen up, Frank. Wouldn't it be the same thing? Think about it. Wouldn't it be almost the same? Would it be fair *(inaudible)?* That's all I try to say. And I love him. And I'm sick I'm even saying what I'm saying. And I love [him,] Frankie. I actually [had] three different appointments the other day. Three people. They think I'm *(inaudible)* around.

LOCASCIO: All *(inaudible)* Sal *(phonetic)*.

GOTTI: Yeah.

LOCASCIO: *(Inaudible)*

GOTTI: *(Inaudible)* they're all "beefs." They're all saying, *(coughs) (inaudible).*

LOCASCIO: It ain't, it ain't no "beef" because nobody *(inaudible)* what I'm telling, John, right.

GOTTI: *Minchia*! Maybe Joe Watts'll be running the whole business. But I feel like a fuckin' hard-on. 'Cause I keep saying, "That's the way I want it." I don't even know what the fuck I'm talking about.

LOCASCIO: We're the only ones that can talk *(inaudible).*

GOTTI: He had the appointment *(inaudible).*

LOCASCIO: *(Inaudible)*

GOTTI: *(Inaudible)* Listen to me.

LOCASCIO: That's it. There nobody else. No *capodecina,* nobody else.

GOTTI: Listen, listen. The guy turned around and said that I was told, "That's a 'Family' company and I'm a 'Family' company. And this is the way it's gotta be." *Minchia*! You know enough to use them terms. The guy didn't make up no terms. "This is a 'Family' company, and this is a 'Family' company." Don't you gotta feed them a little bit, too? I mean you know enough to use that terminology. You get what I'm trying to say? You get this other fuckin' *male minchiata* [lousy fuck]. I wonder when he went to the rug business, this cocksucker. *Minchia!* You giving it to a fuckin' —another guy. He can't have it. I told you this is the one I want to have it. He knew the fuck that he was a rat! I won't give five cents. I swear on my son's grave. And if I did, whose business is it but mine? But today if the best part, if the guy, he says, "Nobody's help to the guy that's in jail." You cocksucker! They got a comp, they're in the business nine years. Joe Gallo told me. What's—when was the last time me and Joe Gallo was together? Four years ago? When that half-ass got sick three years ago? The fuck are you *(inaudible)*? The business, you, you just chasing everybody out of town? *(Pause)* The fuck, I mean, ah, ah, it can't be, Frankie. *(Pause)* It's definitely not fair. It's definitely not fair. And then— *(Pause)* Probably would say, Frankie, he never *(inaudible)*. They chased him out of *(inaudible)* 'cause Danny, after all, was straightened out. Frankie DeCicco took Sammy, *(inaudible)* Danny to me. You know how I felt about him. Probably won't say he never said anything about a bomb, he called the club, big bomb. I'll pluck his fuckin' answer. But they stole from me. I let him go into *(inaudible)* hellacious thing. And, as you see, I gave him "buckwheats." Okay, you're right. Never got nothing, Frankie. Never got five cents. My birthday, they put three thousand. That's what I got from this guy. I swear on my kid, I'd rather die. I never got a fuckin' tie from this guy. I got a jumpsuit I won't even wear because it ain't ours, Frank. *(Coughs)* But why are they such archenemies? These guys were shit and stink, Johnny Gammarano and him. I never saw him without seeing the other.

LOCASCIO: Were always partners.

GOTTI: Yeah! So, now, I'm laying in bed, I said, "Could it be, this guy, who felt he had the strength in each other, would even chase his own fuckin' cousin?" You were sitting at the table that wasn't strong arm, personally get them out for a reason. Now just the effect it had. I said, "Who— Since when are you and Johnny arguing?" When did this rift come—

LOCASCIO: Not on good terms.

GOTTI: Not on good terms *(inaudible)*. "Is this what you want me to do?" I should never see my kids alive. You know, that's *(inaudible)*. You know that's, that's not what this is about. This is not what this is about. Somebody got the wrong concept, this fuckin' guy. And I don't go for it. I don't go for it. I can go for anything. I can tolerate anything. But that I ain't gonna tolerate. What the fuck are we doing here? My own fucking brother comes over to me. He's a fucking "acting *capodecina*," he comes over to me and *(inaudible)* these guys are four or five guys with me that I whacked. Who knows who half these cocks *(inaudible)* anyway. Or Georgie DeCicco, this Louie, the rest of these fuckin' guys. Whoever tried them? Whoever will try them? But mean-fuckin'-time, he comes over to me, when he's got a problem, I tell him, "Go see Sammy, go see Frankie." Tell once, fifty times.

LOCASCIO: He come today. That, you know, that he seen him the other day.

GOTTI: Who?

LOCASCIO: That Eddie!

GOTTI: They gonna hear about this crook.

LOCASCIO: So Pete come over. He's got, "This guys wants to see my brother about that Frank *(inaudible)* remember?" Says chase him! Tell him that your brother doesn't want to see him, anyway. He told ya, he called him.

GOTTI: I told him a million times, "You got anything, unless it's got to do with your mother," meaning my mother, "I don't wanna hear it. See Frankie, or see Sammy. They're always available. Don't bother me!" He could tell you if I turned a little *(inaudible).*

LOCASCIO: And after he told him, here in the back room, and they were still there talking, "Ba, ba, ba." I was gonna *(inaudible). (Pause)* Bossed them around *(inaudible).*

GOTTI: I can push *(inaudible)* because nothing—Well, tell me who? Tell me who benefited by, by, by making me a partner? And I became a piece. I got a piece of something. *(Pause)* I can't, I can name a dozen guys *(inaudible).* I don't service nobody. Absolutely nobody! Purposely don't make my brother Pete service nobody. I purposely don't. The only thing I make my brother Pete do is he picks up about ten thousand every month, or every other month the kid, from, ah *(tapping sound),* ah, ah, Carl. And he brings it to Sammy. You *(inaudible)* Frank? Or you get it *(inaudible)* so sure about Carl *(inaudible)* expose that. No! Nah, ah—I trust Carl with, ah, just about anything. Get what I mean? Because I mean if he was gonna rat, he ain't gonna wait two fuckin' years *(inaudible).* I know three years. But you understand what I'm trying to say, Frankie? If I got five hundred companies that belong to me, when you say, "Well, they belong to you—me, they don't belong to the *borgata!* Yeah. Well, when you're the 'boss!' " So, you were sure that *(inaudible)* eh, eh, Sammy is the *consigliere.* He could turn the whole fuckin' industry into a private playpen. What could I tell you to do? You know what I'm saying? And I could *(inaudible)* if I didn't know. But if I take every fifty companies, and I say, "Frank, these are what we got.

LOCASCIO: *(Coughs)*

GOTTI: "Handle the fifty companies." How bad a guy could I be? Can you see? If I never see, if I never see one, I tell you,

"Frankie, you gonna see that guy?" "Yeah?" "Tell him this, this, and this."

LOCASCIO: You know what *(inaudible)*? I gotta say it. You're telling of all the businesses that he's got, you don't get nothin? *(Inaudible)*

GOTTI: Other than that I know of. Well, let me put it this way, Frankie. I was getting *X* amount of monies, the day I became the "boss," when he had nothing to do with this. And Di B and the other guy, and I said, "Sammy, ah, ah, ya got one, ah, a lump one, these fuckin' guys." We grabbed a hundred thousand, got a, twenty thousand went to DiBono. Twenty thousand went to Bobby Sasso *(coughs) (inaudible)*. Three ways I got maybe twenty or twenty-five thousand. He took the check and I got booked out. Some kind of Chinese checker way. Now, with the money that comes in, that's my business if I wanna distribute it, Frankie. Someday I'll show you what I take out, what I give out.

LOCASCIO: No, but I'm talking about the businesses that he's creatin'.

[. . . .]

GOTTI: Frankie, well, Frankie, let me say something.

LOCASCIO: So I assume that—

GOTTI: Well, let me say something to you, Frankie, a minute. The monies didn't change. Like he said to me, like it was about ten weeks, he turned in, he turned in two ninety. He said, "I turned in two ninety." He didn't turn in two ninety. He turned in sixty-three thousand was my birthday money! Youse gave that to me as a birthday present! Am I correct, Frankie?

LOCASCIO: Right.

GOTTI: You weren't, 'cause that, is that, is that a "Cosa Nostra?" But then I'm in the wrong fuckin' businesses.

LOCASCIO: —*(inaudible)* shouldn't have *(inaudible)*.

GOTTI: Come on! *(Inaudible)*

LOCASCIO: —*(inaudible)* be, anyway!

GOTTI: Yes, well, so that's what I'm saying. So, if the figure's always been around the two bracket. The two forty like that. Unless we make it go longer and longer. But that's not what I'm getting at. I'm not *(inaudible)*—but I don't give a fuck if there's nothing there, Frankie. I don't want nobody get in trouble. Fuck the people, and that's the only way it goes! An end's an end. But what I'm—you were saying these personal businesses, and when I get told there's a thousand from this company and a thousand for me? Not to my knowledge, Frankie, best I can answer you.

LOCASCIO: All right. Well, because this tire business, and we discuss, I discussed it with him. 'Cause if ah, not, not to get into it. He says, "Out of the dollar, John gets thirty cents, I get thirty cents, and there's forty cents left."

GOTTI: Yeah but, but, Frankie, I—

LOCASCIO: What, what it's gonna come about?

GOTTI: *(Inaudible)*

LOCASCIO: *(Inaudible)* the way he's got it.

GOTTI: How did it come about—

LOCASCIO: He's got the car *(phonetic)*—

GOTTI: Ah—

LOCASCIO: The pie cut up already before we even, ah—

GOTTI: *(Coughs)*

LOCASCIO: *(Inaudible)*

GOTTI: I'm not saying the guy forgets me, Frankie. And, ya know, I won't tolerate that, anyway. I'm not saying that, Frank. This whole conversation *(inaudible)*. We know what I'm in here for.

LOCASCIO: *(Inaudible)*

GOTTI: Yeah! Remember that time? You fuckin' *(inaudible)* and I asked you, you told me that's my only livelihood this job. That was three years ago. Couldn't be *(inaudible)*. When I come out of jail. Yeah! So, okay, less than three years. In other words, you told me your only livelihood. Since then, you're in the building business, you in the carpet business, you into this business! You cocksucker! There ain't nothing you ain't into! Where'd ya get this from? Which way? Maybe you become *rappresentante*? *(inaudible)*. Where'd all these come? I mean, do, do you follow me, Frankie? And—

LOCASCIO: Maybe it was wrong for creatin' new—

GOTTI: Yeah, but you're using my fuckin' flag to conquer the fuckin' market. Who the fuck are you? You're creating all these things here. I got made guys that want this business. I got guys in these fuckin' businesses. They, they, they get nothing. *(Sound of something falling to floor)* You know that. *(Sound of something on floor)*

LOCASCIO: But that's what, it came out with this carpet—

GOTTI: Came out with everything, not only the carpet thing. C'mon. Them other kids got thrown out of three jobs for these for, for, for, for Johnny-come-lately company. And Johnny, they can't do the work that they can do. Nobody can do the work Marine does. Don't take my word for it *(inaudible).* You heard me say it. They know the guy does the best work, but they don't like Bosco! Who the fuck cares about Bosco! A guy ain't gonna take it on the chin for a million dollars because he don't like Bosco. Get the fuck outta here! Tell that to somebody else, a *babbeo* [dope] who don't know any better. You don't like Bosco! And I don't blame you, 'cause I'm not crazy about the guy. But let's not, let's not jerk each other off here, ya know what I mean? *(Pause)* But I tell ya, Frankie, for me to get sick, and I'm getting myself to the point where I got myself sick because I told him twice already, I told him, "You're there." I don't butt in. When the fuck do I butt in? This [is] like if you're in charge of something, Frankie. I don't question. *(Coughs)* It's not in my makeup. *(Coughs)* "Cosa Nostra," I wanna know everything. But these things, I don't give two fucks about. Ah, you punish a guy purposely. *Minchia!* You torture the fuckin' guy! You fuckin' hard! Your company gets every job! Everywhere you look. He's got five jobs that they can't even do *(inaudible).* They got [a] brand-new company three times bigger than you, that's my partner, he do one job! Then fuckin' we nuts altogether here or what? And I send him word, I told you, I didn't send another guy to go see Bobby Sasso. I told you to go. You're with me. You're my representative to, to, to Bobby Sasso. Tell Bobby do me a favor and to give him a job. And I'm the *rappresentante* four fuckin' years. I got no companies! The only fuckin' thing I did, I went partners with a company that I put into business five years ago, Albie Trimming, when Paul was alive. Won the permission from him to fuckin' do it. Got a fucking tongue-lashing. It's on the tape. And I just now got on the fuckin' payroll. I'm trying to keep my ass out of fuckin' jail, no other fuckin' reason. And this fuckin' Marine Construction that the guy got chastised for, for having me as a partner. The guy got chased out of the fuckin' country. He used to get five jobs a year. Now he gets none, none a month. Get the fuck outta here! *(Inaudible)* Gotta chase him *(inaudible)*.

LOCASCIO: The association *(inaudible)* got association.

GOTTI: *(Inaudible)* no, me, I got, ah, the only thing I'm on paper. I get forty thousand a year from the *(tapping sound)* plumbing *(inaudible)*. We get, ah, a thousand a week from ah, ah, *(inaudible)*—

LOCASCIO: You're down for a hundred a year.

GOTTI: Nah, that's it, Frank. *(Inaudible)* just now tax purposes eighty-five thousand. At Easter and I'll be like at a hundred twenty-five or thirty-five thousand, is good for me, Frank. I, I *(inaudible)*.

LOCASCIO: You don't—you don't spend more than that shows.

GOTTI: Ah, ah, you know, you know why, why, Frankie? Even though I never touched it *(inaudible)*, my wife gets like thirty-three thousand. So, now it reads another thirty-three on top of it. Huh?

LOCASCIO: Between you and your wife, it's another thirty-three on the top.

GOTTI: Yeah, but not only that, Frank? I don't—we don't have no, ah, mortgage or anything. The only bill, bills that we got is the fuckin' car payments. Ah, four hundred, three hundred and change.

LOCASCIO: *(Inaudible)* this.

GOTTI: Yeah, nothing, I got nothing!

LOCASCIO: That's nothing, yeah.

GOTTI: All my kids are gone. We gotta [get] outta the house.

LOCASCIO: Ya all cover—

GOTTI: Peter, me, and my wife, we pay for that Blue Cross, and, ah, and the fire insurance on the house. Nothing, believe me!

LOCASCIO: Blue Cross? You covered under Blue Cross?

GOTTI: Yeah.

LOCASCIO: Extended coverage or something?

GOTTI: Yeah, special kind of coverage, you know. God forbid *(inaudible)* nine years. But, ah, but then fire insurance on the house, stupid things. Ehh, forget about it! Couple a thousand a month, Frank.

LOCASCIO: You're well within, well within—

GOTTI: *Minchia!* If I was ever, like I saying, I can get up to, me a hundred and thirty, and that other thirty we—make a hundred and sixty a *(inaudible)* we're well within. *(Inaudible)* you want to know the truth, if they followed us. Other, other than if they get a phone conversation with Becca. They followed us. Joe Watts has got the problem, not me! That fuck, he grabs two checks. Yours and the guy under the table you know that.

(Pause. Music in background)

GOTTI: *(Inaudible)* with this cold, coughing *(inaudible)* right? *(Pause)*

LOCASCIO: I know this not the problem. *(Tap sound)*

GOTTI: Huh?

LOCASCIO: I'm thinking about this problem. And it's not a problem. It's—

GOTTI: It's not a problem. He's gotta cut it out!

LOCASCIO: Right.

GOTTI: He's gotta cut it out! And he's gotta cut it out. And he's gotta not treat these couple a guy—now you're in Louie's *decina,* who I "made" a *capodecina,* like they fuckin' special characters, and they get all these jobs that belong to the *borgata.* I mean, but, Frankie, every fuckin' Teamster foreman we got, we got nine of them, they're all from that block. Is that what this [is] all about? What, with the Teamsters came from that club? You, you, I don't know what. You follow me?

LOCASCIO: Does he ever come and say, "I got an opening?"

GOTTI: Never! But I never ask him to, Frankie. Do I, do I have to ask you to do something if I put you in charge of something?

LOCASCIO: Yeah, but if he's got an opening, he should come and—

GOTTI: Yes, Frank.

LOCASCIO: "I got an opening. You got somebody?"

GOTTI: No, never! Never once. *(Steps)* Here's what he tells me. Here's what he tells me. *(Steps)* "Gee, that Joe Brewster, he didn't do such a good job. All the Teamsters foremen told me." "All right, make John Gammarano help to you, if you want it." "Go ahead, put him there." "Gee, Jimmy Brown, all the guys in, in, in the, in the garbage, they're not happy with him, hah? Why don't you put, ah, Joe Francolino?" "Forget about it!" You know, where are we going here? *(Coughs)* And that's it, Frankie. *(Steps)* I mean, the— Like I say, I, I know this life, and I know us, and I know love—but I also have common sense. . . .

(Steps)
(Door is shut)
(Music playing)

JANUARY 4, 1990

FILE NUMBER:	183A-3507
PLACE:	Apartment above the Ravenite Social Club, located at 247 Mulberry Street in Little Italy, Manhattan
TIME:	7:15 P.M.
PARTICIPANTS:	JOHN GOTTI
	SALVATORE GRAVANO
	FRANK LOCASCIO

Getting into the Mafia is not easy. Competition is fierce and few are chosen. Standards (of a sort) are high. As Gotti, in this conversation about potential candidates for induction into America's most exclusive crime club, declares: "I want guys that done more than killing." But good men are hard to find. "Where are we gonna find them, these kinda guys?" Gotti laments. "It's gettin' tougher, not easier!" Gotti worries about the Gambino Family's future should he go to prison. He wonders whether Gravano should remain consigliere *or become official underboss or assume the position of acting boss. He frets about the government's case against him on charges of racketeering. The future of his rule is uncertain and filled with peril.*

■ ■ ■

GOTTI: All right, let me tell you what, Sam. I wanna throw a few names out, five or six. I'm not, I'm trying not to make people *(inaudible)*. I want guys that done more than killing. This Frankie Dap wants to put this "Poncho" *(inaudible)* guys downstairs. But I'm *(inaudible)* I was thinking—

GRAVANO: No *(inaudible)*.

GOTTI: —I was originally thinking of five or six guys . . . that *(inaudible)*.

GRAVANO: I forgot their names.

GOTTI: Yeah, well, I was glad what you said how you felt about *(inaudible)*— I don't care about who we choose. Your mind is where it's supposed to be. That's what I mean. But, but, ah, but, ah, I don't know with this fuckin' "Poncho." Did he ever do anything with us?

GRAVANO: I don't know.

GOTTI: Or anybody?

GRAVANO: I don't know.

GOTTI: Because you know who we got, and this guy would deserve nobody. But the guy that he was replacing *(inaudible)*, he reminded me of, of Johnny Rizzo. You know, I mean it was a shame that me or youse guys, that we know we have to do with that thing. Let me tell you a couple of things before Frank comes up.

GRAVANO: Well, here, you want me to give you the list?

GOTTI: Yeah, I'm gonna do it when Frank is here, too, and I wanna tell you just a couple *(inaudible)*. I've been kicking my brains out, Sammy, what I'm gonna do here. See the plan for them to remand me, and we'll see, and we'll talk. Just the way I call the shot, give them the *(clapping noise)* one postponement, now say can't empanel a jury, they can't prove their case. They're working towards the other case. Pinch us, and beef up bail. I see it coming. Listen, so if I have to, right to the fucking end.

GRAVANO: *(Inaudible)*

GOTTI: *(Inaudible)* I'm hung only, but I don't care. Hopefully, we got time. Tomorrow I wanna call all our "skippers" in. I'm gonna tell them: "I'm the *rappresentante* till I say different. Soon as anything happens to me, I'm off the streets, Sammy is the acting boss. He's our *consigliere*." But I got something that's bothering me, Sammy. I don't wanna start like the "Chin" did with them people, bad precedent. *(Pause)* So, I'm asking you how you feel. You wanna stay as *consigliere?* Or you want me to make you official "underboss"? "Acting boss"? How do you feel? What makes you feel better? Think about it. Think about it tonight. Let me tell you why—

GRAVANO: "Acting boss" really it's . . . it's . . .

GOTTI: That's nothing! I'm gonna tell you why. Here's what I'm talking about.

GRAVANO: *(Inaudible)*

GOTTI: You *(inaudible)* say it. Here's what I'm trying to say to you.

GRAVANO: Go ahead.

GOTTI: The "underboss" should take charge of the "Family." I'm not "breaking" "Joe Piney," by the way. I can't.

GRAVANO: No.

GOTTI: Ya, ya know what I'm saying? You don't need a *consigliere*. We'll put somebody acting there. Know what I'm saying? You're official, Sammy, and that's where it's gonna stay. I, I love Frankie, but I don't wanna *(inaudible) (tap sound)* you know that, too. There's nothing I wouldn't do for the guy. But I don't want *(inaudible)*. And I wanna tell them, if our plan backfires, and they do get me now, they can't help but *(inaudible)*. After that fucking "rat" message. Did Bruce tell ya?

GRAVANO: Yeah.

GOTTI: *(Inaudible)*

GRAVANO: Ah, you know how exactly I read that? And even with some of the bullshit things? The case against me would be a massive RICO racketeering *(inaudible)*.

GOTTI: All right, yeah.

GRAVANO: So, it's probably gonna be like Corky, only a hundred, eighty, indict, eh, counts—

GOTTI: Sammy—

GRAVANO: —of labor racketeering—

GOTTI: Sammy—

GRAVANO: —unless they got—

GOTTI: —they got more than that for you. I don't know what they got for you. But they got more than that for you. It doesn't matter, Sam. This thing here, and I'm gonna make our "skippers" understand that. *(Coughs)* "This is my wishes that if, if I'm in the fucking can, this 'Family' is gonna be run by Sammy. I'm still the 'boss.' If I get fifty years, I know what I gotta do. But when I'm in the can, Sammy's in charge." Now, or you go in the can, God forbid!

GRAVANO: I could go away, too.

GOTTI: You see what I'm saying, Sammy, we gotta fuckin' think, and, and I know what I'm talking about. If I could just get this fuckin' probation I want, you'll get bail. Who gives a fuck! Nobody comes to see ya. They'll send some jerk to see ya *(inaudible)*, like cutting bases with me. Just the fact you're out there. That you could sneak out in the middle of the night and hit a guy in the fucking head with a hatchet. You follow, understand, Sammy? I don't know what he's doing no more. All you're gonna do is, you're gonna have a, a good time, six months, then you're gonna be in the next cell to me. We ain't going nowhere the fuckin' hurry, Sammy. That's *(inaudible)*.

GRAVANO: If they ain't got me already down there *(inaudible)*.

GOTTI: No, I agree with you. But, Sammy, if they ain't got us, they'll never get us. But we feel if they ain't preparing a couple a humdinger cases for you, I'll take it up my fucking ass, Sam.

GRAVANO: Well, I, I believe they are.

GOTTI: And all—

GRAVANO: I believe they are. See last night over there? You know they followed me to my door?

GOTTI: I believe it. Let me tell you what—

GRAVANO: To my door!

GOTTI: You know why, Sammy? They're not stupid. I telegraph my voice. I couldn't help it. But it was, that's the *(inaudible)* run today. You can't do, so you *(inaudible)* today. And they know how I feel. And they know any fucking serious thing that's—that I need done that I can't do, you'll do it. They not—I'm not talking about just this. I'm talking about meeting with people *(inaudible)*. They're not stupid.

GRAVANO: Why would then not put in the ones "underboss" *(inaudible)* fuckin'—

GOTTI: No, I wanted to make it, but that's automatic, he takes over.

GRAVANO: What about Joe Piney? You would send him a message?

GOTTI: I, I would send Ja—er, Jackie to see him. Tell him, "Joey, this is nothing against you. When you come out, you'll be seventy-seven. God bless you! What are you worried about? If when you come out, and everything is okay. People are status quo. Standing here with your hands out if you want, if it makes you happy. And I hope!" Where are we going, here? You know, well, here's what I'm trying to say, Sammy. I'm trying to do this "a Cosa Nostra" way—

GRAVANO: Oh, yeah *(inaudible)*.

GOTTI: Not only that, Sammy, it's, it's, it's right. You see we got people, you know a couple of "skippers" told me right here, Christmas Eve. They says you know *(knocking on door)* . . . Frankie here. Like Sammy says, "Frankie, and then you?" No, you're official, he's not. That's the sequence you put out. And that's the old *(inaudible)* fuck. I got *(inaudible)* a favor, you *(inaudible)*.

GRAVANO: It would be my pleasure. We're all "Family." This is what Joey should tell them, God forbid.

GOTTI: You know why, Sammy? It's the right thing.

GRAVANO: Just in, in, in, in, in history itself.

GOTTI: That's right.

GRAVANO: With you.

GOTTI: Not only that, it's Sammy is the right thing, anyway.

GRAVANO: Well . . .

GOTTI: And I'm not thinking about the way you *(inaudible)*.

GRAVANO: *(Inaudible)*

GOTTI: Yeah. What's the big deal?

GRAVANO: *(Clears throat)* It would be my pleasure to be . . .

GOTTI: Come in, Frankie. Yeah.

GRAVANO: *(Inaudible)* folks from Long Island.

GOTTI: Ah, he'll love it, too, and you know why he'll love it? No, Sammy, may God forbid! Ahh—I think that *(inaudible)*. I'm just thinking, if I got a hundred years, Sammy, and you beat the case *(inaudible)*.

GRAVANO: *(Inaudible)* the door is open.

GOTTI: Yeah, come in! *(Inaudible)* it would be *(inaudible)*.

GRAVANO: I got it.

GOTTI: *Minchia*! I'd be, I'd be in my fucking glory. *(Steps in background) (Coughs)* Let's just *(inaudible)* this here.

LOCASCIO: Well, I hear you out here, "status quo" you were saying?

GOTTI: Yeah, you heard me? *(Door slams)* Either they're right, but I didn't say "status quo." I said, "I'd be the happiest guy." I didn't say "status quo." *(Footsteps)* But you could probably hear us out there. You can't help it with this thing *(inaudible)*. Only thing you can hear is the fucking coughing. You see that there when, when she says I do a lot of whispering? That tape he says they, they themselves said it's inaudible, right. I never say that anyway. Like I just wouldn't say nothin' about poppin' people. I would say everything, but not that. You know what I was telling Sammy, it looks like maybe they're not, they're not—may not even pick a jury next week. So, well, we'll come out. I'll know *(inaudible)* once. We'll probably "make" some *(inaudible)*.

GRAVANO: Right *(inaudible)*.

GOTTI: *(Inaudible)* Christ! No one knows right now, except us three. They might know pretty soon, delay it. I was just telling Sam, talking quick here because, to sign up with these fuckin' guys. We, we gonna put a little list together. You know, Frank, I just didn't wanna make it look like we're nuts. All the heat, going on trial, we don't give a fuck. We just got the list out. You know what I'm trying to say, Sam? I'm trying to make it, those were some nice messages and one or two, another important message from "Chin." One was a guy with Johnny Mash. You probably know the situation, I don't know. Something with Johnny Mash, member of the Family, or something. It's not *(inaudible)* with "Beans," he could explain it *(inaudible)* it's nothin'.

LOCASCIO: That's the one with Prisco.

GOTTI: No, this is with, ah, he's on record. Something with jewelry "beef." That's a bullshit "beef."

GRAVANO: *(Inaudible)*

GOTTI: *(Inaudible)* Yeah, a bullshit. Even told Pete. So, Pete remembers he told, *(inaudible)* right Pete remembers he did tell them?

GRAVANO: *(Inaudible)*

GOTTI: It's all aboveboard. But he's not, he's not talking to a guy with a "beef," or whether, what, what happened. He's talking with the Family members like *(inaudible)*.

GRAVANO: *(Inaudible)* bottom.

GOTTI: They're bottom of the Family, like being a nephew or a brother or whoever. A daughter.

GRAVANO: A daughter and wife.

GOTTI: We got something, but *(inaudible)* your daughter. You know what I'm trying to say? So, well be that as it may, forget about it. With the list, I was telling Sammy here, I wanna make it short and sweet, Frankie. Now, we had said, who you got on the list there?

GRAVANO: Well, I got, on the list that—the kid Richie.

GOTTI: Right.

GRAVANO: With Frankie Loc . . . Tommy . . .

GOTTI: Right.

GRAVANO: Pete . . . Tony from New Jersey—

GOTTI: Right. Fat Tony.

GRAVANO: Mike . . . ah, Johnny Rizzo with Good-Looking Jackie.

GOTTI: Yeah *(inaudible)*.

GRAVANO: Fat Dom—

GOTTI: Yeah.

GRAVANO: —with "Jackie Nose." And Mario with, ah, Louie Ricco.

GOTTI: Yeah, see, now, what I was gonna do is, I was gonna, yeah, I'm, I'm gonna say the first five, and I was gonna do that Louie and Frankie Dap, I'm gonna tell him just do me a favor. Ah, ah . . . seven, you know because it's—Frankie Dap is right. We did have that "Poncho" on the fuckin' list. I keep forgetting his fuckin' name. Three or four times that we pushed him off. So, I was gonna tell him that these two guys that just—they been treated like kings anyway *(inaudible)* and just bear with us a little while. You know what I'm trying to say?

GRAVANO: Yeah.

GOTTI: *Il pozzo* [the well]. Even if, God forbid, I go away youse'll "make" them. On Easter—

GRAVANO: *(Inaudible)*

GOTTI: —ah, we'll just "do" two guys. You see why, what I like about this? I like the Richies, the Tommies, or Dom. They're young, twenty something, thirty something. These guys like Poncho—sixty-one, sixty-two. I mean they're good, but really, eh, ya know, where the fuck are we going? You know what I'm saying, Frankie?

LOCASCIO: Yeah, if I might—

GOTTI: Go ahead.

LOCASCIO: —suggest four and three.

GOTTI: Who?

LOCASCIO: "Make" four and then in a few weeks you, you put on another three.

GOTTI: No, here's what I'm saying.

LOCASCIO: Or, or go all five and—

GOTTI: The reason why I said the five—

LOCASCIO: Four and three I'm saying 'cause—

GOTTI: Yeah, I know what you're saying. I, I . . . here's what I'm—

LOCASCIO: Instead of making it five and two.

GOTTI: Well, here's the reason why I thought we could make it five, and maybe three direct. We got the fuckin' people.

LOCASCIO: Oh, there, you got plenty.

GOTTI: See, see, ah . . . Louie Saccenti, I think the world of him. I don't know him, but I think the world, but I know of him. Sammy put him up. His judgment is as good as mine; and I said "yes," right, Sam? He told me, "I want you [to] think it over a little bit," which is beautiful. I just, I just come out with it. Remember I said that was beautiful, you thinking right, Sam, because . . .

LOCASCIO: And that's the way it came . . .

GOTTI: *(Coughs)* What did I do, Sammy?

GRAVANO: He's a good guy *(inaudible)*.

GOTTI: *(Inaudible)*

GRAVANO: I don't want this to have—

GOTTI: See, see what I wanted to do? Frankie, maybe what we could do, right after Easter. We're not bullying people. This is not the time to "make" twenty guys, but not because they don't deserve it. We got people that deserve it, I think. We got Louie. We got that Tony with Danny Marino. You know, we had—that's right, he's gotta do something, we were gonna use him. We never did use him. Ya know what I'm saying? And, and it's not right. Now, now, now I gotta tell you the fuckin' truth. Out of everything there, that list there, you got "Fat Dom." I'm the comfortablest. I'll tell you why. This kid Tommy was *(inaudible)*? Fuck him! I tell ya, they're beautiful guys, and Richie, I know where you are. But, this Dom *(whispers) (inaudible)* triple scum. I mean . . .

GRAVANO: If they're not . . .

GOTTI: What are we waiting for? You know what I'm saying?

LOCASCIO: Yeah.

GOTTI: But what I'm saying, not only that, he seems like us up *(inaudible)*.

LOCASCIO: Yeah.

GOTTI: You know? He's like giving ya another fuckin' smile, he just eats, makes his fuckin' bets and, ah, so he, he can't be *(inaudible)*.

GRAVANO: He's down when he gets the call.

GOTTI: So, he'll be good. You know, he'll be good—

LOCASCIO: That's what you want. You don't want nothing else but that.

GOTTI: I agree.

LOCASCIO: Somebody that's loyal, faithful, and he's there when you'd need him. That's it. That's it. You don't have no—a guy that makes them the money. You don't want a guy that's a bullshit artist, you don't want that. That's what you need.

GOTTI: So, what you could do is, Frankie, put them five up. We'll put those five guys up. We'll put, we'll put Mario aside. I'll explain to Bracciole. I . . .

GRAVANO: Mario *(inaudible) (steps)*.

GOTTI: Yeah, Mario *(inaudible),* you know why? And then, and then, him I'm gonna explain to Frankie Dap, too. I mean the guy, I don't want, I don't want to break the guy's fuckin' heart, but *(inaudible) (steps)*. Ah, only thing I hate, I'm sorry . . .

GRAVANO: I don't have it right, Frank. I don't have their last names. I don't have the proper spelling. I ain't got, I ain't got the, the guys all down . . .

GOTTI: But, gee, I think we can get it from, from downstairs *(inaudible)*. That Tommy's downstairs. Who do you call, ah, Rizzo, we know Johnny Rizzo.

GRAVANO: Yeah, Johnny Rizzo is Johnny Rizzo.

GOTTI: Ah . . .

LOCASCIO: Richie I know.

GOTTI: Richie you know!

GRAVANO: Tommy, Pete should know.

GOTTI: Yeah. And, ah, these are, he's, he's downstairs. So, *(inaudible)*.

GRAVANO: Tony from New Jersey I don't know.

GOTTI: Proto.

LOCASCIO: Proto.

GOTTI: Proto. I know him. And, ah, the other guy, ah, "Fat Dom," ah, Jackie knows.

GRAVANO: Joey, Joe Watts . . .

GOTTI: Yeah.

GRAVANO: He's downstairs you mean, Jackie.

GOTTI: Yeah. But, what I'm saying, Sam, ah—*(pause)* You give it to the other "Families." And you explain to them, these people—

GRAVANO: Ya know what I do? When I go back to, Benny now—

GOTTI: Yeah *(coughs)*.

GRAVANO: —with your answers—

GOTTI: *(Coughs)*

GRAVANO: I'll give him the list—

GOTTI: Then you could tell him *(inaudible)*, "I just left my friend." You know what I'm saying the, the time for this kind of thing *(inaudible)*. This is something that's been on the shelf only because we, we, we're caught up pretty good. But give 'em in a nice way. You know what to say.

GRAVANO: Yeah, yeah.

GOTTI: Ya know make him *(inaudible)* so it ain't like we jamming people up people's throats. Tell him these people "Go to the bank on." You know what this "Chin" did, ah, he sent me a message: "Fish" is going to testify against me.

LOCASCIO: Against you?

GOTTI: And he, he recommends that I get in touch with Pete Peluso. Which we knew. Pete knows, knows the whole story.

LOCASCIO: I will probably see him tonight.

GOTTI: Yeah, so if you see him, tell him he'll be hearing from me shortly because, obviously, he's aware of it, 'cause—

LOCASCIO: Why should you contact him? Why not *(inaudible)*.

GOTTI: Well, Pete, just send for him.

LOCASCIO: *(Inaudible)*

GOTTI: I mean, I'm gonna send for him. In other words, at our mutual *(inaudible)*.

GRAVANO: He says he was sent to the—if we didn't know him, he would jump right in *(inaudible)*.

GOTTI: Well, I knew, I knew him—

GRAVANO: Yeah, he says—

GOTTI: —pretty good, my *(inaudible)* I don't know him like Frankie does. But I know him from the back . . .

LOCASCIO: He comes with Dennis every Tuesday and Thursday.

GOTTI: Yeah. Good!

LOCASCIO: So, tonight, he'll probably come to the, the restaurant, and he gonna be in Joe and Nina's and then go over there.

GOTTI: You know what you could do, too, Frankie, you could touch on, "Oh, I understand that he's gonna testify . . ."

LOCASCIO: I'll, I'll hear what he's got to say.

GOTTI: All he could say against me, for one, is that he met me *(lowers voice)* as the "boss," 'cause Tony introduced him. But that's about it. I never said a word.

GRAVANO: And what they're saying they got so much shit on him that if he *(inaudible)*.

GOTTI: Yeah, but you know what, Sammy?

GRAVANO: *(Inaudible)*

GOTTI: You know why? Remember when we had the thing, ah, from him from the Crime Commission? He never said nothin' about me. Remember he says—

GRAVANO: That's not mentioned by *(inaudible)*.

GOTTI: Yeah, his ties—

GRAVANO: That you had stopped a—

GOTTI: —stopped them from abusing him, it's, it's all like you said, at my trial. I don't think that hurt me, the other stuff.

Only thing's that's gonna hurt us is with structure, Sam. He's gonna knock our fuckin' brains with the structure. He knows everything. He knows who you are, he knows who he is. At the worst, he's gonna say he's a *capodecina.* He knows them, these guys—

GRAVANO: Good. I know, I know, I know him good.

GOTTI: I'm telling you what he told me in the fuckin' can—*(lowers voice)* Louie Ricco's a *capodecina. (Tap sound)* Lou Monte a *capodecina.* He said, "Meanwhile I got a big size *(inaudible).*" "Man," he says, "that guy, he hated them." "I thought he hated everybody." That, that's all we ever talked. And I never would let on to this motherfucker just once, Sammy.

GRAVANO: *(Inaudible)*

GOTTI: I swear on my kids! I mean, he's not gonna get up and say I fucked him in the ass.

LOCASCIO: *(Inaudible)*

GOTTI: Hopefully! *(Coughs)* Frankie, how, how old is Richie?

LOCASCIO: Thirty-one, thirty.

GOTTI: But that's what I, I, I'm tellin' you. And you guys might think I'm crazy. You know we were fuckin' prisoners *(phonetic),* guys like me and you, when we caught that fuck in '57. We were babies, sixteen and seventeen. You were fifteen and fourteen. But we were fucked. But how old were you when you became a "friend," Frank?

LOCASCIO: Twenty-three.

GOTTI: Twenty-three. You got bred this way! You got, this—He got it rammed down his fuckin' throat.

GRAVANO: Think I musta been, I was only thirty-two.

GOTTI: No, but that ain't what I'm saying.

(Someone clears throat.)

GOTTI: But, Sammy, ya had to be—

(Someone clears throat.)

GOTTI: That, that woulda been at the hiatus— You might have been twenty-five, twenty-two, *(inaudible)*.

GRAVANO: *(Inaudible)*

GOTTI: You know what I'm saying?

GRAVANO: Yeah, that's all.

GOTTI: Guys like us, where was we going? They woulda killed us or made us.

GRAVANO: *(Inaudible)* Yeah, absolutely!

GOTTI: Know what I mean?

GRAVANO: Who the fuck are we kiddin'?

GOTTI: Yeah, but what I'm saying is— That's why these guys —I'm not saying nothing against these guys like, ahh . . . Christ, on, ah, this "Poncho" I asked Frankie Dap. Petie says sixty-two, or sixty-three. Frankie, ah, you know?

GRAVANO: Then *(inaudible)* you're in piss-poor condition even for that age. 'Cause that ain't even that old. Ain't like over-weight even like. *(Inaudible)* out of it. *(Inaudible)* they're out of it like.

LOCASCIO: You remember, ah, Joe Lizza, his name?

GOTTI: Oh, Christ! Jeez, we were just talking about it *(inaudible).*

GRAVANO: I'm gonna go get the list downstairs.

GOTTI: Yeah. We were just talking about it on Wednesday— *(Steps)* Ah, yesterday we were just talking about it. *(Steps)* Mikey Gout was talking about. *(Steps)* No, we *(inaudible)* ah—

LOCASCIO: Well, I ain't got *(inaudible).*

GOTTI: Yeah. *(Coughs)* Don't use Angelo's name, Frank.

LOCASCIO: I'm using '85s, John.

GOTTI: Yeah, ya know why? That's what I'm saying. Looks like we, we're doing what other people were *(inaudible)*— We'll end up getting called the way ya pick "friends."

LOCASCIO: These '85s. In other words, Sam Turone . . . he died in '84 *(inaudible).*

GOTTI: Yeah.

LOCASCIO: *(Inaudible)*

GOTTI: Frank, you mind after we leave we take a little weight get off my back. You grab Lou maybe, "Bracci . . . ?" Or do you want me to do it? Which *(inaudible)*? You explain to him, Frank. I give him my word, by May, that's right after Easter. If I'm not home, you might not be home, either. But whoever is home will do it.

LOCASCIO: All right, then, these are the names: Sam Turone . . . Sal . . . Sam Turone was with Mario. In case, you know, if there's any discrepancies. Sal D'Acquisto was with

Georgie DeCicco; John Riccobono with Georgie DeCicco; Pietro Angelo . . . I guess Tommy Gambino.

GOTTI: Yeah.

LOCASCIO: And, ah, and Gaspare Romano—

GOTTI: Yeah, make it with *(inaudible)* ya goin' back to '80—

LOCASCIO: Eighty-five.

GOTTI: For me that's plenty.
(Pause)

LOCASCIO: Let me make a good copy. And I'll give it to Sammy.

GOTTI: I think we gonna have, ah, pretty soon we gonna have a . . . if you know. Because *(steps) (inaudible) (steps)* was just tellin' Sam about that meet at Maxim's and a few other things *(steps)* very important. But just before we go now I'll talk to you. I was kicking something around with Sam, I just wanted, if we go out *(inaudible)* go over my head. And then we'll deal, we'll sit these "skippers" down. *(Pause)* Fuckin', I tell you what a fuckin' heartbreak. You know you feel like you're being raped with these fuckin' tapes.

GRAVANO: I know. I hate it. I, I listened to a couple a tapes of mine. I was sick.

GOTTI: But, Sam, you know the truth, this is the bread and butter. This—the waste of time being, and really, other than . . . we are being raped! But what the fuck are we doing wrong? Like, like Bruce heard every tape and, and Gerry, you heard what they said. Says there's a lot of structure. What am I gonna do? You don't think we commit a crime when

[we] brag about a wedding. Hey, motherfucker, what are we saying bad?

LOCASCIO: You want me to put down—

GOTTI: *(Coughs)*

LOCASCIO: —where they're from these guys, Bronx, or this and that?

GRAVANO: No.

GOTTI: Nah *(inaudible)*.

GRAVANO: They never said, because the, the best they ever did was nicknames, Frank.

GOTTI: Not only that, if Sammy, er, if they ask Sammy, he knows where the fuck they come from, anyway.

GRAVANO: Nobody else does it.

LOCASCIO: Yeah, well, I, I remember one time he remarked, "Who the fuck are these guys? Nobody ever even heard of 'em. How we going, supposed to know who they are?"

GOTTI: If he goes there's three people ain't heard of 'em, you know, if he goes, they'll never say that to us. He's been sending me messages. Did you see yesterday when Jackie whispered in my ear?

GRAVANO: Yeah.

GOTTI: And he sent that other guy over. And he says, "I just left him, himself." He said he took him for a walk. He took him in the park where he told him, "Give, tell Jackie to go himself, see my friend. Give him a big kiss, a hug. Tell him any shape or form he needs me for his trial, or anything he wants to do, or any messages he wants to send, pertaining to the 'Family' to me, I'm here a hundred percent."

GRAVANO: That's almost word for word, what you just said.

GOTTI: Yeah. But you know between me and you, Sammy, I, ya, you know I'm not a fucking jerk. Eh, he smells his "Family's" pretty shaky. And we're keeping him strong here, too *(inaudible).*

GRAVANO: Keeping John strong?

GOTTI: If we—

(Inaudible—all talking)

GRAVANO: —*(inaudible)* could topple him in three seconds fuckin' flat. You couldn't topple him in three seconds fuckin' flat? *(Inaudible)* we'd be putting our necks out there.

GOTTI: But then we, that fuckin' tables *(inaudible)* so that—

GRAVANO: I don't even think so. Even, even a few other guys.

GOTTI: Sammy, every day, for two weeks, Joe Glitz came to see me, or to catch me before you went on vacation. I purposely said I'd be here eleven, twelve o'clock. I never go there eleven, twelve o'clock, just to miss him. You know and now you want us to *(inaudible)* vacation *(inaudible).*

GRAVANO: Same thing *(inaudible)* got in there.

GOTTI: Yeah.

GRAVANO: Because and Tito *(phonetic)* says, "Well, well, you know we can get to him through Joe Glitz he got a good relationship." So, and I heard the whole thing. I know that, that they know. And they figure sending Joe Glitz there—

GOTTI: *(Inaudible)* do it.

GRAVANO: —they . . .

GOTTI: They already touched the two guys. I told you what he did. And he told me. *(Tap sound)* He says, "John, isn't he a fucking nut?" He says, "Why should I be subject to follow a nut?" And, then he said, "If he ain't a nut, he's faking it. He'll do this to stay out of jail. He'll do anything, you know, he'll put you in a Catch-22." So, I told him, "Listen, Joey, you said it, and got it off your chest, okay? That's that. Don't say it no more." You know. So, he said, "But I gotta be able to talk to you," he says. "A lot of 'friends of ours' know my relation with you. You got, but you still gotta open the door. If you people got a problem, you can come here. But this is not a problem. You don't wanna hear anything out of his bedroom, you know what I mean? I don't think nobody does." But *(inaudible)*. *(Tap sound)* What's this? *(Inaudible)*

GRAVANO: They don't do this here? They don't do this?

GOTTI: He ain't going *(inaudible)*.

GRAVANO: I know they ain't. They're, they're buzzing. In other words, he ain't doing this for his protection.

GOTTI: Remember I told you and Frankie? I says, "He's keepin' it out of the bag with that phony hope that he's gonna 'make' forty or fifty guys *(inaudible)*" sixty that time at the wedding?

LOCASCIO: And then after I come back and I told you what—

GOTTI: Yeah, he ain't good. But I mean remember, I'm talking about a wedding a couple a months ago. Remember we paid forty and then the guy told us sixty.

GRAVANO: Are you writing that out four times, Frankie?

GOTTI: *(Coughs)*

LOCASCIO: I got it twice. You want it four times?

GRAVANO: Yeah, please. But we got everybody.

LOCASCIO: Yeah, but we gotta get the other names in there.

GRAVANO: Put a note.

LOCASCIO: Well, ya need Tommy's name here. You need Tommy . . .

GOTTI: Cacciopoli. But you better get the right spelling. It's Cacciopoli.

LOCASCIO: That, that's what I mean. Tommy?

GOTTI: Cacciopoli.

LOCASCIO: Tommy and Dom. I need their names.

GOTTI: "Fat Dom," I think it should be.

GRAVANO: When we go down, when we, when we go down.

LOCASCIO: Yeah, well *(inaudible)*.

GOTTI: Hey, Sam, ah, did the rest of them respond with that guy and Gerry *(phonetic)*?

GRAVANO: No.

GOTTI: Nobody responded? The Bonanno's people, I'm saying.

GRAVANO: No, "Gas" or the Bonanno.

GOTTI: With the Bonanno people I told you what Sally told me when he came here—

GRAVANO: Gave it to you.

GOTTI: —the other day. I told him, I says, "I sent Sammy into Spero, in case he forgets, Spero forgets. Tell him, make sure he gives an answer here. Tell him, 'Listen, it's a one-shot deal so not to feel bad, nothing like that.' " He says, "We'll, we'll see Cass . . ." It was Anthony who called Spero. What does he care? He just wants to make us happy. So I took that as a yes. *(Inaudible)*

GRAVANO: If we don't fall with this thing, it will exist.

GOTTI: The way we know it will, yeah. But not the way we know it. The way we know it? It could never happen.

GRAVANO: —fall? No, it would never fall—

GOTTI: Huh?

GRAVANO: If we fall?

GOTTI: Yeah.

GRAVANO: No.

GOTTI: It'd be a—this, gangs, forget about it.

GRAVANO: Yeah. They'll never resolve things. It'll linger on. I, I, I think the chances . . .

GOTTI: No talk, we'll have no talking.

GRAVANO: I think that we'd have talking. Because the guys who are a little bit active in . . .

GOTTI: As long as we're here, there'll always be an accounting. See, when—even he recognized that this fucking—

GRAVANO: *(Inaudible)*

GOTTI: *(Inaudible)* a piece of paper that you're not sissies.

GRAVANO: All right.

LOCASCIO: There's another *(inaudible)*.

GOTTI: Sam *(inaudible)*.

LOCASCIO: *(Inaudible)*

GOTTI: *(inaudible)* paper you're not sissies.

LOCASCIO: Different handwriting here. Looks like—Right?

GRAVANO: Huh?

LOCASCIO: If their last names are totally different handwriting, then it looks like we don't know what we're doing.

GOTTI: *(Coughs)*

LOCASCIO: *(Inaudible)*

GOTTI: Yeah.

LOCASCIO: You know what I mean?

GRAVANO: Yeah.

GOTTI: He's like a fucking perfectionist, this guy; a ninny. You see, only he—

LOCASCIO: Well—

GOTTI: —would think of that.

LOCASCIO: Well—

GOTTI: You're right. You happen to be right. But only you would think of that is what I'm saying.

LOCASCIO: If you see a list and they say, "Look—

GOTTI: Yeah.

LOCASCIO: —one guy wrote this, one guy wrote that, one guy wrote the other thing."

GOTTI: Well, how about them other people? You gonna ask them who's coming and who's going. You don't wanna be disrespectful about it.

LOCASCIO: Eh, you want me to put common known—

GOTTI: No.

LOCASCIO: You know a Donny?

GOTTI: No, Sam tells this guy *(inaudible)*.

LOCASCIO: Yeah, yeah, on the bottom, they're down, they're down.

GOTTI: Yeah.

GRAVANO: They're on, they're on. The top is *(inaudible)*.

GOTTI: Fucking, I was telling, ya, you—you could feel bad, like some guys you know real good, we're in love with something, you know I use their fucking name, you replace it, but, ah *(inaudible) (background noise)*.

GRAVANO: Hold on. Tellin' ya top . . . That's it.

LOCASCIO: That's it. This one, then they'll think—

[. . . .]

GRAVANO: I hope a good guy is replacing my name. Like, you know.

LOCASCIO: Better than me.

GOTTI: Well, let me tell you something, it's pretty tough—

GRAVANO: Better than—

LOCASCIO: Better than me. Better than me. He's gotta be better than me.

GRAVANO: Equal.

GOTTI: And where are we gonna find them, these kinda guys? Frank, I'm not being a, a pessimist. It's gettin' tougher, not easier! We got everything that's any good. Look around, ask your son someday, forget who you are, what you are. Talk to your son like his age. Put yourself in his age bracket, and let him tell you what good kids in the neighborhood other than the kids that are with you. Or good kids in the neighborhood other than with him. You know what I'm trying to say? I told you a couple a weeks ago, we got the only few pockets of good kids left. Look at this fucking bum. Your father's a cop, the uncle's a cop, the mother's a pain in the ass. Well, well, somewhere along the line, we may have this, maybe. I don't know if we ain't got it. Somewhere down the line there's gonna be a foul ball or somethin'. But even if a *(inaudible)* what I'm saying, we'll, but we okay.

GRAVANO: I think they made a big blunder, *(tap sound)* without taking the brother.

GOTTI: Well, I thought they told us *(inaudible)*, the big *(inaudible)*.

GRAVANO: A matter of fact—

GOTTI: —*(coughs)* . . . didn't they say to you?

GRAVANO: —when he asked me, I'm gonna be honest with you, later on, he said, "You know the three of us *(inaudible)* tell them, a job well done. Don't say nothing where you're going! Dress proper! Da, da, da. Da, da, da."

LOCASCIO: Tell them we're gonna "make" six. They have three with them, take one at a time. And, as they come—

[. . . .]

GRAVANO: We have no resistance to this. We were wiped *(snap sound)* out. There's no—they're no threat to ya. You wipe three guys *(inaudible)*. What the fuck were they gonna do? And they—they're helpless.

GOTTI: But maybe, maybe we should wait. *(Inaudible)* one or two. *(Inaudible)* Maybe this guy just showed up. You know what I'm saying? Could it be?

GRAVANO: I, I hope so. Because I, I think it won't end. I think it won't end, especially with a "Family" like that. If they didn't get your brother, then he's bumping his father and the uncle. I'm sure, ah . . .

GOTTI: At the worst . . .

GRAVANO: Then you're gonna tell them, this is what the fuck. They buy it.

GOTTI: See, by worst, I says, I even told them, you know, "He's like our closest 'Family.' I know him like I know *(inaudible)*. Touch base with Sammy right away." He shoulda been to you, to let you know, two, one, three, no one.

GRAVANO: Soon as I picked up the paper—

GOTTI: *(Inaudible)*

GRAVANO: —most likely I think he'd connect with you. Soon as I picked up the paper, I see exactly what I had to say, look at this fucking guy. I knew he was looking. He's a good guy. But he's fucking not in that position.

GOTTI: He's a fucking mope. Here's why, Sam.

GRAVANO: He's a mope.

[. . . .]

GOTTI: What fuckin' heartaches we got. And with all the heartaches when you hear these things like "Louie Fat" *(inaudible) (tap sound)* at which we seem to be. As soon as we feel sorry for one guy, we have another guy *(inaudible)* expired. The other guy goes *(inaudible)*.

GRAVANO: Well, what are we gonna do? Let's assume they don't let, ah, Johnny Gambino out. Whoever meets *(inaudible)* will have to meet him. Really, they're all *(inaudible)*.

GOTTI: They'll, they'll let him out *(inaudible)*. We're gonna have to *(inaudible)*. Then you gonna see him and his fuckin' brothers here.

GRAVANO: His brother's *(inaudible)*.

GOTTI: Well, ya know what we do, we'll just send him word if they get in any trouble just to shoot by Louie, and, er, touch base with Louie. Because it's clear that they, they got stronger old-timers. The youngest guy is fifty-one.

LOCASCIO: They got another two, that's all they got, no?

GRAVANO: Three. Where? *(Inaudible)*

GOTTI: Three.

GRAVANO: What "friends of ours"?

GOTTI: Yeah, yeah. Three, Sam. He's got five. Him, his brother and three guys. Three other guys! The youngest guy is that guy, what's his name, Filippo, his name is? That big gray-haired guy. The guy's about a hundred and twelve. He's the youngest. I'll tell you—

GRAVANO: No, there's more than three, John. Didn't we accept the guys when we were out, when we went around with the committee, and made him a *capodecina,* and there was about five, six, seven guys there. Didn't they accept the guys—

GOTTI: Well, he told me that guy—

GRAVANO: —Paul *(inaudible)* brought in?

GOTTI: —he lost that one guy and he told me, the guy—

LOCASCIO: The guy that went to Italy?

GOTTI: Yeah. He told me he had six, he got five now. This was two weeks before Christmas. But we—you gotta check to see—

GRAVANO: *(Inaudible)*

GOTTI: —what I'm saying?

GRAVANO: *(Inaudible)* I remember, remember, remember when there was eight guys around Paul who were "friends of ours" they never came in? And he had asked. And we "made" him the *capodecina* that day he sent us over there? We "made" him the *capodecina.* We called them in? There was a whole bunch of 'em.

GOTTI: I'll tell you the fuckin' blunder we made, and I knew I was making a blunder.

GRAVANO: Remember?

GOTTI: But I did it, anyway.

LOCASCIO: *(Inaudible)*

GRAVANO: Even "Joe Butch" went. He called, didn't they decide in the little room? Then we went outside there near the table *(inaudible)*.

GOTTI: But Joe would remember, he would remember, too.

GRAVANO: "Joe Butch," he'll remember. "Joe Butch" was there.

GOTTI: You know when I knew I made a fucking mistake?

GRAVANO: There was a guy there?

GOTTI: When, when, when, when he put up his brother, and Lorenzo, I knew—

LOCASCIO: Who's Lorenzo?

GOTTI: —Lorenzo was a *(inaudible)* a real fucking man. You, you see Friday, over there, he's one of us.

GRAVANO: Yeah. And he's more Ameri—I don't know, he's more Americanized. He's fifty percent.

GOTTI: More Americanized, and I like what I hear from a lot of our "friends," young "soldiers," what I hear about the guy . . .

GRAVANO: And he's exposed to a lot of that shit. Like Stymie's son *(inaudible)*—

GOTTI: *(Coughs)* Not only that.

GRAVANO: He's exposed to a lot more people. He's not as clannish as the other guy.

GOTTI: The other—the other guy is. If he was any worth his fuckin' oats, if somebody else would've suggested straightening him out. They notice. Come on, you know that, and I know it. He's a little bit a *cacumbero* [cucumber]. *(Inaudible)* You know he's a—

GRAVANO: Yeah, John.

GOTTI: I don't wanna insult—

GRAVANO: He is. That's what he is! *(Inaudible)*

GOTTI: Lorenzo, you heard him, ah—

GRAVANO: He's a diehard.

GOTTI: "Mr. Gotti," this is when I told him, me and Frankie was there. "John is fine," I said to him. "You realize I can't *(inaudible)* fucking *(inaudible)*" you could see, but even he was proud to see us.

[. . . .]

GRAVANO: They'll get it right.

GOTTI: Fine, you know why? You see, he's one of—excuse the expression, he's "a friend of ours." Continental slime, that's what he is. And European, ah, a, not smarter than you'll ever be.

GRAVANO: I know, because of the joints. That was wrong. That's what he is.

GOTTI: Not this kid Lorenzo.

GRAVANO: No.

GOTTI: Well, breaks my fuckin' heart, this guy. See, Sammy, if for, if . . . we're not in a fuckin' fuckin' can in a year. Ten years from now, a guy like a Lorenzo, these young guys that we straightened out, they're gonna be really proud of these cocksuckers.

GRAVANO: Yeah.

GOTTI: You know why?

GRAVANO: A lot of them are gonna plug there.

GOTTI: Yeah, and the right way! And they're gonna—and they're gonna get stronger and stronger by our mistakes. Stronger and stronger, know what I mean?

GRAVANO: Yeah. No, they *(inaudible)*.

LOCASCIO: *(Inaudible)*

GRAVANO: We "made" a lot of good guys. Carmine, from "Top Tomato," he's developing nice.

GOTTI: They're all!

GRAVANO: Carmine, there's a lot of them.

GOTTI: I went there, I went to see the store the other day. He got lights. I went there day before, I went the other day. He stole that fuckin' joint. Thirty-three thousand square feet, for thirty thousand dollars *(inaudible)* a month, there on Broadway. You gotta see the fuckin' action. He fuckin' iced the guy *(inaudible)*. I gotta tell him after. There was a horse going today. I don't know how it made out, "Top Tomato" . . . in New York. Yeah, I *(inaudible)*—

GRAVANO: You got an appointment with this guy? *(Inaudible)*

GOTTI: —And I learned to keep my mouth shut. The original way, I would've paid less than open my big mouth. Ya know that, don't you?

GRAVANO: Sure.

GOTTI: All three of them. Actually four of them, with this fuckin' Pollok. I know when to keep my fuckin' mouth shut.

GRAVANO: I like *(inaudible)* three figures. I like *(inaudible)* the best.

GOTTI: *(Coughing)* Yeah, but—

GRAVANO: I hate them—

GOTTI: You know these are "rats," er, Sam. And I gotta say, they all want their money up front. And then you get four guys that want sixty-five, seventy-five thousand a piece, up front. You're talking about three hundred thousand in one month, you cocksucker. Take it easy, you motherf . . . I don't give a fuck, Frankie. But it ain't gonna end for you. This is gonna end here—

LOCASCIO: *(Inaudible)*

GOTTI: Where you guys going? Once you get hit with a fuckin' *(inaudible)*—who's on trial? Where we going here? You think I'm gonna break my "Family" for them. There! I go see J. B. I'll go in there, and I'll moon the fuckin' judge, you know what I mean? *(Snickers)* Kiss my fuckin' ass! *Minchia*! These *babania* guys. They go, they get a, a 848, one hundred fifty years. They're in there. A lawyer's living in Greenwich, Connecticut, and their family's at the mercy of [the] welfare department. Hey! You got motherfucker if you want. But that's where it ends, you cocksucker.

GRAVANO: *(Inaudible)*

GOTTI: Fuckin'—*(Pause)* And not only that. See what I told him last night? I hadda tell him where to lie. Where to look *(inaudible)*, Sammy, and not to talk about it. Because this [is] what brothers are for *(inaudible)*. I paid a hundred thirty-five thousand for their appeal. For Joe Gallo and, and "Joe Piney's" appeal, I paid thousands of dollars to Pollok. That was not for me. I paid seventeen thousand five hundred for printing. I just got hit with another twelve thousand eight hundred for pri— That's one hundred seventy *(inaudible)* printing these fuckin' minutes and [to] prepare briefs, whatever you fucking call 'em.

LOCASCIO: You can throw 'em in the fucking toilet.

GOTTI: *(Coughs)* Yeah.

LOCASCIO: That's how much good they done.

GOTTI: Yeah, right, that's right. That's one hundred seventy thousand. Then I gave him twenty-five thousand for Carneg's appeal. The only reason why I done that—*(whispers)* because away. Johnny's a wealthy kid, thank God, and he, he don't want none of my money. But he refused to pay. So there wasn't even no appeal. What, what do we do? So, I says, "What do you mean? How much is it? Gerry can tell you." He says, "Twenty-five." "Well, you got it. Pete, bring him fifteen. And then, you got ten in two weeks." He got that *(clap sound)* fuckin' twenty-five. The other guy's appealing. I'm paying John, I paid his fifty. Where the fuck are we going down here? You give these motherfuckers, and what I'm trying to say, that's what I told him last night, "I gave youse three hundred thousand in one year. Youse didn't defend me. I wasn't even mentioned in none of these fucking things. I had nothing to do with none of these fucking people. What the fuck is your 'beef'? 'Beef,' ya, ya, ya, youse, youse gonna defend me here? Before youse made a court appearance, youse got forty thousand, thirty thousand, and twenty-five thousand. That's without counting John Pollok. He's brand-new on the scene." They each need backup fuckin' lawyers. He needs that, that Schulman, that little guy. I gotta see if he's gonna get *(inaudible)* to him five thousand a week. And this guy needs Pollok. You know, you know what I'm trying to say, Sammy? I don't give a fuck who's *(inaudible)* but I gotta take the motherfucker. But where are we going here? Youse wanna laugh at us? You know what it felt like? You standing there in the hallway with me last night, and you're plucking me. How are you? Tony Lee's lawyer, but you're plucking me. I'm paying for it. You got Sammy, you got one hand in his pocket. You got both your hands in "Joe Butch's" pocket. Where does it end? Gambino Crime Family? This is the Shargel, Cutler, and whattaya call it Crime Family. You wanna go steal? You and your fuckin' mother.

GRAVANO: They wind up with the money.

GOTTI: The fuckin' you kiddin'? You know what I mean?

LOCASCIO: They're overpriced, overpaid, and, and underperformed.

GOTTI: The only thing I could say is, er, Frankie, is that I get my shit off them.

GRAVANO: I don't even know, I don't even know about underperformed. They just can't win, Frank. They just ain't got the . . .

GOTTI: Yeah, but you know why, too, they can't—

GRAVANO: They can't win.

GOTTI: —you know why they can't win, Sammy? They got no fuckin' cohesion. They got no unity. It's like us.

LOCASCIO: And they ain't got the balls to do what they supposed to do.

GOTTI: *(Inaudible)* They can't come in. Right.

LOCASCIO: They ain't got the balls with doing what they're supposed to be—

GOTTI: Don't you know why?

LOCASCIO: Go up there and holler and holler.

GOTTI: Don't you know why they ain't got the balls, too? I told them yesterday, I told them why. That's why Tommy was laughing. Ah, ask Tommy. "You don't get up and holler when you could because nothin' you couldn't do it. You can't even come to court six hours? You write a stay and you're out automatically. They got you for six hours, tops, they keep you. You don't wanna do it because, you cocksucker, you know and I know that they know that you're taking the money under the table. Every time you take a client, another one, one of us on, you're breaking the law."

GRAVANO: And . . .

GOTTI: And it's, it's a, it's a bullshit agreement. They don't fuck with youse and youse don't go all out in court, you know that. If they wanna really break Bruce Cutler's balls, what did he get paid off me. He ain't defending me three years ago. I paid tax on thirty-six thousand. What could I have paid him? *(Pause)* You follow what I'm saying? They didn't ask him, he didn't answer them. And then he sees them behind our back, "Hello, Mrs. Giacalone."

LOCASCIO: "Hi ya, Robbie."

GOTTI: Yeah, Robbie. And this is what it is. Then, and that's why— But you get a guy like Melvin Belli right now, that,

that files two million a year. He, his client's paying him with a tac, with a—

LOCASCIO: Check.

GOTTI: —check—He'd get in there and tell the judge to "Go fuck yourself!" Two times, not once! Once now, and once for your answer, you cocksucker. The judge looks, "*Minchia,* this guy's gonna come and fight. Let me give him, this fucker. We get him out of the court, and get to the next fuckin' trial." Forget it, Sam. Believe me, we *(inaudible). (Slap sound)*

GRAVANO: We got the worst of it.

GOTTI: *(Inaudible) (coughs)* here.

GRAVANO: Yeah. And we got the worst of it. Every which way.

LOCASCIO: *(Inaudible)*

GRAVANO: We got the worst ones.

GOTTI: When Johnny Carneg told me what he gave these fucking guys, in two and a half years, gave 'em a fuckin' mill. "What [the] fuck you talking about? You what?" You get pulled back two and one half, three and one half years ago. What the fuck, are youse nuts? *(Pause)* The indictment should read, then, "John Carneglia and Lawyer!" He's your fuckin' partner. And he's the senior partner. If you gave him . . .

GRAVANO: But they have a good, a good hunk of it.

GOTTI: *Minchia!*

LOCASCIO: All of it!

(Tap sound)

(Pause)

GOTTI: No good. It's no good, Sam. But more worse than that is— You, you see me talk for ten minutes in the hall? What do we talk about? Nothing. I say, "Go find out information what's going, when, when the pinch is coming, you cocksucker!" We're making you an errand boy. High-priced errand boy. Bruce, worse yet! They got a routine now, the two lawyers. "Muck" and "Fuck" I call them. When I see Bruce, "Hi, Gerry loves you," he says. "He's in your corner one hundred percent." When I see Gerry, "Hi, Bruce loves you. He's in your corner a hundred percent." "I know youse both love me!" Both fuckin' *(inaudible)*. I didn't think *(laughter)* dumb fucks you know?

GRAVANO: They keep doing it *(inaudible)*. They must really like ya.

GOTTI: Sure, Sammy. What's not to like about us? They see you and you. And you ain't kiddin' me. You duke 'em pretty good. He was hollering. He dukes them pretty good. Ahh . . . A guy like Joe Watts, I'd like to kill all the lawyers. He triple dukes them. Who the fuck we kiddin'? So they write—

GRAVANO: *(Inaudible)*

GOTTI: Why not to like 'em?

GRAVANO: Well, they hit you with the number *(inaudible)* you know, you can push 'em a little bit. But—they won't, ah . . .

GOTTI: Yeah, but, Sammy—if we didn't break them in this way, I don't mean me, and I don't mean us three here. We didn't get broken in this way. When you were a "button," we used to pay them five hundred a week. I'm talking about a tough trial, not this fuckin' shit here. "On the come if . . . See, I'm, I'm expecting a score next week." *(Laughs)*

GRAVANO: I had, I had a . . .

GOTTI: *(Inaudible) (coughs)* Cocksuckers!

LOCASCIO: *(Inaudible)*

GOTTI: I had . . .

LOCASCIO: What about the case . . .

GRAVANO: I had *(inaudible)* with the murder case. My original fee I think was, was, was we started off with twenty thousand. It was that case in Brooklyn.

GOTTI: Yeah, but see, Sammy—

GRAVANO: Double murder.

GOTTI: —Sammy, see if you only went—

GRAVANO: Twenty thousand.

GOTTI: Yeah, but see Sammy, if you win, let the guy whatever the fuck he wants *(inaudible)*.

GRAVANO: Oh, I mean, it went more than that.

GOTTI: Yeah.

GRAVANO: But, I was just saying, look at the difference in numbers.

GOTTI: Yeah. But how about a case—I'll give you a case in point, "Ernie Boy." He accused—whattaya call it now? This is ten years ago, nine years ago. Two hundred twenty-five thousand—that's under the table. That's like a million today, like a million today. Loses! Gets a million years. The guy comes back and charges him two hundred thousand for an appeal? You rat motherfucker. That's like, at today's standards, a million and a half? And the guy's got an absolute fuckin' nothing. Where's it end? Where's compassion come?

GRAVANO: Not there. Not there.

(Pause)

GOTTI: If you win the case, hey, I win the case, I know I gotta do the right thing by you. You win, I promise you fifty—you get seventy-five! You got a fuckin' bonus, fifty percent, because we're here now. Now we go up the corner, hustle a buck. Man, you, you just got me a hundred fifty years. You want me to leave my son destitute and my family destitute. What the fuck is it all about? Was it you that put me on this earth to rob and make you rich and me poor? Go fuck yourself!

[. . . .]

(Steps)
(Door closes—radio in background)

JANUARY 17, 1990

FILE NUMBER:	183A-3507
PLACE:	Apartment above the Ravenite Social Club, located at 247 Mulberry Street in Little Italy, Manhattan
TIME:	7:26 P.M.
PARTICIPANTS:	JOHN GOTTI
	SALVATORE GRAVANO
	FRANK LOCASCIO
	DANNY MARINO

The secret ceremony in which new members of the Mafia are "made" is an object of more than anthropological curiosity. For many decades, little was known of this criminal rite of passage. Members swore an oath of unquestioning loyalty and eternal silence. The penalty for betrayal was death. In this meeting, Gotti and his men gather to induct new members into the Gambino Family. It is not a matter for levity, and Gotti determines to conduct the ritual with dignity and sobriety: "I'm not in the mood for the toys or games or kidding, no time . . . This is gonna be a Cosa Nostra till I die. Be it an hour from now or be it tonight or a hundred years from now when I'm in jail. It's gonna be a Cosa Nostra."

■ ■ ■

GOTTI: What's the matter, Sam?

MARINO: Heard noise out there.

LOCASCIO: Open the door.

GOTTI: *(Inaudible)*

LOCASCIO: Open—

GOTTI: Fuckin'.

LOCASCIO: Open the door.

(Door opens.)

GOTTI: You might as well look. You might as well check it now, anything.

MARINO: Yeah, so did I.

GRAVANO: You heard it there?

(Door slammed shut, locked.)
(Steps)

LOCASCIO: Is that a radio up there? Let's put that radio on.

(Steps)

GOTTI: We got one here, Frankie.

LOCASCIO: No, no, but, ah, what I'm saying is—

GOTTI: Door *(inaudible)*.

LOCASCIO: —stand by that door and hear you talk.

(Steps)

GOTTI: Yeah.

[. . . .]

GRAVANO: Everything this year is all set. We notified everybody. Everything is done, set. There's nothing more. Just . . . told them everything, look, tie, everything.

GOTTI: Make sure that—well, I'm gonna tell them all, anyway. Make sure they don't say something. Make their—it's not like a fuckin' *stunatu* [dopey] "make."

GRAVANO: Yeah.

GOTTI: I mean, get these guys *(slap sound)*.

LOCASCIO: Is it all right if I ask them, "Is there any reason why you shouldn't be a member?"

GOTTI: Well, sure, you could ask them that. But, ah, like how, when you ask them—

LOCASCIO: Just say well, "Ya know, when Sammy opens up, ya know, we got this club and all. This and that." You know.

GOTTI: "You know why you're here?"

LOCASCIO: Yeah. "Is there any reason why you shouldn't be here?"

GOTTI: "You feel—"

LOCASCIO: "If you know of any reason that we don't know about?" Something, ya know, just to—

GOTTI: Well, if the guy's shaken up *(inaudible)*.

GRAVANO: *(Inaudible)*

GOTTI: *(Inaudible)*

GRAVANO: —reason fuck, we gotta fuck *(inaudible)*.

GOTTI: Kill him and the others down there.

GRAVANO: Right there, Bo *(laughs)*—

GOTTI: *Minchia!*

GRAVANO: *(Laughing)* He says, "Yeah, I'm a fucking agent." *(Laughs)* God forbid! *(Laughs) (inaudible)* over there, he said, *(inaudible)* we just tell ya—

GOTTI: All right, what do you wanna, you got anybody in mind you wanna *(inaudible)*?

GRAVANO: *(Inaudible)* no, no.

LOCASCIO: I'm not, I'm not squeezing *(phonetic)*, I'm not ah—

GOTTI: Trying to hold you or nothing, Frank. Because I ain't got time for games.

LOCASCIO: No, I know that.

GOTTI: I mean it in my heart. I got—

LOCASCIO: No, I, I, I'm just saying. That's a serious—

GOTTI: I'm not giving gifts away here.

GRAVANO: Yeah.

LOCASCIO: Just a serious question.

GOTTI: It's not a toy. I'm not in the mood for the toys or games or kidding, no time. I'm not in the mood for clans. I'm not in the mood for gangs, I'm not in the mood for none a that stuff there. And this is gonna be a Cosa Nostra till I die. Be it an hour from now or be it tonight or a hundred years from now when I'm in jail. It's gonna be a Cosa Nostra. This ain't gonna be a bunch of your friends are gonna be "friends of ours," a bunch of Sam's friends are gonna be "friends of ours." It's gonna be the way I say it's gonna be, and a Cosa Nostra. A Cosa Nostra! You might, because a guy's nice to you. And I'm not controlling the way you are. Just saying, you might being a guy brings you a basket, makes him a good guy. It makes him a motherfucker to me. Don't make him a good guy. It makes him a good guy when he's one [of] us and he proves he's right for us. And I'm the best judge of that, I think, right now. So, you got a reason, Frank, say it. "I love you," say it. I mean, that's not the point—ah, ah . . . This thing here, I'm not so sure the five guys that I'm putting in are the first five guys that should be going. But we're doin' it. I'm doing it because I want this thing to be proper. Ah, we got some guys that deserve it. And they'll be here forever! They won't be having the secret fuckin' parties when people won't be around. That we don't want, and that we don't need. That's for sure! I wanna see an effort. I gotta see an effort for, starting now, a Cosa Nostra. I don't need a guy who come, tell, tell me, "I feel sorry you got trouble." I don't need—I don't need that. I ain't got no trouble. I ain't got no trouble. I'm gonna be all right. They got the fuckin' trouble. And I don't mean the cops. I mean the people, the people who can make this a joke. You know what I mean? That's not a fucking joke. And I *(inaudible)* some guys. See even, even, even some guy, some of the people downstairs now. You know I know whose fuckin' stomach is rotten. And I know whose stomach ain't rotten. You think I, I could smell it. The way a dog senses when a guy has got fear in him, you know what I mean? You think I'm being a *(inaudible)* fuckin' guy's causing the "Family" trouble? So they can leave that shit where the fuck, where they found it. Like Jimmy Brown today with, ah, he thinks he "ducking." What could he duck? What reason would Danny have to tell me this fuckin' nonsense? What purpose are they serving? Jimmy knows his fucking place. I'll get in my car, we'll meet him anywhere he wants me to meet him. What is he worried, that he's gonna go to jail?

GRAVANO: That's what he's worried.

GOTTI: All right. This "grim reaper," where is he, this fuckin' bum? And get him outta the way, no?

JANUARY 24, 1990

FILE NUMBER:	183A-3507
PLACE:	Apartment above the Ravenite Social Club, located at 247 Mulberry Street in Little Italy, Manhattan
TIME:	7:41 P.M.
PARTICIPANTS:	JOHN GOTTI
	SALVATORE GRAVANO
	FRANK LOCASCIO
	JOHN D'AMATO

Government surveillance makes Mob business hard to conduct. Wiretaps and bugs force the Mafia to virtually speak in tongues. But euphemism and code only go so far. The desire to speak plainly is often overwhelming. The problem of loose lips begins to obsess Gotti. In this conversation, Gotti confesses that he is a prime offender. He admits his naïveté, acknowledging that "This [is] how we get in trouble—we talk." And yet, just minutes later, he boasts that he will "whack" anyone who dares to oppose his regime.

■ ■ ■

[. . . .]

GOTTI: And from now on, I'm telling you if a guy just so mentions "La," or if he wants to say, "La, la, la, la." He just says "La," the guy, I'm gonna strangle the cocksucker. You know what I mean? He don't have to say, "Cosa Nostra," just "La," and they go. No, you know why *(inaudible)*. Look, I heard other people's—I heard nine months of tapes of my life. Gambling, I put the guy's head up his mother's cunt, and I'll kill him about this, *(inaudible)* all that shit. It, er, once in a while you heard "a nice fellow," something like that. It bothered me, but it didn't bother me. This actually is fucking bothering me today. I was actually sick and I don't wanna get sick. Not sick for me—sick for this "thing of ours." Sick for that—how, how naive we were five years ago. This was '85. This is fuckin' April '85, ah, up until, ah, till May of '86. And, I'm, I'm sick that we were so fucking naive. Me number one!

D'AMATO: Well, if it makes you feel any better, there was a Vito in this "thing of ours." *(Lowers voice) (Inaudible)*

GOTTI: *(Inaudible)*

D'AMATO: That makes—and that's the truth. That's not just we're buddies.

GOTTI: John, after make me feeling—

D'AMATO: *(Inaudible)*

GOTTI: Johnny, Johnny—

D'AMATO: *(Inaudible)* you doing great!

GOTTI: Yeah, but let me give ya an example. I'm telling Angelo, "Hey, you gotta do me a favor," I tell him. "Don't make nobody come in. Don't make nobody talk. This [is] how we get in trouble—we talk. You don't have to be in this club." I'm talking about Mike or Jose now *(clap sound),* naturally. *(Coughs)* He says, "I know." We just got through talking, me, Frankie, and "Joe Butch." What we're gonna do is, we're gonna insulate all the disputes from all the guys. We get all the "skippers." The, the main "skippers." Then I grab, ah, Jimmy Brown, grab "Frankie Loc," grab Sam, grab this guy, Lou *(inaudible)* and they say—right in the mike—and I'm telling, "Don't forget! Don't let them bother Joe . . . er, Frank DeCicco, either. That means the 'underboss.'" Hey! *(Inaudible)* bother me about. We doing right here, right now. One-two-three, we end it. *(Inaudible)* in here. *(Inaudible)* go work next week. But I'm telling you, I'm sort of more guilty than any of you are simply because, I'm telling you, I know better. "Get the fuck out!" I'm supposed to tell them. "I wanna talk to you." Two blocks up I'm talking to you. Six blocks around I'll talk *(inaudible) (coughs)*. And this was as much as a couple of months ago.

[. . . .]

GRAVANO: Johnny Gambino— *(Clears throat)* Mr. Gambino, what happened, he's now, Tommy grabs me when he walks in. So he says, "I got a message." "From who?" "Johnny Gambino." He says, "They understand that you were reaching out for him. He's almost under, like, a house arrest," he says. "I got in touch with him. He'd like to make an appointment. If youse wanna see him, in the lawyer's office." So, I says, "Well, Joey was looking to make the arrangements with his son." Says, "I know." Whatever which way you wanna do it *(inaudible)* which way I wanna do it. When he comes, I'll, I'll see what, what you want him. You want me to meet him in the lawyer's office, I'll meet him Wednesday.

GOTTI: *(Clears throat)*

GRAVANO: I don't know what position, you know, how you felt, ya know?

GOTTI: No, I'm willing to sit. But when I hear, I heard it again today—

GRAVANO: *(Clears throat)*

GOTTI: I heard this guy that's ratting over there is a "friend" from over there. He was the "mixologist." He's a "friend." They just "turned" another guy, another "friend" ratted. Two "friends of ours," from over there. An old-timer and the guy about our age, he's like, he's a forty-seven bracket, and an old-timer. I don't know what they mean, er, by an "old-timer." They're bringing the both of them over here. And they got depositions and/or tapes. They got a video surveillance caught with "a *minchia.*" *(Lowers voice) (Inaudible)* over here in the corner and he's *(inaudible).*

(Tap sound)

GRAVANO: Not only that—

GOTTI: *(Coughs)*

GRAVANO: —I understand we have a forewarning when they hear you. Some fucking thing in Italy. Your people . . . Italian people. That's gonna come out. They got "friends" are in Italy, and here, back and forth.

GOTTI: Ya know, ya know what we gotta do—

GRAVANO: I wouldn't be surprised if this fucking kid—

GOTTI: —but if true . . . if it's him—

GRAVANO: He's gotta—

GOTTI: —the liaison, the liaison guy's getting "whacked." Because—

GRAVANO: *(Clears throat)*

GOTTI: —that's not, that don't belong to us. That's their fucking "crew." And he's gotta get "whacked"! Because he's getting the same, for the same reason that "Jelly Belly's" getting it. You wanna, you wanna challenge the "administration"? Well, we'll, you will meet the challenge. And you're "going," you motherfucker!

The Testimony of Salvatore Gravano

A Note to the Reader

John Gotti and Frank Locascio went on trial in the United States District Court for the Eastern District of New York on January 21, 1992. They were charged with running the Gambino Family, New York's most notorious crime clan. Gotti, said the government, was the boss; Locascio was his devoted advisor. In addition to charges of labor racketeering and tax evasion, Gotti and Locascio were accused of several murders, including the shooting deaths of former Gambino boss Paul Castellano and Tommy Bilotti, his bodyguard.

The prosecution's star witness was Salvatore (Sammy the Bull) Gravano, Gotti's underboss and close friend. Along with Gotti and Locascio, Gravano was arrested in December 1990 and charged with many of the same crimes. Ten weeks before the trial began, however, Gravano became a witness for the government—and the most important American Mob defector since Joseph Valachi testified before the Senate in the early 1960s. Gravano agreed to plead guilty to a single count of racketeering with a maximum twenty-year sentence in exchange for the government dropping all the other charges against him. He had faced a maximum sentence of imprisonment for life without parole. Gravano spent nine days on the stand answering questions from John Gleeson, the assistant United States attorney, and enduring cross-examination from Albert Krieger, representing Gotti, and Anthony Cardinale and John Mitchell, representing Locascio. Gravano's testimony, frequently startling in its brutal candor, was delivered with a deadpan demeanor.

The testimony reprinted here (as well as the cross-examination) has been edited for reasons of space. Excised material is indicated by the use of four dots enclosed by brackets. All subtitles are provided by the publisher and are not part of the original trial transcript.

DIRECT EXAMINATION: JOHN GLEESON, ASSISTANT U.S. ATTORNEY

Salvatore Gravano, called as a witness, having been first duly sworn, was examined and testified as follows.

■ ■ ■

THE CLERK: Please give your name.

GRAVANO: Salvatore Gravano.

GLEESON: May I begin, Your Honor?

GLEESON: Do you have a nickname?

GRAVANO: Excuse me?

GLEESON: Do they call you Salvatore?

GRAVANO: Sammy.

GLEESON: Mr. Gravano, do what you can to keep your voice up, okay? That microphone is not on. Would you do that, please?

GRAVANO: Sure.

GLEESON: How old are you?

GRAVANO: Forty-six.

GLEESON: Are you married?

GRAVANO: Yes.

GLEESON: How long?

GRAVANO: Twenty-one years.

GLEESON: Do you have children?

GRAVANO: Yes.

GLEESON: How many?

GRAVANO: Two.

GLEESON: How old are they?

GRAVANO: Nineteen and a half and sixteen and a half.

GLEESON: Where does your family live?

GRAVANO: In Staten Island.

GLEESON: Where were you born?

GRAVANO: In Brooklyn.

GLEESON: Where were you raised?

GRAVANO: In Brooklyn.

GLEESON: Do you have any brothers or sisters yourself?

GRAVANO: Two sisters.

GLEESON: Are they older than you or younger than you?

GRAVANO: Older.

GLEESON: How much education do you have?

GRAVANO: Eighth grade.

GLEESON: Did you drop out of school then?

GRAVANO: Yes.

GLEESON: How old were you when you stopped going to school?

GRAVANO: Sixteen.

GLEESON: What year were you born?

GRAVANO: 1945.

GLEESON: You dropped out of school when you were sixteen, correct?

GRAVANO: Yes.

GLEESON: That would be approximately 1961, fair to say?

GRAVANO: Yes.

GLEESON: Were you ever in the military?

GRAVANO: Yes.

GLEESON: What branch?

GRAVANO: The Army.

GLEESON: Did you enlist or were you drafted?

GRAVANO: I was drafted.

GLEESON: When did you go in the Army?

GRAVANO: 1964 to 1966.

GLEESON: What type of discharge did you have from the Army?

GRAVANO: Honorable discharge.

GLEESON: Mr. Gravano, between 1961 and 1964, '61 you left school, correct?

GRAVANO: Yes.

GLEESON: '64 you went in the Army?

GRAVANO: Yes.

GLEESON: During that period, what did you do?

GRAVANO: I worked on and off, I hung out.

GROWING UP CRIMINAL

GLEESON: Did you commit any crimes during that period?

GRAVANO: Yes.

GLEESON: More than one?

GRAVANO: Yes.

GLEESON: What types of crimes did you commit?

GRAVANO: Armed robbery. Burglary.

GLEESON: Okay. Armed robberies, you used a gun?

GRAVANO: Yes.

GLEESON: You robbed people?

GRAVANO: Yes.

GLEESON: Did you commit crimes with other people?

GRAVANO: Yes, I did.

GLEESON: After you were discharged from the military in 1966, where did you go?

GRAVANO: Back to Brooklyn.

GLEESON: What did you do then?

GRAVANO: The same thing, on and off I did some work and I went back to the life of crime.

GLEESON: Did you continue that life of crime?

GRAVANO: Yes.

GLEESON: What neighborhood in Brooklyn did you grow up in?

GRAVANO: Bensonhurst.

GLEESON: As you were growing up, did you meet people who were involved in organized crime?

GRAVANO: Yes.

GLEESON: Did you associate with them over the years?

GRAVANO: Yes, I did.

[. . . .]

GLEESON: You said you were the underboss of the Gambino Family when you were arrested in December of 1990, correct?

GRAVANO: Yes.

GLEESON: When you left the MCC [Metropolitan Correctional Center] in November of 1991, what position did you hold?

GRAVANO: I was the underboss.

GLEESON: Have you ever heard the term "administration"?

GRAVANO: Yes.

GLEESON: To you what does that mean?

GRAVANO: There is the boss, the underboss, and the *consigliere,* it's the higher up in the family. The administration.

GLEESON: Were you part of the administration of the Gambino Family in November of 1991?

GRAVANO: Yes.

GLEESON: Who was the rest of the administration?

GRAVANO: John was the boss, I was the underboss, and Frank —and Joe Piney was the *consigliere,* Frankie was acting *consigliere.*

GLEESON: Fair to say when you you say "John," you are referring to John Gotti?

GRAVANO: Yes.

GLEESON: And Frankie is Frank Locascio?

GRAVANO: Yes.

GLEESON: And in November of 1991, where was Joe Piney?

GRAVANO: He was in jail.

GLEESON: Did you know his last name?

GRAVANO: Armone.

GLEESON: What's below the administration?

GRAVANO: Captains.

GLEESON: Were there captains in the Gambino Family in November of 1991?

GRAVANO: Yes.

GLEESON: During your debriefings, have you had an opportunity to tell the people who have debriefed you who those captains were?

GRAVANO: Yes.

GLEESON: Before coming into court today to testify, were you shown a chart depicting the names and photographs of the administration and those captains?

GRAVANO: Yes.

GLEESON: Was it accurate?

GRAVANO: Yes.

GLEESON: Mr. Gravano, together with the defendants and with the captains on that chart, did you help run the Gambino Family?

GRAVANO: Yes.

GLEESON: Let's go back in time, if we can. When you came home from the service in 1966, where did you go?

GRAVANO: Bensonhurst, Brooklyn.

GLEESON: You testified already that then you began basically a life of crime, correct?

GRAVANO: Yes.

GLEESON: Did you have any jobs during that period beginning in 1966?

GRAVANO: Did I have any jobs?

GLEESON: Yes. Any jobs other than committing crimes?

GRAVANO: Yes. I was in the construction field.

GLEESON: Was there a particular person who got you involved in the construction field?

GRAVANO: I worked on and off with my brother-in-law Eddie.

GLEESON: How is he your brother-in-law, Eddie?

GRAVANO: Married to my sister.

GLEESON: What's his last name?

GRAVANO: Garafolo.

GLEESON: Did there came a point in time when he became a made member of the Gambino Family?

GRAVANO: Yes.

GLEESON: Have you ever heard the expression, Mr. Gravano, "to be with somebody"?

GRAVANO: Yes.

GLEESON: What does that expression mean to you?

GRAVANO: When you are with somebody, you are with a made person of an organized crime family and just with them, you're under their umbrella, under their protection.

GLEESON: Did there come a point when you became with somebody in an organized crime family?

GRAVANO: Yes.

GLEESON: When was that?

GRAVANO: In '68.

[. . . .]

GLEESON: Okay. In that two-year period between when you got home from the Army and '68 when you were with Shorty Spero, what did you do for a living?

GRAVANO: The same thing. I worked on and off. I committed —committing crimes.

GLEESON: Did you commit lots of crimes?

GRAVANO: I guess so.

GLEESON: Well, what is your recollection?

GRAVANO: Yes.

GLEESON: Okay. Did you use guns?

GRAVANO: Yes.

GLEESON: Did you commit armed robberies?

GRAVANO: Yes, I did.

GLEESON: Were there people you committed crimes with regularly during that period?

GRAVANO: Yes.

GLEESON: Mr. Gravano, were there people who you committed crimes with regularly for long periods of time?

GRAVANO: Yes.

[. . . .]

GLEESON: Can you tell us what types of crimes you committed to make money during that period?

GRAVANO: The same thing, armed robberies, burglaries, shylocking. I had a club. I ran a game.

GLEESON: What kind of game?

GRAVANO: Card game.

GLEESON: A gambling game?

GRAVANO: Gambling.

GLEESON: Okay. You mentioned armed robberies, correct?

GRAVANO: Yes.

GLEESON: Did you commit those alone or with other people?

GRAVANO: With other people.

GLEESON: I think you mentioned shylocking?

GRAVANO: Yes.

GLEESON: Is that criminal activity?

GRAVANO: Yes.

GLEESON: Have you been engaged in that for a long period of time?

GRAVANO: Yes.

GLEESON: Basically your whole adult life?

GRAVANO: Yes.

GLEESON: Can you tell the jury what it is?

GRAVANO: It is just lending somebody money out at a very high interest rate.

GLEESON: And did you make those loans?

GRAVANO: Yes, I did.

GLEESON: Okay. In those circumstances, when you made those loans, Mr. Gravano, did the people you lent the money to, as far as you knew, were they under the impression that if they didn't pay the money back they might have some physical problems?

GRAVANO: Yes, I would imagine so.

GLEESON: Did you deliberately create that impression on their part?

GRAVANO: Yes.

[. . . .]

GLEESON: You said you were with Shorty [Spero of the Colombo Family] for four years, correct?

GRAVANO: Yes.

GLEESON: What happened at the end of those four years?

GRAVANO: I had a dispute with Shorty's brother and I had a meeting with Toddo from the Gambino Family, with Shorty and Alley Boy Persico, and I was released and put into the Gambino Family.

GLEESON: You had a dispute with Shorty Spero's brother?

GRAVANO: Yes.

GLEESON: You mentioned the name Toddo. Who is Toddo?

GRAVANO: Toddo was captain in the—in the Gambino Family.

[. . . .]

GLEESON: You mentioned a term that you were "released." Am I correct?

GRAVANO: Yes.

GLEESON: What does that mean?

GRAVANO: When I was on record with the Colombo Family, they had to do it formally, release me. There was a "beef" and there was an argument. They sat down. They formally released me to Toddo. Toddo intervened and talked for me.

GLEESON: I'm sorry? Toddo what?

GRAVANO: Intervened in the problem and talked for me.

GLEESON: You used the term a minute ago, you were "on record" with the Colombo Family. What does that mean?

GRAVANO: It means when you are with somebody, you are on record. It's the same thing.

GLEESON: Okay. Does that give you any advantage if you happen to be with somebody?

GRAVANO: It gives you that umbrella, yes.

GLEESON: Okay. Did you just give us—briefly, what does the umbrella mean?

GRAVANO: If I had a card game or a disco or a club, no other Family or made member or anybody could move in on it. I had the protection of who you were with.

GLEESON: And did you go from being with Shorty Spero to being with Toddo?

GRAVANO: Yes . . .

GLEESON: After you switched to the Gambino Family in approximately 1972, did you continue to commit crimes?

GRAVANO: Yes, I did.

GLEESON: What types of crimes?

GRAVANO: Murder, shylocking, construction—I was in the construction industry. I moved with unions.

GLEESON: Wide variety of crimes?

GRAVANO: Yes.

GLEESON: Did you commit them with other people in Toddo's crew?

GRAVANO: Yes.

GLEESON: Did you commit them with people who were associated with other crews in the Gambino Family?

GRAVANO: Yes.

GLEESON: Did you commit crimes with people who were associated with other crime Families?

GRAVANO: Yes.

GLEESON: During that period, after you switched to Toddo's crew, did you share the proceeds of your crimes with anyone?

GRAVANO: Yes.

GLEESON: With whom?

GRAVANO: With Toddo.

[. . . .]

GLEESON: Now, did there come a point when you became a made member of the Gambino Family?

GRAVANO: Yes.

GLEESON: When was that?

GRAVANO: '76. In '76.

[. . . .]

GLEESON: At that point, who was the boss of the Gambino Family?

GRAVANO: Paul.

GLEESON: What was Paul's last name?

GRAVANO: Castellano.

GLEESON: Was he related in anyway to Carlo Gambino?

GRAVANO: He was his brother-in-law.

GLEESON: At that point, when you got made in 1976, who was the underboss and who was the *consigliere?*

GRAVANO: Neil [Dellacroce] was the underboss and Joe Gallo was the *consigliere.*

GLEESON: So the only change was that there was a different boss, correct?

GRAVANO: Yes.

GLEESON: Back before Carlo Gambino was replaced by Paul Castellano, what position did Castellano have?

GRAVANO: He was a captain in the Family.

GLEESON: Where were you made?

GRAVANO: In Brooklyn.

GLEESON: How was it arranged?

GRAVANO: Toddo told us we're having an appointment, to come by the club, come by dressed up. I went by his club. I got in the car with his son.

GLEESON: Was his son dressed up, too?

GRAVANO: Yes.

GLEESON: What was his son's name?

GRAVANO: Charlie Boy. And we drove to somebody's house, Frankie Wop's house.

GLEESON: Did you know Frankie Wop?

GRAVANO: No.

GLEESON: Was he associated with the Gambino Family?

GRAVANO: Yes.

GLEESON: How?

GRAVANO: He was a made member.

GLEESON: Had you ever been to his house before?

GRAVANO: No.

GLEESON: Have you ever been there since?

GRAVANO: No.

GLEESON: What happened when you got there?

GRAVANO: We went there. There was a few other people with suits. They told me to wait upstairs.

Toddo went downstairs, and they would send for us one by one.

GLEESON: The few other people in suits, did you know who they were?

GRAVANO: I recognized some of them.

GLEESON: You had seen some of them before?

GRAVANO: Yes.

GLEESON: Did there come a point when you were asked to go downstairs?

GRAVANO: Yes.

GLEESON: Did you go down alone or with someone else?

GRAVANO: I went down alone.

GLEESON: What did you see when you got down there?

GRAVANO: There was a table with a bunch of guys sitting around.

There was Paul, and on one side of him was Neil, and on the other side was Joe Gallo, a couple of captains, and some other guys who just went down before me, were sitting there and there was a chair next to Paul.

They told me to sit down next to Paul.

GLEESON: Let me interrupt you. Throw your voice a little bit so all of the jurors can hear you, okay, Mr. Gravano? Did you sit down next to Paul?

GRAVANO: Yes, I did.

GLEESON: What happened then?

GRAVANO: He asked me if I knew what I was doing there. I told him no. He asked me to look around, if I knew everybody that was sitting down at the table. I told him I knew them. He told me that this was a society, and he was about to induct me as a made member in the Gambino Family.

GLEESON: By the way, when he said to you—what was the first thing he said to you?

GRAVANO: He asked me if I knew what I was doing.

GLEESON: Did you know what you were doing there?

GRAVANO: Basically, I knew.

GLEESON: What was your answer?

GRAVANO: No.

GLEESON: Did there come a point later in time when you, yourself, conducted this type of ceremony?

GRAVANO: Yes.

GLEESON: Is that the first question that's asked at such a ceremony?

GRAVANO: Yes.

GLEESON: I interrupted you. What else happened when he was asking you these questions?

GRAVANO: He asked me if I liked everybody there. I told him yes. He asked me a few questions. One of the last questions he asked me was would I kill, if he asked me to. I told him yes.

He told me what was my trigger finger. I pointed to my trigger finger. He pinched it, blood came out. He put it on the saint, and started to burn the saint and my hand. He said, honor the oath. He said, to me, that if I divulge any of the secrets of this organization, that my soul should burn like the saint.

I kissed him on both cheeks. I kissed everybody. I went around the table and kissed everybody. I sat down. They got up. They locked hands. They unlocked hands. They made me get in the middle of it.

They locked hands again, and told me, at that point, I was part of the brotherhood. I was a made member and I belonged.

GLEESON: Let me back up a little bit. He said—what's the saint? What did the saint look like?

GRAVANO: Just a little piece of paper with a saint on it.

GLEESON: And who set fire to the saint?

GRAVANO: One of the guys standing there. I don't remember who.

GLEESON: What was the oath that you were asked to give?

GRAVANO: That if I divulge any of the secrets of this secret society, that my soul should burn like this saint.

GLEESON: Mr. Gravano, is it fair to say that you're violating that oath by your cooperating with the government?

GRAVANO: Yes.

GLEESON: After the ceremony was over, what happened?

GRAVANO: I went and sat at the table, and they called out another guy and we did the same exact thing with another guy.

GLEESON: Were you told of any rules of the society at the time you were made?

GRAVANO: Yes.

GLEESON: What were you told?

RULES OF THE GAME

GRAVANO: That we weren't allowed to deal junk, we weren't allowed to kill with bombs, we weren't allowed to violate one another's wives or kids, we weren't allowed to raise our hands to one another, and they skipped by a few other rules. They told us that you would be placed with a captain, and you'll eventually be told all the rules.

GLEESON: I am sorry, you'll eventually be told what?

GRAVANO: All of the rules and regulations.

GLEESON: Were you told anything about the administration of the Gambino Family?

GRAVANO: We were told who the boss was, who the underboss was, who the *consigliere* was, who the captains were who were there. We were told there was other families, who the administration was, who the bosses were, who the underbosses were, who the *consiglieres* were, we were told there was a commission.

GLEESON: What's a commission?

GRAVANO: A commission is the five families in New York, the boss of every Family is a commission.

[. . . .]

GLEESON: Mr. Gravano, were you told anything, when you were made, about introductions?

GRAVANO: Yes. We were told how to introduce one another.

GLEESON: What do you mean by that, how to introduce one another?

GRAVANO: When you introduce one made member to another made member, you say he's a friend of ours or *amico nostro*. If the guy is not a made member, you introduce him as a friend of mine.

GLEESON: You mentioned that one of the rules you were told when you were made was there's no dealing in junk. Is that the term you used?

GRAVANO: Yes.

GLEESON: What does that mean?

GRAVANO: No drugs.

GLEESON: Was there a penalty for that rule?

GRAVANO: Death penalty.

GLEESON: In 1990, at the time you were arrested, you mentioned that your role was underboss, correct?

GRAVANO: Yes.

GLEESON: Did you have—what was your role as underboss? What did you do?

GRAVANO: First of all, I ran the construction industry and I helped John run the Family. I spoke with some of the captains and took care of some of the problems in the Family.

GLEESON: When you spoke to the captains, did you talk about their criminal activity?

GRAVANO: Some of them.

GLEESON: Did you discuss their criminal activity with the other members of the administration?

GRAVANO: Yes.

GLEESON: As a result of that, did you become familiar with the criminal activity of the various crews in the Family?

GRAVANO: Yes.

GLEESON: Were any of the crews involved in dealing narcotics?

GRAVANO: Not with any kind of okay.

GLEESON: They didn't have an okay to do it, correct?

GRAVANO: No.

GLEESON: Some of them were involved in it, nevertheless?

GRAVANO: We assumed so.

GLEESON: Was it overlooked?

GRAVANO: Yes.

[. . . .]

MEETING JOHN GOTTI

GLEESON: Do you recall when you first met John Gotti?

GRAVANO: I met John about a year later.

GLEESON: When you were introduced to him, were you introduced as a friend of ours?

GRAVANO: No.

GLEESON: How were you introduced to him?

GRAVANO: John had just gotten out of jail. I met him in an after-hours club. Frankie DeCicco and Frankie DeCicco's father introduced me to him and told me he's a good guy, he just come out of the can, he's up and coming, and he wants me to meet him, and I met him.

GLEESON: And you met him?

GRAVANO: Yes.

GLEESON: From time to time after that, did you see him?

GRAVANO: Yes.

GLEESON: Did there come a point when John Gotti got made?

GRAVANO: Yes.

GLEESON: Was it long after you first met him?

GRAVANO: No.

GLEESON: Whose crew was he in?

GRAVANO: He was in Charley Wagons's crew.

GLEESON: Charley Wagons?

GRAVANO: Yes.

GLEESON: Did he have a brother?

GRAVANO: Danny.

GLEESON: Was he also in that crew, Danny Wagons?

GRAVANO: I believe so.

GLEESON: Do you know whether Wagons was a nickname or real name?

GRAVANO: It was a nickname.

GLEESON: Where was that crew? Where did that crew spend most of its time?

GRAVANO: Queens.

GLEESON: From time to time after you met him, where would you see John Gotti?

GRAVANO: Weddings, funerals, sometimes in the neighborhood.

GLEESON: When you say the neighborhood, which neighborhood are you referring to?

GRAVANO: Brooklyn, Manhattan.

GLEESON: What was down in Manhattan?

GRAVANO: Sometimes a crap game. I was with Frankie DeCicco, and sometimes I would bump into him at a crap game.

GLEESON: Were there particular people you saw him with regularly?

GRAVANO: Yes.

GLEESON: Who?

GRAVANO: Angelo [Ruggiero], his brother Gene.

GLEESON: Do you recall when you met "Frankie Loc"?

GRAVANO: I don't recall the exact day. I met him after I met John, I believe.

GLEESON: Were you introduced to him as a friend?

GRAVANO: Yes.

GLEESON: At the time you met him, what position did he have in the Family?

GRAVANO: He was a made member.

GLEESON: What crew was he in?

GRAVANO: He was in the Bronx, someplace. I don't know what crew.

GLEESON: Is that where his crew hung out, in the Bronx?

GRAVANO: Yes.

[. . . .]

TERMINATOR

GLEESON: During that period [1976–1986] did you commit murders?

GRAVANO: Yes.

GLEESON: Did you commit more than one?

GRAVANO: Yes.

GLEESON: Did you commit those murders alone or with other people?

GRAVANO: With others.

GLEESON: Were those other people members and associates of the Gambino Family?

GRAVANO: Yes.

GLEESON: Mr. Gravano, were there some people that you committed more than one murder with?

GRAVANO: Yes.

GLEESON: When you were doing this stuff, being involved in murders, was there an expression that you and the people who you associated with used to describe a murder?

GRAVANO: Yes. To do a piece a work or whack somebody out.

GLEESON: Did you and the people in your crew, a crew you were a member of, become skilled at this kind of work, as you put it?

GRAVANO: Yes.

GLEESON: Were you known for that?

GRAVANO: Yes.

GLEESON: Were there other people, other made members of the Gambino Family, who were also known for that?

GRAVANO: Yes.

GLEESON: Are any of them here in the courtroom?

GRAVANO: Yes.

GLEESON: Who?

GRAVANO: John, Frankie, myself.

GLEESON: Did people rely on you to commit murders?

GRAVANO: Yes.

GLEESON: Who?

GRAVANO: Paul Castellano, John.

GLEESON: During that period between when you became a made member of the Gambino Family and when you were made a captain, shortly after the murder of Paul Castellano, you were involved in eight murders, correct?

GRAVANO: Yes.

GLEESON: And did you commit those murders with other members and associates of the Gambino Family?

GRAVANO: Yes.

GLEESON: Are those among the murders you told the government about after you decided to cooperate?

GRAVANO: Yes.

LABOR RACKETEERING

GLEESON: Now, you testified that you were involved in labor racketeering, correct?

GRAVANO: Yes.

GLEESON: Mr. Gravano, over how long a period were you involved in that activity, beginning approximately when?

GRAVANO: I've been in the construction industry, on and off, all my life.

GLEESON: In the early '80s, did you have your own business?

GRAVANO: Yes.

GLEESON: What kind of business was it?

GRAVANO: Drywall business, plumbing business.

GLEESON: By drywall, you mean like Sheetrock?

GRAVANO: Yes.

GLEESON: Were there other people who you were in that business with?

GRAVANO: Yes, there was.

GLEESON: Who?

GRAVANO: Joe Madonia and my brother-in-law Eddie Garafolo.

GLEESON: Now, were you, yourself, skilled at hanging drywall?

GRAVANO: No.

GLEESON: Were either of the other two people you mentioned skilled at that?

GRAVANO: Yes.

GLEESON: Who?

GRAVANO: Joe Madonia.

GLEESON: How about your brother-in-law Eddie? His last name is Garafolo, correct?

GRAVANO: I don't think he could hang it, drywall.

GLEESON: Was he in the construction business?

GRAVANO: Yes.

GLEESON: During that period in the early '80s, did you become familiar with various labor unions and union officials?

GRAVANO: Yes.

GLEESON: Did you—what was your role with respect to the drywall company that you had with Joe Madonia and Eddie?

GRAVANO: I would go out and solicit and get work for the company and take care of the union problems, some of the union problems.

GLEESON: Did you make payments to union officials?

GRAVANO: Yes, I did.

GLEESON: Was that illegal?

GRAVANO: Yes.

GLEESON: During that period, did you become familiar with Gambino Family control over particular unions?

GRAVANO: Yes.

GLEESON: Did you, yourself, use that control in order to make money with the drywall company?

GRAVANO: Yes, I did.

GLEESON: Were there particular unions in the construction industry that were controlled by the Gambino Family?

GRAVANO: Yes.

GLEESON: Which ones?

GRAVANO: 282 the Teamsters, Mason Tenders Union Local 23, and a few others.

GLEESON: Now, Teamsters 282, back in the early '80s, was there a particular official at 282 through whom the Gambino Family exercised control?

GRAVANO: Yes.

GLEESON: Who was that?

GRAVANO: Cody. John Cody.

GLEESON: What was his position?

GRAVANO: He was the president of the union.

[. . . .]

GLEESON: Now, Mr. Gravano, can you give us an example of how you used the control over Local 282 to make money?

GRAVANO: We would talk with contractors and if they had to hire a Teamster foreman or two Teamster foremans, we would like let the Teamster foreman come in late, rather than start the job right away, come in a couple of months later and leave the job a couple months early, which would save the contractor money and, in turn, we would get some money and share it with the union.

GLEESON: And for that example who would you get the money from?

GRAVANO: The contractor.

GLEESON: The contractor gets a break by not having to have a Teamster foreman on the job?

GRAVANO: Yes.

GLEESON: Did you ever use the union to get work for companies?

GRAVANO: Yes, we did.

GLEESON: How did you go about doing that?

GRAVANO: We would have the union ask certain companies, when jobs were coming out, to recognize us and our companies and give the work to our companies.

GLEESON: When that happened, when the companies—did the companies pay any money to the Family?

GRAVANO: Yes.

GLEESON: Was that money shared with anyone?

GRAVANO: Yes.

GLEESON: With whom?

GRAVANO: With me and the administration.

GLEESON: Did the union officials get any of that money?

GRAVANO: Sometimes.

[. . . .]

THE PLOT TO KILL CASTELLANO

GLEESON: You already testified that you participated in the murder of Paul Castellano, correct?

GRAVANO: Yes.

GLEESON: Did you know Tommy Bilotti?

GRAVANO: Yes.

GLEESON: Who was he?

GRAVANO: He was a captain in the Gambino Family.

GLEESON: Was there anybody with whom he was particularly close to when he was a captain?

GRAVANO: He was very close with Paul Castellano.

GLEESON: Was anybody murdered along with him?

GRAVANO: Tommy and Paul were murdered together.

GLEESON: Did there come a point before Tommy and Paul were murdered, that you became unhappy with Paul Castellano?

GRAVANO: Yes.

GLEESON: Did you hear others express their unhappiness as well?

GRAVANO: Yes.

GLEESON: Was there one reason for that or more than one reason?

GRAVANO: There's quite a few reasons.

GLEESON: Are there any reasons that you would describe as germane reasons why people were unhappy with Paul Castellano as boss?

GRAVANO: He was selling out the Family for his own basic businesses. He had a captain who was in our Family, Piccolo, killed and he used another Family to do it. He used certain unions and certain companies that belong to our Family, he made other Families service them and take care of them.

. . . There was a number of reasons that Paul was eventually having a lot of problems with a lot of different people.

[. . . .]

GLEESON: Another problem you mentioned was Paul had had a captain killed. You mentioned the name Piccolo?

GRAVANO: Yes.

GLEESON: How long before Paul was murdered did this happen?

GRAVANO: Quite a while. I don't remember the exact dates.

GLEESON: Did Piccolo have a particular responsibility within the Gambino Family?

GRAVANO: He was a captain in Connecticut, controlled our interests in Connecticut.

GLEESON: What was it about the handling of the Piccolo situation that made people unhappy with Paul?

GRAVANO: You just don't let another Family kill a captain within your own Family. That's against our rules, and nobody was happy with that.

GLEESON: You mentioned a problem relating to Angelo. Which Angelo were you referring to?

GRAVANO: Angelo Ruggiero.

GLEESON: What was the nature of that problem?

GRAVANO: Angelo Ruggiero had gotten caught with some tapes. Paul wanted the tapes, and there was a beef or a problem with the tapes. Angelo didn't want to give it to him, and he wanted the tapes.

GLEESON: Was anybody taking Angelo's part, as far as you were aware, in that period of time. Do you understand my question?

GRAVANO: Yes, I do. I believe John was taking his part and I believe Neil was taking his part.

GLEESON: At that point, what was Neil's position?

GRAVANO: In the beginning, it was that they were arguing with Paul. Paul was trying to get the tapes from Angelo. When he refused, he was trying to get them off from Neil.

GLEESON: What was his position in the Gambino Family?

GRAVANO: Neil?

GLEESON: Yes.

GRAVANO: Underboss.

GLEESON: Was there anything about the tapes that made this a big problem other than it might otherwise have been?

GRAVANO: There was a lot of conversations about drugs.

GLEESON: Was this problem discussed within the Family?

GRAVANO: Yes.

GLEESON: Who did you discuss it with before Paul's murder?

GRAVANO: Frankie DeCicco and other people.

GLEESON: Did you learn who Paul had spoken to in order to get the tapes?

GRAVANO: I believe he spoke with his lawyer to get the tapes.

GLEESON: Did you learn whether he had spoken to anyone within the Family?

GRAVANO: No, I don't know.

GLEESON: Did you learn why he wanted the tapes?

GRAVANO: I think he wanted to prove to Neil that Angelo was in the drug business.

GLEESON: Did he finally get the tapes?

GRAVANO: I believe so.

GLEESON: Did you hear that, at that period of time?

GRAVANO: Yes.

GLEESON: Did there come a point, Mr. Gravano, when you participated in discussions about murdering Paul Castellano?

GRAVANO: Yes.

GLEESON: Was there one such discussion or more than one?

GRAVANO: There was a lot of different discussions.

GLEESON: Approximately how long before Paul Castellano and Tommy Bilotti were murdered was the first discussion about murdering him?

GRAVANO: About eight, ten months before.

GLEESON: Can you describe the circumstances of the first conversation you had along that line?

GRAVANO: Di B came to me and told me Angelo Ruggiero wants to talk to me in Queens about Paul, and I went down to talk to Angelo about it.

GLEESON: Where did you go in Queens?

GRAVANO: On 101st Avenue.

GLEESON: What was there?

GRAVANO: There's a club there.

GLEESON: Whose club was it?

GRAVANO: John's.

GLEESON: When you went there, did you speak to Angelo alone, or were there other people present?

GRAVANO: Alone.

GLEESON: Where were you, inside or outside?

GRAVANO: Outside.

GLEESON: Could you tell the jury what the conversation was?

GRAVANO: Angelo had told me that it came time, he wanted to know if I was with him, as far as killing Paul Castellano. At that time, I asked him where John was. What his opinion was. I asked him where Frankie DeCicco was. We were just alone in the meeting. It didn't just strike me right.

GLEESON: What was his response when you said that about John and Frank?

GRAVANO: "John is with us," he said, "you can go talk to Frankie." And I told him I would get back to him.

GLEESON: Did you go talk to Frankie?

GRAVANO: Yes.

GLEESON: Where did you speak to him?

GRAVANO: I believe I spoke to him on Bath Avenue.

GLEESON: What was there?

GRAVANO: A club.

GLEESON: When you spoke to Frankie, what did he say?

GRAVANO: Well, at this time there was a lot of different conversation about Paul, nobody was too happy, it didn't come as any shock we were going into this direction. And he asked me what my feelings and my position was and we had a serious conversation and we sent messages back and forth through Di B to John and Angelo and we decided to back their play.

GLEESON: You mentioned you sent messages through Di B?

GRAVANO: Yes.

GLEESON: What was Di B's position?

GRAVANO: A soldier in the Family who answered directly to Paul in the administration, the high-level business end.

GLEESON: Mr. Gravano, at that point in time were there factions within the Gambino Family?

GRAVANO: Yes.

GLEESON: Did the discussions that you had, that you described in part, did they continue over a period of time?

GRAVANO: Yes.

GLEESON: At any time did you discuss obtaining support of other people within the Family?

GRAVANO: Yes.

GLEESON: What did you discuss in that regard?

GRAVANO: Once we discussed that we were going to go along with it, we discussed which captains would go along with it, which Family would go along with it, what problems we would have either from the commission, from his immediate family, what fraction would be against us, and which would be with us. We had a lot of different discussion about that.

GLEESON: Were there any particular captains within the Family whose support you wanted?

GRAVANO: Looking for old-timers' support which we understand "Joe Piney" was with us. "Joe Piney" assured he would be able to reach Joe Gallo, who was *consigliere*, and do the right thing after it was over.

GLEESON: Let me stop you there.

Who assured you of that?

GRAVANO: "Joe Piney" assured John and Angelo, and they told us—

GLEESON: When you say they told us, who are you referring to?

GRAVANO: Myself, Frankie DeCicco.

GLEESON: Did you do anything to speak to "Joe Piney" about this directly, you and Frank DeCicco?

GRAVANO: We had one meeting before we finally went forward; we sat in a house in Staten Island, Joe Watts's house.

GLEESON: Was Joe Watts present for the meeting?

GRAVANO: He was excused.

GLEESON: Who was present at that meeting?

GRAVANO: Frankie, myself, "Joe Piney," John, and Angelo.

GLEESON: What was discussed?

GRAVANO: Exactly what I just said—"Piney" would talk to the old-timers and it wouldn't be a problem with them and they would be able to control Joe Gallo. And he had a relationship with the West Side people.

GLEESON: When you say the West Side people, who do you mean?

GRAVANO: The Genovese people.

GLEESON: When you said "Piney" would be able to control Joe Gallo, control him how?

GRAVANO: He would go along with what we were doing.

GLEESON: Did "Piney" give you that assurance?

GRAVANO: Yes.

GLEESON: Did there come a time later on, Mr. Gravano, when "Joe Piney" had a way of referring to the people who were involved, the fractions that were involved in this plan to murder Paul?

GRAVANO: A couple of times, five different fractions that got involved.

GLEESON: Who were the heads of those five fractions?

GRAVANO: John was the head of his, I was the head of mine, Frank DeCicco the head of his, "Joe Piney" the head of his, and Di B was the head of his.

GLEESON: At that time you were a soldier?

GRAVANO: Yes.

GLEESON: Di B was a soldier?

GRAVANO: Yes.

GLEESON: Did you tell any of the other people in your crew that you were involved in these discussions before the plan to murder Paul was carried out?

GRAVANO: Only one.

GLEESON: Who was that?

GRAVANO: This guy, old man Paruta.

GLEESON: Do you know his first name?

GRAVANO: Joe Paruta.

GLEESON: After this discussion with "Joe Piney" were ways discussed to kill Paul Castellano, ways that weren't used?

GRAVANO: Yes.

GLEESON: More than one?

GRAVANO: Yes, a couple.

GLEESON: Can you tell us the ones you remember?

GRAVANO: One time looking into killing him near his house, either going out or coming home. At one point this is why old man Paruta was involved, he had a case and stopped by a diner at Seventh Avenue and 65th Street before they went to the lawyer, and they didn't know the old man and he would be able to walk in the diner and shoot the two of them. The meeting came to us at Sparks that he was going to have.

GLEESON: That meeting resulted in a plan that was used, is that correct?

GRAVANO: Yes.

GLEESON: Go back to the ones that weren't. You said that he had a case, who had a case?

GRAVANO: Paul.

GLEESON: What kind of case?

GRAVANO: A racketeering case.

GLEESON: You mentioned that they stopped at a diner, when you say they, who are you referring?

GRAVANO: Paul and Tommy.

GLEESON: Did you see Tommy Bilotti in Paul's company?

GRAVANO: Yes.

GLEESON: Often?

GRAVANO: All the time.

GLEESON: The diner that you mentioned they stopped at that was on their way where?

GRAVANO: To see their attorney, Jimmy La Rossa, in Manhattan.

GLEESON: At the time he was eventually murdered was Paul Castellano on trial?

GRAVANO: Yes.

GLEESON: By the way, was there a particular reason that the idea of killing Paul near his home wasn't used?

GRAVANO: There was a couple of reasons. One, there was a lot of FBI surveillance by his house and if there was another option to kill we would use that option.

GLEESON: Was Neil Dellacroce still alive while the plans were being considered to murder Paul?

GRAVANO: Yes.

GLEESON: Was he still the underboss?

GRAVANO: Yes.

GLEESON: Did he have a role in this plan?

GRAVANO: No, not really; he was sick.

GLEESON: Did he eventually die?

GRAVANO: Excuse me?

GLEESON: Did he eventually die before—

GRAVANO: Yes.

GLEESON: You mentioned one of the things discussed was other Families, is that correct?

GRAVANO: Yes.

GLEESON: Was anything done to contact other Families about the plan to murder Paul?

GRAVANO: Yes.

GLEESON: What was done?

GRAVANO: We reached "Vic" and "Gas" with the Lucchese Family, and the boss and underboss was on trial. We weren't concerned with them. Asked "Gas" to reach Christy Tick with the Lucchese Family.

GLEESON: "Vic" and "Gas" were who?

GRAVANO: One captain and one made member in the Lucchese Family.

GLEESON: Christy Tick?

GRAVANO: *Consigliere* in the Lucchese Family.

GLEESON: Did you have a close relationship with any of these people?

GRAVANO: Yes.

GLEESON: With who?

GRAVANO: "Vic" and "Gas."

GLEESON: Who contacted "Vic" and "Gas"?

GRAVANO: Frankie DeCicco and myself.

GLEESON: What was their response?

GRAVANO: They were behind it.

GLEESON: Were any of the other Families contacted?

GRAVANO: Colombo Family spoke with Angelo and sent a message with Angelo—What is John waiting for to kill Paul? We knew they were behind us and wouldn't be a problem.

GLEESON: Who were the people that were contacted in the Colombo Family?

GRAVANO: "Gerry Lang" was the underboss and "Donny Shacks" was the captain helping "Gerry" run the Family. Carmine Junior Persico was in jail at the time.

GLEESON: Who contacted them?

GRAVANO: Angelo spoke to them.

GLEESON: Lucchese and Colombo Families, any other Families?

GRAVANO: Bonanno, Joe Messina was the underboss and had a close relationship with John and they would be behind us without a problem. The only people we didn't reach was the Genovese people.

GLEESON: Any reason?

GRAVANO: Paul was already partners back and forth; we didn't trust them.

GLEESON: You began to say a moment ago, I believe, you came up with a plan that was used. Is that correct?

GRAVANO: Yes.

GLEESON: What was that plan?

GRAVANO: The plan was to kill him out of Sparks Steak House.

GLEESON: How long approximately before the murders took place did you come up with this plan?

GRAVANO: About a week, ten days.

GLEESON: Was Dellacroce dead or alive when you came up with the plan?

GRAVANO: Dead already.

GLEESON: Did Dellacroce's death have anything to do with this plan to murder—

GRAVANO: It may have heightened it.

GLEESON: Why?

GRAVANO: One, that Paul showed disrespect and didn't go to the funeral of his own underboss, and we were wondering if Paul, if and when, because he had the tapes already he might make a move.

GLEESON: Paul might make a move?

GRAVANO: Yes.

GLEESON: By that, what do you mean?

GRAVANO: He might strike.

GLEESON: What do you mean by "strike"?

GRAVANO: He might have somebody whacked.

GLEESON: Were there any particular people he might whack?

GRAVANO: John and Angelo.

GLEESON: Did Neil Dellacroce have a crew?

GRAVANO: John and them were basically his crew. Even though an underboss don't have a crew. They were close associates.

GLEESON: Did Castellano express any intentions to the people close to Neil after Neil died?

GRAVANO: Excuse me?

GLEESON: After Dellacroce died, did Castellano express any plan or intention to the people close to Dellacroce?

GRAVANO: John's crew—he was going to break it up.

GLEESON: You were aware of that before Castellano was murdered?

GRAVANO: I believe so.

GLEESON: Did you subsequently have a conversation with John Gotti about that?

GRAVANO: Yes.

GLEESON: Was there a particular event that gave rise to the plan that was eventually used?

GRAVANO: Found out he had an appointment with a few people in the restaurant, and we made arrangements to kill him outside the restaurant.

GLEESON: How did you find out about the meeting?

GRAVANO: Quite a few people knew he was meeting with Frankie DeCicco and already disclosed to us as one of the people to attend.

GLEESON: He was part of the plan to kill him?

GRAVANO: Yes.

GLEESON: Was there anybody else a part of the plan to kill him who was going to be at the meeting?

GRAVANO: No, I don't believe so.

GLEESON: Who were the other people who were going to be at that meeting?

GRAVANO: "Jimmy Brown," John Gammarano, I believe Danny Marino, Frank DeCicco, Tommy Gambino, himself, Tommy Bilotti, and I don't know who else.

GLEESON: And of those, just Frankie DeCicco was involved in the plan to kill both?

GRAVANO: Yes.

CHOOSING THE ASSASSINS

GLEESON: Was there a meeting to plan the murder?

GRAVANO: Yes, that was the night before we had a serious meeting.

GLEESON: Where was the meeting?

GRAVANO: In my office in Brooklyn.

GLEESON: Who was present?

GRAVANO: There was myself, Frankie DeCicco, Joe Watts, John Gotti, Angelo [Ruggiero], Eddie Lino, Fat Sally, Vinnie Artuso, Johnny Carneglia, "Tony Roach," Iggy.

GLEESON: Anyone else?

GRAVANO: I believe that is it.

GLEESON: Of those people, until that time, that meeting in your office, of those, how many previously had been involved in the plan to murder Paul?

GRAVANO: Just myself, John, Angelo, and Frankie.

GLEESON: Were the other people who came to that meeting, the new people, were they with anybody?

GRAVANO: Yes, they were with—some with John, Joe Watts with Frankie. Vinnie Artuso was with Frankie Lo [Botz] and a couple of people.

GLEESON: You mentioned Eddie Lino, Fat Sally. Who were they with?

GRAVANO: With John.

GLEESON: John Carneglia and "Tony Roach"?

GRAVANO: John.

GLEESON: Vinnie Artuso was with whom?

GRAVANO: Frankie Lo [Botz] in the Bronx.

GLEESON: At that point, was Frankie Lo a soldier or captain?

GRAVANO: A soldier.

GLEESON: Was Vinnie made?

GRAVANO: No.

GLEESON: Joe Watts?

GRAVANO: Frankie DeCicco.

GLEESON: You mentioned Iggy. Who was he with?

GRAVANO: John.

GLEESON: Who chose the new people to come to this meeting to plan the murder of Paul?

GRAVANO: John and Angelo.

GLEESON: You didn't mention Di B?

GRAVANO: No. He was excluded from all of these meetings.

GLEESON: Was there a particular reason he was excluded?

GRAVANO: He was more of a conduit between all of us while the talking was going on, high-level business guy, wasn't regarded in that fashion to do work, and we excluded him from the hit.

GLEESON: One of the people you mentioned was "Tony Roach," that is a nickname or his real name?

GRAVANO: Nickname.

GLEESON: Do you know his real name?

GRAVANO: Rampino.

GLEESON: I am sorry?

GRAVANO: Rampino.

GLEESON: What is inside your office at Stillwell Avenue? You go in the door, what do you see?

GRAVANO: Reception area, desk.

GLEESON: What is there? What is housed in that building?

GRAVANO: Construction office. Offices and downstairs is a big table, a place to have conferences, and a big conference room.

GLEESON: The conference room is below street level?

GRAVANO: Yes.

GLEESON: Where in the building was the meeting to plan the murder of Paul Castellano?

GRAVANO: Downstairs.

GLEESON: What happened at the meeting?

GRAVANO: We discussed that we were going to go on a piece of work the following day and we couldn't miss, it had to be done. We discussed who the shooters would be, what positions different people would take, and what time we would meet the following day, and that is about it. We didn't tell them who it was.

GLEESON: Did you tell them where it would take place?

GRAVANO: I believe just New York.

GLEESON: As far as you knew did they know who the subject of the hit was going to be?

GRAVANO: I am not really sure at that particular point, no. After we left they might have.

GLEESON: Who presided over the meeting? Who did the talking?

GRAVANO: John, Frankie.

GLEESON: You say you discussed who the shooters would be. Was a decision made as to who the shooters would be?

GRAVANO: Yes.

GLEESON: What was the decision?

GRAVANO: Eddie Lino, Fat Sally, Vinnie Artuso, and John Carneglia.

GLEESON: I am sorry. How many names did you mention—

GRAVANO: Four.

GLEESON: Eddie—

GRAVANO: Fat Sally, Vinnie Artuso, John Carneglia.

GLEESON: Any people made members of the Family?

GRAVANO: Only one, just John Carneglia.

GLEESON: I believe you testified a moment ago you discussed what the positions would be at that meeting?

GRAVANO: Yes.

GLEESON: What did you discuss in that regard?

GRAVANO: Shooters would be right outside of Sparks restaurant. We didn't tell them the exact restaurant. They would be right outside the restaurant. [We discussed] who was going to be backup and what role they were going to play and actually get into it the following day.

GLEESON: Did you discuss specifically where the backup people would be?

GRAVANO: Not specifically, we didn't get into it too much.

GLEESON: Did you do it the following day?

GRAVANO: Yes.

GLEESON: Did you make arrangements to meet the following day?

GRAVANO: Yes.

[. . . .]

FINAL ARRANGEMENTS

GLEESON: Where did you arrange to meet the following day?

GRAVANO: Down New York near the water, there was a little park, downtown.

GLEESON: By the way, where is Sparks?

GRAVANO: It is on, I believe 46th Street and Third Avenue.

GLEESON: Had you ever been there before you went there to kill Tommy and Paul?

GRAVANO: Yes.

GLEESON: Where in relation to the park, in terms of blocks or miles, was the park that you arranged to meet at?

GRAVANO: About a mile or little more downtown and over toward the water.

GLEESON: Do you recall the name of the park?

GRAVANO: No.

GLEESON: Did you in fact go there the next day?

GRAVANO: Yes.

GLEESON: Who did you go there with?

GRAVANO: I went with Joe Watts, and we met everybody over there, other than Frankie DeCicco, he wasn't there.

GLEESON: Why wasn't DeCicco there?

GRAVANO: He was going to the meeting with Paul. He went to the restaurant.

GLEESON: Other than DeCicco did you meet all the other people you had met the night before at Stillwell?

GRAVANO: Yes.

GLEESON: . . . Did you bring anything with you?

GRAVANO: A gun and walkie-talkies.

GLEESON: Where did you get the gun?

GRAVANO: I had it.

GLEESON: Did you have guns at your disposal throughout your life in crime?

GRAVANO: Yes.

GLEESON: Joe Watts have anything?

GRAVANO: A gun and some—a walkie-talkie.

[. . . .]

GLEESON: You say you brought walkie-talkies to the park?

GRAVANO: Yes.

GLEESON: What was the purpose of bringing walkie-talkies?

GRAVANO: So we could communicate with one another.

GLEESON: Is that something you discussed the night before at Stillwell?

GRAVANO: Yes.

GLEESON: When you got to the park, did you drive there?

GRAVANO: Yes.

GLEESON: In whose car?

GRAVANO: I came with Joe Watts.

GLEESON: When you got there, who did you see?

GRAVANO: Everybody that I saw the night before excluding Frank DeCicco.

GLEESON: Was there any discussion at the park?

GRAVANO: I believe we told them exactly who was going and it had to be done.

GLEESON: When you say you told them who was going, what do you mean?

GRAVANO: We told them Paul and Tommy Bilotti was going.

GLEESON: By that you meant they were going to be killed?

GRAVANO: Yes.

GLEESON: Was there any other discussion at the park?

GRAVANO: Not really.

GLEESON: Did there come a time when you left the park?

GRAVANO: Yes.

GLEESON: Before you left the park, was it decided where people would position themselves in the vicinity of Sparks Steak House?

GRAVANO: We went over it real quick.

GLEESON: What did you go over real quick?

GRAVANO: We knew who the shooters were, they would be right outside. Because they usually parked there and pulled up, "Tony Roach" was going to be across the street, Joe Watts, Angelo, Iggy, and them up the block.

GLEESON: Toward where?

GRAVANO: Second Avenue. They were going to take a backup position and me and John Gotti in the car and we went on the other side of the Third Avenue side, and we were taking that position.

GLEESON: What was your role going to be?

GRAVANO: I was the backup shooter.

GLEESON: What was the role of Rampino?

GRAVANO: We were all backup shooters.

GLEESON: Rampino was going to be directly across the street?

GRAVANO: Yes. If they got away, ran across the street, or somebody interfered, Tony would whack them.

GLEESON: What was the role you mentioned the three people going to be up the block, who were—

GRAVANO: Watts, Angelo, and Iggy.

GLEESON: They were up 46th Street toward Second Avenue?

GRAVANO: Yes.

GLEESON: What was their role?

GRAVANO: Backup shooters and getaway drivers.

GLEESON: Where were you and John Gotti going to be?

GRAVANO: On 46th Street and Third Avenue. Across the avenue on the other side. And we had Sparks Steak House sandwiched in.

GLEESON: You were going to be on 46th Street but across Third Avenue?

GRAVANO: Yes.

[. . . .]

GLEESON: Now, were the shooters at the park in Manhattan, were they dressed distinctively?

GRAVANO: Yes.

GLEESON: Can you tell the jury how they were dressed?

GRAVANO: They had white trench coats and black Russian hats.

GLEESON: Now, did all four of them, all four of the shooters, were they dressed that way?

GRAVANO: Yes.

GLEESON: Okay. Did you participate in any discussions regarding how they should dress?

GRAVANO: No.

GLEESON: Did you know before you arrived at the park that that's how they would be dressed?

GRAVANO: No.

GLEESON: Do you recall what the other people, not the shooters, but the other people at the park involved in the plan to kill Paul and Tommy Bilotti, do you recall what they were wearing?

GRAVANO: Not really.

GLEESON: Were they dressed like the shooters?

GRAVANO: No.

GLEESON: Approximately how long were you at this park before you left it?

GRAVANO: Fifteen, twenty minutes.

GLEESON: From there, where did you go?

GRAVANO: Right to the restaurant.

GLEESON: Okay. You testified that you went to the park with Joe Watts, correct?

GRAVANO: Yes.

GLEESON: Did you leave the park with Joe Watts?

GRAVANO: No.

GLEESON: With whom did you leave, if anyone?

GRAVANO: I left with John.

GLEESON: John Gotti?

GRAVANO: Yes.

GLEESON: Fair to say, when you refer to John in your testimony, unless you otherwise indicate, you are referring to John Gotti?

GRAVANO: Yes.

GLEESON: Whose car did you leave in?

GRAVANO: John's car.

GLEESON: Was it his personal car?

GRAVANO: I don't know. I don't think so.

GLEESON: What kind of car was it?

GRAVANO: It was a Lincoln.

GLEESON: Okay. Who drove?

GRAVANO: John drove.

GLEESON: Where were you seated in the car?

GRAVANO: In the passenger side.

GLEESON: Was there anyone else in the car?

GRAVANO: No.

GLEESON: Where did you go when you left the park in the car with John Gotti?

GRAVANO: Across the street from the restaurant. On the corner of Third Avenue and 42nd Street.

GLEESON: You said 42nd Street. Is that where—

GRAVANO: 46th Street. I'm sorry.

GLEESON: Did you go there directly from the park?

GRAVANO: Yes.

GLEESON: Approximately how long did it take?

GRAVANO: Ten minutes.

[. . . .]

GLEESON: Mr. Gravano, were there a lot of people in the vicinity when you first pulled up to the corner of 46th Street and Third Avenue?

GRAVANO: Yes.

GLEESON: And was it busy?

GRAVANO: Yes.

GLEESON: When you first pulled up, did you see—by the way, did your car have—what kind of windows did it have, the car you were in with John Gotti?

GRAVANO: Tinted.

GLEESON: From where you were when you first pulled up to that corner, could you see the vicinity of Sparks Steak House?

GRAVANO: Yes.

GLEESON: Were there people in the vicinity of Sparks Steak House?

GRAVANO: Yes.

GLEESON: Did you see any of the others who were involved in the plan to kill Paul and Tommy?

GRAVANO: I saw some of the people with the white coats near the restaurant. Across the street, I saw "Tony Roach."

GLEESON: Okay.

GRAVANO: We weren't parked too good on the corner, so we circled around the block once.

GLEESON: Okay. Before you circled around the block, let me ask you, you mentioned that the plan was for three other people to be down the block, correct?

GRAVANO: Yes.

GLEESON: Could you remind the jury of who the three people who were going to be down the block were?

GRAVANO: Angelo, Joe Watts, and Iggy.

GLEESON: Now, when you first pulled up to the corner, could you see them?

GRAVANO: No.

GLEESON: Do you know where on the block they were?

GRAVANO: No.

GLEESON: Their role, though, was to be where?

GRAVANO: Up the block. Toward Second.

GLEESON: Toward Second Avenue?

GRAVANO: Toward Second Avenue.

GLEESON: You mentioned that you went around the block. Correct?

GRAVANO: Yes.

GLEESON: Why?

GRAVANO: Because the car was sticking out too far, so we went around the block. When we came back, the spot was a little bit better. We pulled in. I looked to the right and stopped for the light. There was a Lincoln just pulled up with Paul and Tommy.

[. . . .]

GLEESON: Which direction was the car facing?

GRAVANO: Going from Third Avenue to Second Avenue.

GLEESON: So you were facing—you looked across Third Avenue?

GRAVANO: Yes.

GLEESON: How long after you pulled into that spot—by the way, were you right on the corner?

GRAVANO: Right on the corner.

THE HIT

GLEESON: How long after you pulled into that spot did you see the Lincoln pull up to the right of you?

GRAVANO: A couple of minutes.

GLEESON: What did you see?

GRAVANO: The Lincoln pulled up with Paul and Tommy Bilotti in it.

GLEESON: They pulled up on where, what street were they on?

GRAVANO: Right on 42nd Street. They stopped for the light. They had their dome light on. They were talking.

GLEESON: Were they on the same street you were parked on?

GRAVANO: Right next to us.

GLEESON: You mentioned 42nd Street. You mean—

GRAVANO: 46th Street.

GLEESON: They were right next to you and John?

GRAVANO: Yes.

GLEESON: Did their car have tinted windows?

GRAVANO: Yes.

GLEESON: Could you see into their car?

GRAVANO: Yes.

GLEESON: Why?

GRAVANO: They had the light on. The dome light in the car.

GLEESON: Now, they were on 46th Street facing Third Avenue, correct?

GRAVANO: Yes.

GLEESON: Had they yet crossed Third Avenue?

GRAVANO: No.

GLEESON: Was the light red or green when they pulled up?

GRAVANO: It was red.

GLEESON: Where were you in relation—who was driving that car, by the way?

GRAVANO: Tommy.

GLEESON: Where was Paul seated?

GRAVANO: In the passenger seat.

GLEESON: In the front passenger?

GRAVANO: Yes.

GLEESON: Where was Tommy in relation to you when they pulled up to the light?

GRAVANO: He was right next to me. In the next car.

GLEESON: Could you see whether they were doing anything in the car?

GRAVANO: They were just talking. I don't know what they were doing.

GLEESON: Okay. So you remember the dome light was on?

GRAVANO: Yes.

GLEESON: Okay. Did you look over and see Tommy?

GRAVANO: Yes.

GLEESON: At that point did you do anything?

GRAVANO: I just turned and I told John they were right next to us. I got on the walkie-talkie and told them that they were stopped at the light, the first car, and they were coming through.

GLEESON: Who did you tell that?

GRAVANO: To the people on the other end who were waiting, the shooters and whoever had the walkie-talkie.

GLEESON: Did you know which of those people that were at the scene had the walkie-talkies?

GRAVANO: No.

GLEESON: What happened then?

GRAVANO: The light turned. They pulled up. There was a parking space in front of the restaurant. They pulled into the spot.

The shooters, Tommy got out. The shooters ran over to them, started shooting them.

They watched the surrounding people. We pulled up. I looked at—at Tommy on the floor. I told John he was gone.

We went to Second Avenue, made a right, and went back to my office.

GLEESON: Let's back up a little bit. After they go through the light, where specifically did they park?

GRAVANO: Right in front of the restaurant.

GLEESON: From that vantage point, could you see the shooters?

GRAVANO: Yes.

GLEESON: What were you watching as this was happening?

GRAVANO: The people, the people on the street. The surrounding people.

GLEESON: Why?

GRAVANO: Because I was a backup shooter. If anybody would interfere with them, I would come into play.

GLEESON: Did you see who shot who?

GRAVANO: No.

GLEESON: Did you see Paul get out of the car?

GRAVANO: No.

GLEESON: Did you see Tommy get out of the car?

GRAVANO: Yes.

GLEESON: Did you see which one was shot first?

GRAVANO: I believe Paul was shot first.

GLEESON: Why?

GRAVANO: Tommy squatted down to look through the window, kind of squatted down. And then somebody came up behind him and shot him. He was actually watching Paul get shot.

GLEESON: Did you watch the shooting the whole time it was occurring?

GRAVANO: No.

GLEESON: Did you see who shot who?

GRAVANO: No.

GLEESON: Later on, did you discuss who actually did the shooting of the four shooters who were on the scene?

GRAVANO: Just the four shooters.

GLEESON: Did all of them fire their guns? Did you discuss this later on?

GRAVANO: No. We discussed it later on. They didn't all fire their guns. Supposedly, Eddie Lino had reported back that Vinnie Artuso's gun jammed and that he didn't shoot.

GLEESON: You say "supposedly." Who told you this?

GRAVANO: John had told me that Eddie Lino reported it back in.

GLEESON: That Vinnie Artuso's gun had jammed?

GRAVANO: That Vinnie's gun jammed and he didn't shoot.

[. . . .]

GLEESON: Were Bilotti and Castellano shot basically as—right after they parked in front of Sparks Steak House?

GRAVANO: Yes.

GLEESON: Did it take a long period of time?

GRAVANO: No.

THE GETAWAY

GLEESON: What did you and John Gotti do after the shootings occurred?

GRAVANO: We pulled straight up the block.

GLEESON: By that, do you mean straight across Third Avenue and into that block?

GRAVANO: Right.

GLEESON: Did you see where the shooters went after the murders took place?

GRAVANO: They went straight up the block toward Second Avenue.

GLEESON: You mentioned that you and John Gotti drove through that intersection and into the block on which Sparks is located, correct?

GRAVANO: Yes.

GLEESON: Did you drive fast or slow?

GRAVANO: Slow.

GLEESON: As you drove past the restaurant, what did you do?

GRAVANO: I noticed, I looked down at Tommy Bilotti. I said he was gone. We drove a little faster to go to Second Avenue. We made a right. We went back to my office in Brooklyn.

GLEESON: As you drove past Tommy Bilotti, could you see Castellano?

GRAVANO: No.

GLEESON: As you drove down 46th Street—by the way, when you went down 46th Street, did you make a turnoff off 46th Street?

GRAVANO: When we hit Second Avenue, we made a turn.

GLEESON: Okay. What kind of a turn?

GRAVANO: Right turn on Second Avenue.

GLEESON: Then you testified you drove back to your office on Stillwell Avenue?

GRAVANO: Yes, in Brooklyn.

GLEESON: On the way down 46th Street to Second Avenue, did you see any of the shooters?

GRAVANO: No.

GLEESON: Did you see them at all after you saw them head down toward Second Avenue after the shooting?

GRAVANO: No.

[. . . .]

AFTERMATH

GLEESON: Now, after these murders, were there any meetings of the captains in the Family?

GRAVANO: A couple of days later.

GLEESON: Where?

GRAVANO: Down in New York, at Caesar's East Restaurant.

GLEESON: Where is that?

GRAVANO: On 58th Street and Third Avenue.

GLEESON: Okay. Whose restaurant was that?

GRAVANO: It was mine, my brother-in-law Eddie's, and this guy named Caesar.

GLEESON: Sorry?

GRAVANO: And a guy named Caesar.

GLEESON: Who came to the meeting?

GRAVANO: Joe Gallo, all the captains in the Family. Myself, Angelo, and most of the captains had somebody drive them down to the restaurant.

[. . . .]

GLEESON: Was anyone else present besides Joe Gallo and the captains for that meeting?

GRAVANO: Just myself and Angelo.

GLEESON: You weren't captains at that point in time?

GRAVANO: No.

GLEESON: Were you armed?

GRAVANO: Excuse me?

GLEESON: Did you have guns, you and Angelo?

GRAVANO: I believe so.

GLEESON: What was the purpose of your being there, you and Angelo?

GRAVANO: Probably for some intimidation purposes.

GLEESON: Is that what you understood your reason for being there was?

GRAVANO: Yes.

GLEESON: Who presided at this meeting in the downstairs at Caesar's East?

GRAVANO: Joe Gallo did.

GLEESON: What did he say?

GRAVANO: He told all the captains that we didn't know who killed Paul, we were investigating it. He was in charge of the Family at that point. He told all the captains not to discuss this out of the Family, not to have any of the members carry guns or overreact to anything, to anything that they would hear they would come back to—to Joe Gallo through either John or Frankie, and report everything back in place.

[. . . .]

GLEESON: You testified that Joe Gallo said that we don't know who did it?

GRAVANO: Yes.

[. . . .]

GLEESON: They [the captains at the meeting] weren't told who did it, correct?

GRAVANO: No.

GLEESON: You testified earlier that Joe Gallo had been approached by "Joe Piney" before the murder?

GRAVANO: Yes.

GLEESON: Was there a reason that the other captains weren't told who killed Paul and Tommy?

GRAVANO: Because there is a commission rule about killing a boss. And we broke that rule. And we weren't ever going to admit it.

GLEESON: What's the penalty for killing your boss?

GRAVANO: Death penalty.

GLEESON: At that point, there was no boss of the Family, correct?

GRAVANO: No.

GLEESON: Was a new boss elected at that meeting?

GRAVANO: No.

GLEESON: At the time, the time of that meeting, were you familiar with the procedures for appointing a new boss?

GRAVANO: Some of them.

GLEESON: After the Caesar's East meeting, were there any meetings to discuss that procedure?

GRAVANO: Yes. We had a meeting with Joe Gallo in a hotel, a small little coffee shop.

GLEESON: Where was the hotel?

GRAVANO: Uptown someplace, in Manhattan.

GLEESON: You say "we had a meeting with Joe Gallo." Who is the "we"?

GRAVANO: Joe Gallo, "Joe Piney," John, Angelo, Frankie DeCicco, and myself.

GLEESON: What was discussed at that meeting?

GRAVANO: We discussed some of the positions of the other Families, how we were going to make the new boss, and what some of the rules and regulations were. Joe Gallo informed us that we could never tell the truth as far as killing Paul. We'd have to come up with a story sooner or later. We'd have to make up some sort of a story on what happened. And basically that was it.

GLEESON: Okay. Did you discuss how you would go about electing a new boss or appointing a new boss?

GRAVANO: Yes.

GLEESON: What did you discuss in that regard?

GRAVANO: That the captains vote, they—they have an election. They take a vote and we vote a boss in.

GLEESON: Mr. Gravano, you testified just now that Joe Gallo said you could never talk about or admit the murders, correct?

GRAVANO: Right.

GLEESON: Yesterday afternoon you testified that before the murders, three of the other four Families in New York were contacted?

GRAVANO: Yes.

GLEESON: Why were they contacted?

GRAVANO: Just to see, it was an off-the-record contact, just to see where and what direction they were going to go, what position they were going to take off the record. We weren't asking for permission on the record. We couldn't do that. It would take a formal meeting and all the Families would be involved. It would be a commission meeting to take a boss down.

GLEESON: After the murder, were there any on-the-record contacts with the other Families?

GRAVANO: Yes.

GLEESON: Can you describe those?

GRAVANO: After that, we sent out people to talk to other Families. We told them that we didn't know what happened to Paul, but our Family was intact. We weren't in a position that a war was going to break out. We had no internal trouble. And we didn't want anybody to get involved in our problems.

GLEESON: Were those messages off the record or on the record?

GRAVANO: Those were official messages.

GLEESON: Were those messages sent to the same Families that had been spoken to unofficially before the murder?

GRAVANO: Yes.

GLEESON: To the same people within those Families?

GRAVANO: Yes.

GOTTI BECOMES BOSS

GLEESON: Was there a meeting to appoint a new boss?

GRAVANO: Yes, later on Wednesday a meeting.

GLEESON: Approximately how long after the murders did that take place?

GRAVANO: A couple of weeks.

GLEESON: Do you recall where?

GRAVANO: It was in Manhattan, lower Manhattan someplace, in a building in a basement.

GLEESON: Do you recall what kind of building it was?

GRAVANO: It was a big complex. It was a recreation basement for an entire building. Somebody knew somebody in the building and we had access to this area.

GLEESON: Who came to that meeting?

GRAVANO: All the captains.

GLEESON: Anyone else besides all the captains?

GRAVANO: A few other people. Angelo, myself, John's brother Genie, Georgie DeCicco, a few other people.

[. . . .]

GLEESON: Who presided at that meeting?

GRAVANO: Joe Gallo.

GLEESON: At that point his role was what?

GRAVANO: He was the *consigliere* of the Family and he was in control of the Family.

GLEESON: What happened at the meeting?

GRAVANO: They talked a bit. They talked about electing a new boss. I believe Frankie DeCicco got up and nominated John. They went right around the table. Everybody nominated John. John was the boss.

GLEESON: Before the murder of Paul and Tommy, did you have any discussions with Frankie DeCicco as to who would be boss if Paul was killed?

GRAVANO: Yes, there were conversations about it.

GLEESON: Can you tell the jury the substance of those conversations that you had with DeCicco?

GRAVANO: In the beginning, we were thinking about Frankie DeCicco becoming the boss.

GLEESON: Did he speak to you about that?

GRAVANO: Yes.

GLEESON: What did he say?

GRAVANO: He said he would be able to be John's underboss, John would not be able to be his underboss, and leave it alone like that.

GLEESON: Did he say—did he tell you anything about what would happen if John was his underboss?

GRAVANO: John wouldn't be able to live with it. His ego would bother him and they would clash.

GLEESON: At that time, the time of that meeting when John was appointed boss, what was his position before he was appointed boss?

GRAVANO: He was acting captain.

GLEESON: What was Frankie DeCicco's position before he was appointed underboss?

GRAVANO: He was a captain.

GLEESON: Was anything done to replace the two of them, once they were elected to boss and underboss?

GRAVANO: Yes. Once it was done, John made his underboss, which was Frankie DeCicco. He kept Joe Gallo as his *consigliere*. He replaced Frankie DeCicco with his uncle Georgie DeCicco. And John was replaced by Angelo Ruggiero.

GLEESON: Was that done at the meeting?

GRAVANO: That was done at the meeting.

GLEESON: Did there come a point shortly after the meeting when additional captains were made?

GRAVANO: About a week after that, I became a captain and Sonny Ciccone became a captain.

GLEESON: Who did you replace?

GRAVANO: The old man Toddo.

GLEESON: During the years leading up to your becoming captain, what you just described, could you describe the old man Toddo's activity? Do you understand my question?

GRAVANO: No.

GLEESON: He was in charge of a crew?

GRAVANO: Yes.

GLEESON: When you replaced him as captain, was that against his wishes?

GRAVANO: No, not really.

GLEESON: Why?

GRAVANO: He was old. He was tired. He was looking to retire anyway. We had a close relationship. When he was asked to step down, he stepped down gracefully.

GLEESON: Who did Sonny Ciccone replace?

GRAVANO: Scotto.

GLEESON: What was Scotto's first name?

GRAVANO: Anthony Scotto.

GLEESON: After John Gotti was voted boss by the captains, was there anything else to be done?

GRAVANO: We sent out committees again to other Families and notified them that we had elected a new boss, who our new boss was, who our new administration was, and we wanted their approval, for one thing, that we had no sanctions against our Family and we would be able to have no restrictions against our commission seat.

GLEESON: Was there anything you were concerned about in terms of not wanting to have sanctions against the Family?

GRAVANO: I don't understand that.

GLEESON: What sanctions might have been imposed as a result of what?

GRAVANO: Restrictions, that we couldn't sit and have a vote on the commission.

GLEESON: Were you concerned about why a sanction might be imposed?

GRAVANO: Because a boss was killed and there was no explanation of it as yet and we thought there could be a possibility of somebody putting sanctions on us.

GLEESON: Was the approval to have John Gotti on the commission without sanctions sought?

GRAVANO: Yes.

GLEESON: How?

GRAVANO: We went to each Family and we notified them that we have a boss, we have an administration. We have no problems within our Family. Every captain is in total agreement. We were still investigating the Paul situation, and we didn't want any restrictions on our Family.

GLEESON: Was a response received back? By the way, what other Families were contacted in this regard?

GRAVANO: All four Families were contacted.

GLEESON: All four in New York?

GRAVANO: Yes.

GLEESON: Was a response received from those four Families?

GRAVANO: Yes.

GLEESON: What was the response?

GRAVANO: It was a positive response. Every Family sent their blessings and they accepted it. Except for the Genovese Family. They accepted it but they told "Joe Piney" that to the exception, there was a rule broken, someday somebody would have to answer for that if and when the commission ever got together again.

GLEESON: And by that, what did you understand them to be referring to?

GRAVANO: The rule with a boss being killed.

GLEESON: Did there ever come a point when the administration of the Gambino Family had to answer for breaking that rule?

GRAVANO: No.

GLEESON: After John became the boss, Mr. Gravano, as far as you knew, did the rest of the Gambino Family, did the captains, know who had killed Paul and Tommy?

GRAVANO: We never told them.

GLEESON: That wasn't my question. You became part of the administration, correct?

GRAVANO: Yes.

GLEESON: As part of the administration, did you have regular contact with other people in the Family?

GRAVANO: Yes.

GLEESON: Did the other people include the captains?

GRAVANO: Yes.

GLEESON: Did you speak to them from time to time about the prior administration?

GRAVANO: Yes.

GLEESON: Did you speak about Paul Castellano?

GRAVANO: Yes, we did.

GLEESON: You mentioned that there was unhappiness within the Family before the murder of Paul?

GRAVANO: Yes.

GLEESON: Was that unhappiness discussed from time to time?

GRAVANO: Occasionally.

GLEESON: After the murder, did you ever admit directly to anybody else in the Family that you had been involved in the murder of Paul Castellano?

GRAVANO: No.

GLEESON: Why not?

GRAVANO: Because of that rule, we would never talk about it or admit.

[. . . .]

THE TAPES

GLEESON: From time to time over the years, did you have occasion to discuss the events leading up to Paul Castellano's and Tommy Bilotti's murders with other people?

GRAVANO: Again, I'm losing you.

GLEESON: Okay. Did you learn that you were caught on tape at the Ravenite Social Club?

GRAVANO: Yes.

GLEESON: Did you learn that after you got indicted?

GRAVANO: Yes.

GLEESON: At the Ravenite Social Club, and specifically up in the apartment above the club, did you learn subsequently that you had been recorded speaking to John Gotti regarding Paul Castellano and the events leading up to his murder?

GRAVANO: Yes.

GLEESON: You had an opportunity to listen to that tape [recorded in the apartment above the Ravenite Social Club on November 30, 1989]?

GRAVANO: Yes.

GLEESON: Your Honor, we are going to play this all the way through and then I will come back and do my questioning.

JUDGE GLASSER: Okay. Do you have a headset?

GRAVANO: Right here.

JUDGE GLASSER: You can put it on and listen, if you'd like. All right.

(Tape plays.)
(Tape concludes.)

GLEESON: Before we go on, Mr. Gravano, let me ask you a few questions based on what we heard so far. Mr. Gravano, this conversation is approximately four years after the murder of Paul and Tommy, correct?

GRAVANO: Yes.

GLEESON: Gotti says: "When that bum asked for the tapes, you were there. I'm best friends with Frankie." Who did you understand him to be referring to when he said the bum asked for the tapes?

GRAVANO: Paul.

GLEESON: And which tapes did you understand Gotti to be referring to?

GRAVANO: Angelo's tapes.

GLEESON: Gotti says: " 'Hey, Frank, don't start. Tell him not to give them the tapes.' What was he, what was he gonna do, Sam? What was he gonna do if five of us got mad? What was he gonna do?" Who did you understand Gotti to be referring to when he said, "What was he gonna do?"

GRAVANO: Paul. What was Paul gonna do.

GLEESON: In [the FBI transcript of the November 30, 1989, tape], Mr. Gravano, you say: "Well, you know, that and there's an 'inaudible.' He would've, he would've tried to make a move from outside, I think." What were you referring to when you said: "He would've tried to make a move from outside"?

GRAVANO: Possibly from outside the Family.

GLEESON: Who would have made a move?

GRAVANO: Paul.

GLEESON: Against whom?

GRAVANO: Against John and Angelo.

GLEESON: When you say outside the Family who, in your opinion, would he have gone to?

GRAVANO: The Genovese Family. Possibly, the Westies.

GLEESON: Who are the Westies?

GRAVANO: A small little Irish gang that was associated with us.

GLEESON: Gotti said, to you: "He couldn't succeed because, Sam, he felt, and you know what we heard. He felt he hadda hit me first." Is he referring to Paul there?

GRAVANO: Yeah.

GLEESON: When he says, "he hadda hit me first," what did you understand him to mean? First, before whom?

GRAVANO: Before Angelo.

GLEESON: And he continues: "But if he hits me first, he blows the guy who really led the ring, Angelo and them. Supposedly, that's the guys on the tapes." When he says "led the ring," what type of ring did you understand him to be referring to?

GRAVANO: Where they're concerned with the drug dealing.

GLEESON: You immediately said to him: "I think he would've hit Angelo, and not you."

Gotti responded: "No."

You said: "No."

And then he said: "And what was he going to do with us?" Did you understand him to mean that he thought Paul was going to kill him and Angelo?

GRAVANO: Yes.

GLEESON: [Later on,] you said: "But I'm saying this guy was stark raving nuts." Who are you referring to there?

GRAVANO: Paul.

GLEESON: And then Gotti responded: "And Neil was another one. Neil would've told him just like this, 'What? What are we cops here?' Let's kill all the cocksuckers that *(inaudible),* in the whole Family. Every Gambino, every Castellano." Mr. Gravano, what did you understand Gotti to be referring to when he said that?

GRAVANO: Kill the Gambinos and every Castellano's involved in drugs.

GLEESON: Were there Gambinos and Castellanos involved in drugs?

GRAVANO: There were people, yes, who were arrested for it.

GLEESON: [Later you say:] "Well, how, how could he have conversations with us?"

GRAVANO: Yes.

GLEESON: You continue: "Me and Frankie and Angelo. We were sitting there. 'Yeah, I'm gonna go down to Neil's— Christmas part—' ah, he looked at me like I had five heads. Frankie was there. 'You're on our side! Where you going?' " What were you referring to there, Mr. Gravano?

GRAVANO: I was going down to Neil's Christmas party to wish him a merry Christmas.

GLEESON: Is this something you're relating to Gotti and Locascio on November 30, 1989?

GRAVANO: No, I am not referring to Locascio at all. I am talking about Frankie, Frankie DeCicco.

GLEESON: This is a conversation in 1989 with Gotti and Locascio, correct?

GRAVANO: Oh, yes.

GLEESON: Who are you referring to in the conversation?

GRAVANO: I am referring to Paul, as the first time when he actually turns around and says to me that why go down to Neil. You're on my side, and I tell Frankie DeCicco that did you hear what he said? See, he's referring to us as sides, now.

GLEESON: Did that have significance to you?

GRAVANO: It had significance to me. You couldn't go down and see your underboss and wish him a merry Christmas. He was already distinguishing sides.

GLEESON: How long before the murder of Paul and Tommy did this happen?

GRAVANO: This is the Christmas before.

GLEESON: In the next attribution to you, you say: "I says, 'Frankie, what happened? What's he have a problem? What do you mean on our side? What's he talking about?' " What were you referring to there?

GRAVANO: Just what I just said.

GLEESON: And the Frankie that you're speaking to, you're relating this conversation to the Frankie you're referring to as whom?

GRAVANO: Frankie DeCicco.

GLEESON: [Later] there's a long attribution to Gotti where he says: "This rat brother was, the brother-in-law was a rat, a back door motherf. He wouldn't, he purposely wouldn't make him *consigliere*. He didn't wanna make him no underboss. He wouldn't make nobody official." When he says the brother-in-law was a rat, who did you understand John Gotti to be referring to?

GRAVANO: Paul's brother-in-law, Carlo Gambino.

GLEESON: Gotti says: "Neil would've never—he would've never tolerated Angelo with the tapes. He would've tolerated, put him on the shelf."

When he said Neil would have put him on the shelf, what did he mean?

GRAVANO: If Neil would have heard the tapes, he would have been very, very disturbed with Angelo. We don't think that Neil would have killed Angelo, but he would have put him on the shelf, meaning put him on the side, maybe strip him of any position of talking or anything, just put him on the side. That's what he would have done.

GLEESON: In response to that, Gotti says: "Using hindsight now, ourselves—he deserved to have his tongue cut out. If nothing else, his tongue cut out." Who did you understand him to be referring to?

GRAVANO: Angelo.

GLEESON: Gotti [goes on to say] to you and Locascio: "Paul, let me tell you about Paul, Sammy. He didn't—he was a fish on the desert. He was a fish outta water! He don't know this life! . . . He was a piece of shit! Rat, rat, yellow dog, yellow dog, right? What *(inaudible)*, Sammy? All this guy needed was a little whack in the mouth."

Is he referring to Paul Castellano in that portion of the conversation?

GRAVANO: Yes.

GLEESON: At any point during the period of time when you discussed murdering Paul Castellano, did you ever consider just giving him a little whack in the mouth?

GRAVANO: No.

GLEESON: Is there a reason for that?

GRAVANO: I don't think it would have lasted him too long, if you whacked him in the mouth.

[. . . .]

GLEESON: Before I go further, you mention a term, you say "Nasabeak." What were you referring to?

GRAVANO: Paul.

GLEESON: Why "Nasabeak"? Why did you use that term?

GRAVANO: He's got a big nose.

[. . . .]

GLEESON: [Much later on the tape] you mention the name Nino. "Nino found out." First, who are you referring to there?

GRAVANO: Nino was a captain in our Family.

GLEESON: What was his last name?

GRAVANO: Gaggi.

GLEESON: You continue: "He had trouble, right after the trial he was going." What trial were you referring to?

GRAVANO: Paul was on trial at that particular time.

[. . . .]

GLEESON: What did you mean by that? Going where?

GRAVANO: More than likely, he would have been killed.

[. . . .]

GLEESON: And could you explain to the jury what you were explaining to John Gotti and Frank Locascio?

GRAVANO: I was explaining to Nino that I knew that Paul wasn't going to carry out any plot against him because I already knew he was going himself.

GLEESON: Did you tell Nino you were going to kill Paul?

GRAVANO: No.

GLEESON: But you told him that you knew Paul wasn't going to be able to kill Nino?

GRAVANO: Yes.

GLEESON: And you continue: "How come you didn't say nothin' when he was talkin' about all of us? Me, John, Angelo." Are you still relating a conversation with Nino?

GRAVANO: Yes.

GLEESON: What were you telling them?

GRAVANO: I was tellling him just the opposite. I put the ball back in his court. Why didn't he warn us? He didn't have no plot to do anything [to] Paul. Why didn't he come to us and warn us about him talking behind our backs?

GLEESON: And you continued: "How come you never said nothing? You didn't have no plans where he was going? I knew he wasn't doing nothin' to you!" Again, are you continuing explaining the same conversation to John Gotti?

GRAVANO: Yes.

GLEESON: Then John Gotti says: "Yeah. But, no, I'm saying. Well, whoever done it, I don't know who done it." What was he referring to there?

GRAVANO: Who did it with Paul.

GLEESON: Who did what with Paul?

GRAVANO: Who killed him.

GLEESON: And he said, "I don't know who done it." Did you commit to murder Paul?

GRAVANO: Yes.

GLEESON: Did you commit it with John Gotti?

GRAVANO: Yes.

GLEESON: At this point in the conversation John Gotti states: "I don't know who done it." He's referring to the murder of Paul, correct?

GRAVANO: Yes.

GLEESON: Had you heard such statements before?

GRAVANO: I just got done telling Nino almost the same thing. We never admitted it.

GLEESON: Have you heard statements like this before?

GRAVANO: Yeah.

GLEESON: Often?

GRAVANO: Whenever we referred to him.

GLEESON: If you did it, why did you say you didn't do it?

GRAVANO: Because we broke the rule, and we were never gonna really admit it. We were never openly going to admit it.

GLEESON: Gotti states: "But, anyway, here's a guy, whoever done it, probably the cops done it to this guy. Whoever killed this cocksucker, probably the cops killed this Paul. But whoever killed him, he deserved it."

Did you understand him to believe that probably the cops killed Paul Castellano?

GRAVANO: No.

GLEESON: Is this another denial?

GRAVANO: It's not a denial. It's just a way of talking.

GLEESON: Gotti states: "We had nothin' to do with it; no reason to do it." Were there reasons to kill Paul Castellano?

GRAVANO: Yes.

GLEESON: Have you already described them in your testimony?

GRAVANO: Yes.

GLEESON: Are some of the reasons referred to in this very conversation?

GRAVANO: Yes.

GLEESON: After Gotti asks what time is it, you say: "I love it when he does that, Frank." Do you recall what you were referring to?

GRAVANO: He makes some sort of a motion, body language.

GLEESON: Who did?

GRAVANO: John did.

GLEESON: What kind of body language?

GRAVANO: It's hard to explain. It's just an expression, just the way he moves.

GLEESON: The denials, you mentioned that it's a way of speaking. You mentioned that a moment ago. When that occurred, what was the demeanor of the people who were speaking that way? Do you understand my question?

GRAVANO: No.

GLEESON: You mentioned body language here and that it's hard to explain. Do your best. Try to explain to the jury what you're referring to.

GRAVANO: When he says that the cops did it, probably the cops did it, he'll do an expression and move his hands, give a smirk.

JUDGE GLASSER: Indicating a shrug of the shoulders and extension of the arms.

GLEESON: Is that something you had seen before?

GRAVANO: Yes.

GLEESON: Is that something you, yourself, did?

GRAVANO: Yes.

[. . . .]

DI B GETS "WHACKED"

GLEESON: Mr. Gravano, was Robert DiBernardo present that night when Paul Castellano and Tommy Bilotti were murdered?

GRAVANO: No.

GLEESON: Do you know where he was?

GRAVANO: I think he was in Florida.

GLEESON: You testified earlier that he was a soldier in the Family at that point, correct?

GRAVANO: Yes.

GLEESON: Prior to the murder, what responsibility, if any, did DiBernardo have within the Family?

GRAVANO: He was directly with the boss. He handled unions, construction, certain businesses.

[. . . .]

GLEESON: [By early 1990] did you see Di B regularly?

GRAVANO: Yes.

GLEESON: In what circumstances would you see Di B?

GRAVANO: I would see Di B three, four times a week. We handled the construction, the unions.

GLEESON: Did you ever hear him express views on who should replace [Frank] DeCicco as underboss?

GRAVANO: Yes, he did.

GLEESON: What were his views?

GRAVANO: His view is that I should be underboss.

GLEESON: Did you express any views on the issue, at that point?

GRAVANO: No.

GLEESON: Now, you testified that you spoke regularly with Angelo and "Joe Piney," right, after John went to jail, correct?

GRAVANO: Yes.

GLEESON: By the way, does there come a point later on when one of those two went to jail?

GRAVANO: Yes. Angelo went to jail.

GLEESON: Before that happened, you spoke regularly with Angelo and "Joe Piney," correct?

GRAVANO: Yes.

GLEESON: During that conversation, did Di B's opinion about who should be underboss come up?

GRAVANO: Yes, it did.

GLEESON: Can you tell us how?

GRAVANO: It came up at a meeting with "Joe Piney," myself, and Angelo. Angelo said that Di B expressed an opinion that I should be the underboss. He was telling "Joe Piney," and then he asked me if it was so.

GLEESON: Who asked you if it was so?

GRAVANO: Angelo.

GLEESON: What did you say?

GRAVANO: Yes.

GLEESON: At the time, did you think much of it?

GRAVANO: No.

GLEESON: While John was in jail, did you speak to anybody about killing Di B?

GRAVANO: I spoke to Angelo.

GLEESON: How did that conversation come about?

GRAVANO: Angelo came to me and told me that John sent out an order to kill Angelo—Di B.

GLEESON: Did Angelo say why?

GRAVANO: He said that he was talking behind his back, and there was other reasons.

GLEESON: Approximately how long after John Gotti went to jail did this happen?

GRAVANO: Soon.

GLEESON: Did you respond to Angelo when he told you this?

GRAVANO: Yes. I asked Angelo to reach John and see if we couldn't hold up on it, and when he came out, we would discuss it. Di B was just talking a lot and not meaning anything. He wasn't dangerous. It was something we could hold up on.

GLEESON: You said this to Angelo?

GRAVANO: Yes.

GLEESON: Did he respond to you?

GRAVANO: He immediately responded to me that this had to be done, that John was steaming. We already had a location to kill him, which was in Tony Lee's mother's basement, and I was just gonna sit in this meeting and my role was actually going to be when Di B came to me, I was gonna explain to him there's a meeting, something to do with the Family, some construction, if Di B checked with me.

GLEESON: Before we get to the proposed meeting, you said to Angelo, Di B is not dangerous. Is that what you just testified to?

GRAVANO: Right.

GLEESON: What did you mean by that?

GRAVANO: Well, Di B was just a talker. He had no crew. He wasn't a shooter. He was no threat.

GLEESON: You mentioned that Angelo had said that there was already a plan?

GRAVANO: Yes.

GLEESON: And could you tell us again what the plan was that Angelo mentioned to you?

GRAVANO: Angelo told me that there was gonna be an appointment at Tony Lee's mother's house in the basement. I would be sitting there with a few other people, and when Di B came down, whoever was behind him, would shoot him in the head. If Di B came to me and questioned me if there was a meeting, I would tell him yes, there was a meeting, it was about construction and about Family policy.

GLEESON: By the way, who's Tony Lee?

GRAVANO: He's a soldier in our Family.

GLEESON: Do you know his last name?

GRAVANO: No.

GLEESON: By the way, Mr. Gravano, did you refer to each other by your last names?

GRAVANO: No.

GLEESON: Are there a lot of people in the Family whose last names you just don't know?

GRAVANO: Yes.

GLEESON: Was the plan, the plan you mentioned about Tony Lee's mother's house, was that ever carried out?

GRAVANO: No.

GLEESON: Did you have a conversation with Angelo about a different plan?

GRAVANO: Angelo came back to me, soon after the first conversation, and told me that John was hot, we couldn't get the house. We had to get it done right away, if I could take care of it myself.

GLEESON: Did you agree?

GRAVANO: Yes.

GLEESON: Did you formulate a plan as to how you would take care of it?

GRAVANO: Yes. I told him that if it had to be done right away, Di B sees me a couple of times a week, that I would kill him right in my office.

GLEESON: Who did you discuss this with?

GRAVANO: Angelo.

GLEESON: And was he going to have any role in this plan?

GRAVANO: He was gonna get rid of the body and call Di B and assure him that there was a meeting with me, which I told him wasn't necessary anyway.

GLEESON: Why wasn't it necessary?

GRAVANO: Because Di B saw me three, four times a week.

GLEESON: Did there come a point when you carried out the plan?

GRAVANO: Yes.

GLEESON: Could you tell us what you did?

GRAVANO: Di B came down in the morning to meet me as usual and told me he couldn't spend too much time, that he had an appointment in New York. I told him I had an appointment. I told him if we could meet five-thirty, six o'clock, by my office. We'll have a cup of coffee and discuss a few things that came up. He told me fine, and then he left. I got my crew together and we set the hit up in my office.

GLEESON: When you say you got your crew together, who did you get together for this hit?

GRAVANO: I got in touch with Angelo and told him that I spoke to Di B already, that it was on for five-thirty, six o'clock. I had my brother-in-law Eddie, old man Paruta, who's around me, and a guy name Huck.

GLEESON: Do you know—is Huck a friend of yours?

GRAVANO: Yes.

GLEESON: What's his real name?

GRAVANO: Thomas Carbonaro.

GLEESON: Was he also in business with you?

GRAVANO: No.

GLEESON: Was Angelo in your crew?

GRAVANO: No.

GLEESON: Did the plan include Angelo being at your office when the murder took place?

GRAVANO: No. He would be at a Burger King in Coney Island at six o'clock on and, if I succeeded, I would go to the Burger King and see him over there.

GLEESON: Did Di B come back to your office later that day?

GRAVANO: He came about five, five-thirty.

GLEESON: Did he come alone or with others?

GRAVANO: He came alone.

GLEESON: When he came, where were you?

GRAVANO: I was downstairs.

GLEESON: Is this the same location where you had the meeting to plan the murder of Paul Castellano?

GRAVANO: Yes.

GLEESON: Were you with anybody else downstairs?

GRAVANO: I was with my brother-in-law and old man Paruta.

GLEESON: Your brother-in-law being?

GRAVANO: Eddie Garafolo.

GLEESON: Was anyone upstairs when Di B came?

GRAVANO: Huck was upstairs.

GLEESON: What happened when Di B came?

GRAVANO: He told Di B that we were downstairs. Di B came in. He came downstairs. He said hello. He sat down.

Then old man Paruta got up and I told him to get Di B a cup of coffee. He got up.

In the cabinet there was a .380 with a silencer. He took the gun out, walked over to Di B, and shot him twice in the back of the head.

Me and Eddie picked him up and put him in the back room, locked it up. We left the office. We locked the office up and I went and met with Angelo and I told him it was done.

GLEESON: Where did you meet with Angelo?

GRAVANO: In the Burger King in Coney Island.

GLEESON: You mentioned your brother-in-law Eddie, the old man Paruta and Huck. Had you committed murders with them in the past?

GRAVANO: Yes.

GLEESON: When you met with Angelo, were you alone? Did you go there alone?

GRAVANO: I believe my brother-in-law drove me.

GLEESON: When you got there, was Angelo alone?

GRAVANO: I don't know.

GLEESON: Did you have a conversation with him?

GRAVANO: Yes.

GLEESON: What did you tell him?

GRAVANO: I told him it was done, that he came down with a brand-new Mercedes with a sophisticated alarm system.

GLEESON: Who had?

GRAVANO: Di B. I told him I had the keys. He told me don't worry about it, he'll see me tonight, meaning that night, eight-thirty, nine o'clock, at Tali's, and he would get rid of the body and the car.

GLEESON: At that point, did he tell you how he was gonna get rid of the body and the car?

GRAVANO: No.

GLEESON: Where was the car, by the way?

GRAVANO: Half a block away from my office.

GLEESON: Did you go to Tali's later that evening?

GRAVANO: Yes, I did.

GLEESON: Did you meet people there?

GRAVANO: Yes.

GLEESON: Who did you meet?

GRAVANO: It was Angelo, Johnny Carneglia. Johnny Carneglia was with a bunch of young kids. I don't know who they are, Bobby Borriello and it was my brother-in-law Eddie, Huck, and there might have been some other people there.

GLEESON: There were some other people there, as well?

GRAVANO: Yeah.

GLEESON: Did there come a point when you left Tali's?

GRAVANO: Yes.

GLEESON: What is Tali's?

GRAVANO: It's a bar that's more like a club.

GLEESON: Was it your club?

GRAVANO: Yes.

GLEESON: Did you hang out there regularly?

GRAVANO: Yes.

GLEESON: Was there a particular night of the week where people who were close to you would go to Tali's?

GRAVANO: Every Tuesday night we would get together at Tali's.

GLEESON: When you got to Tali's that night, did you learn what arrangements had been made to dispose of the body?

GRAVANO: Frankie was there. He was supposedly gonna receive the body and John—

MITCHELL: I object, Your Honor.

JUDGE GLASSER: Overruled.

MITCHELL: May I have a continuing objection to this line?

JUDGE GLASSER: Yes.

GLEESON: Which Frankie?

GRAVANO: Frank Locascio.

GLEESON: He was at Tali's in addition to the people you mentioned before?

GRAVANO: Yes.

GLEESON: When you left Tali's, where did you go?

GRAVANO: I went to my office.

GETTING RID OF THE CORPSE

GLEESON: At that point, was Di B's body still down in the basement of your office?

GRAVANO: Yes.

GLEESON: Did you take steps to remove the body?

GRAVANO: Yes.

GLEESON: What happened in that regard?

GRAVANO: We went downstairs, we went back into the office. We went downstairs; me, my brother-in-law Eddie, Johnny Carneglia, and Bobby Borriello and took the body upstairs.

Frankie pulled up on the sidewalk, opened up the trunk. And we put the body in the trunk. Frankie left, John Carneg went over with a bunch of kids and took the car and left.

We went back to Tali's and closed up the office.

GLEESON: Johnny Carneg took what car and left?

GRAVANO: Di B's car.

GLEESON: You say Frankie pulled up the car to the office?

GRAVANO: Yes.

GLEESON: Was he in the car alone or with others?

GRAVANO: Alone.

GLEESON: Did he get out of car?

GRAVANO: No.

GLEESON: Who opened the trunk?

GRAVANO: I don't really know if it opens from the inside.

GLEESON: Did you have help bringing the body up from the basement?

GRAVANO: Yes.

GLEESON: Where was the body placed?

GRAVANO: In the trunk.

GLEESON: After that, what happened?

GRAVANO: The car left, Johnny Carneg left with these kids taking the other car, we locked up, and left.

GLEESON: Did you see either Johnny Carneg, or the kids who took Di B's car, later that night again?

GRAVANO: I don't believe so.

GLEESON: Did you see Frankie Loc later that night again?

GRAVANO: No.

GLEESON: When he left in the car, was there anyone else in the car with him?

GRAVANO: No.

GLEESON: Just Di B's body in the trunk?

GRAVANO: Yes.

GLEESON: Did he tell you where the body was taken?

GRAVANO: No.

GLEESON: Did you ever ask him?

GRAVANO: No.

GLEESON: Was there a reason why you didn't ask him?

GRAVANO: It was none of my business.

[. . . .]

GLEESON: Did you ask for permission to kill Di B?

GRAVANO: No.

GLEESON: Was he a friend of yours?

GRAVANO: Yes.

GLEESON: You testified at the beginning of your testimony that evidence was presented at a hearing where the government sought to detain you pending trial. Do you recall that?

GRAVANO: Yes.

GLEESON: What did the evidence consist of?

GRAVANO: Part of it was the taped conversation about killing Di B.

GLEESON: Did you hear that? Did you hear part of that conversation played right here in open court?

GRAVANO: Yes.

GLEESON: That was back in December of 1990?

GRAVANO: Yes.

GLEESON: Did they reveal anything about the murder of Di B? What is your recollection of what—

JUDGE GLASSER: By "they," you are referring to the tapes?

GLEESON: The tapes that we heard at the detention hearing.

GRAVANO: Said that I talked—I told John that he was talking behind his back and I asked permission basically to kill him.

GLEESON: After that hearing, did you have an opportunity to speak to John Gotti about that conversation?

GRAVANO: Yes.

GLEESON: Were you alone when you spoke about it?

GRAVANO: I was alone with John.

GLEESON: What did you say to him?

GRAVANO: I told him it wasn't true.

GLEESON: That what wasn't true?

GRAVANO: What was said on—in the tape when he was explaining to Frankie on tape wasn't true.

GLEESON: What part?

GRAVANO: I never asked permission to kill Di B. I never said he talked behind his back. I said that whatever Angelo told him, wherever he got this from, wasn't true. What I did was an order. I was ordered to kill Di B. An order came out of prison and I killed him.

GLEESON: What did he say to you?

GRAVANO: He says he heard it from "Joe Piney" as well.

GLEESON: Heard what?

GRAVANO: That Di B was talking behind his back and that I agreed with it.

GLEESON: Di B was your friend?

GRAVANO: Yes.

GLEESON: You didn't ask permission to kill him?

GRAVANO: No.

GLEESON: But is it fair to say, Mr. Gravano, that you didn't have any qualms in killing your friend once you were ordered to do so?

GRAVANO: No.

[. . . .]

THE FATE OF LOUIE MILITO

GLEESON: Over the years, did you commit murders with Louie Milito?

GRAVANO: Yes.

GLEESON: More than one?

GRAVANO: Yes.

GLEESON: When you were released in 1972, in or about 1972, to Toddo's crew in the Gambino Family, who was Louie Milito with?

GRAVANO: He was with the old man Johnny Rizzo. He was a made member in that crew.

GLEESON: Were you both in the same crew?

GRAVANO: Yes.

GLEESON: Did you continue to commit crimes with him even going back that far?

GRAVANO: Yes.

GLEESON: What types of crimes did you commit with Louie Milito?

GRAVANO: Murder, shylock, we ran games, auto-theft ring.

GLEESON: When you got made, was he already made?

GRAVANO: No.

GLEESON: Did there come a point after you became a made member that he did?

GRAVANO: Yes.

GLEESON: Did you have anything to do with that?

GRAVANO: Yes.

GLEESON: What?

GRAVANO: I actually pushed it. He became made through me.

GLEESON: Was he a friend of yours?

GRAVANO: Yes.

GLEESON: Did you know his family?

GRAVANO: Yes.

GLEESON: Did you know his son and daughter?

GRAVANO: Yes.

GLEESON: Before the murder of Paul Castellano and Tom Bilotti, did you have any construction interests with Louie Milito?

GRAVANO: Yes.

GLEESON: Could you tell the jury what they were?

GRAVANO: We were partners in a company named Gem Atlas Steel. We handled them together.

[. . . .]

GLEESON: Did there come a point when your partnership ended?

GRAVANO: Yes, it did.

GLEESON: Who ended it?

GRAVANO: He did.

GLEESON: Is this before or after the murder of Castellano and Bilotti?

GRAVANO: Before.

GLEESON: Did he tell you why?

GRAVANO: No.

GLEESON: Did you find out later why Louie Milito ended your shylock business with him?

GRAVANO: Yes, I did.

GLEESON: What did you find out?

GRAVANO: I found out that he spoke with Paul and in a conversation with Paul he became very concerned and broke up partnerships.

GLEESON: What did he become concerned about?

GRAVANO: Paul was angry about a discotheque that I was involved in and that he wasn't used to dealing with Paul. The conversation obviously scared him, and he broke up the conversation, the partnership.

GLEESON: Who wasn't used to dealing with Paul, Milito?

GRAVANO: Milito.

GLEESON: Did he tell you that that was the reason he was breaking up the partnership?

GRAVANO: No.

GLEESON: After the murders of Paul and Tommy, did you find out anything about Louie Milito?

GRAVANO: We found out through Frankie DeCicco that he was partners with Tommy Bilotti.

GLEESON: That Louie Milito was?

GRAVANO: Yes.

GLEESON: How was that found out?

GRAVANO: He had broke up with me. He went partners with Tommy Bilotti in shylock business, and what he basically did was he betrayed us. He went behind our back and went partners with Paul and Tommy.

GLEESON: How was it found out that he had gone partners with Tommy Bilotti?

GRAVANO: When Tommy had died, we went into his interests—what he had, what he didn't have, what they were doing.

GLEESON: Did you go into those interests for the same reason that you had gone into Di B's interests?

GRAVANO: Yes.

GLEESON: After you found out that Milito had become partners with Tommy Bilotti, did you have any discussions with Frankie DeCicco?

GRAVANO: Yes, I did.

GLEESON: Can you tell the jury the nature of those discussions?

GRAVANO: Frankie was upset. I told Frankie that when Louie came out, I could talk to him, tell him that we know what he did. Put him on the side, and that I could live with it.

Frankie responded that he betrayed us. It was something he couldn't live with, and the minute Louie got out he was going to get killed.

GLEESON: Got out of where?

GRAVANO: He was in jail.

GLEESON: Was he in jail when Castellano and Bilotti were murdered?

GRAVANO: Yes.

GLEESON: What was your response to DeCicco's stated plan to kill Milito when he got out of jail?

GRAVANO: I didn't have any at that point.

GLEESON: Did you agree with it?

GRAVANO: Not really.

GLEESON: Did there come a time when Louie Milito finally got out of jail?

GRAVANO: Yes.

GLEESON: At that point was Frankie DeCicco still alive?

GRAVANO: No.

GLEESON: When he got out of jail, whose crew was Louie Milito in?

GRAVANO: He was in my crew.

GLEESON: Did you have a discussion with him when he got out of jail about the fact that according to you he had betrayed you?

GRAVANO: Yes. I told him that we knew. We found out exactly what he did, why he did it, and he was to stay in Staten Island, mind his business, be low-key, and he would be all right. I was going to give him a pass. I gave him my word I wouldn't hurt him.

GLEESON: When you say "gave him a pass," you mean you weren't going to kill him?

GRAVANO: Right.

GLEESON: What was Louie Milito's response to that when you had that conversation?

GRAVANO: Fine. He understood at that point.

GLEESON: When you told him to stay in Staten Island, could you explain to the jury what you mean by that?

GRAVANO: Just stay in his small little circle and mind his business and he had nothing coming. He couldn't expand. He would just stay in a small little area and just do his business, shylock or whatever.

[. . . .]

GLEESON: Did you have any problems with Milito after that conversation?

GRAVANO: Yes.

GLEESON: Could you tell us what the nature of the problems were?

GRAVANO: Milito didn't believe the conversation, so what he was doing was going behind my back, going to people who were close to me to try and find out what I was thinking, what my attitude was when he left. Different things like that.

GLEESON: Was that upsetting to you?

GRAVANO: Checking on me was a little upsetting to me, yes.

GLEESON: Why?

GRAVANO: Louie was relatively dangerous. He would be somebody I would pay attention to.

GLEESON: Had you committed multiple murders with him in the past?

GRAVANO: Yes.

GLEESON: When he came out of jail, you said you were a captain, correct?

GRAVANO: Yes.

GLEESON: During this period, where you found out that Louie was talking about you, did you change position in the family?

GRAVANO: Yes. I became the acting *consigliere* of the family.

GLEESON: Who replaced you as captain?

GRAVANO: Big Louie.

GLEESON: Who is Big Louie?

GRAVANO: Big Louie Vallario.

GLEESON: Was he a member of your crew when you were captain?

GRAVANO: Yes.

GLEESON: Did Louie Milito have anything to say about the selection of Big Lou Vallario to take over your crew?

GRAVANO: At that time Big Lou came to me, he was bad-mouthing Big Lou. He felt that he should be the captain in that crew, and then he was bad-mouthing our administration, our judgment, and what we were doing.

GLEESON: Who is doing the bad-mouthing?

GRAVANO: Louie Milito.

GLEESON: During this period, how regularly did you see John Gotti?

GRAVANO: Five days a week, six days a week.

GLEESON: Did you keep him apprised of these problems with Louie Milito?

GRAVANO: In the beginning, it wasn't a big problem. Toward the end, it became a big problem, and I started to talk to John about it.

GLEESON: When you talked to John about it, did you describe to him the problems that you have described to the jury?

GRAVANO: Yes.

GLEESON: Did there come a point when you made a decision as to what to do about Louie Milito?

GRAVANO: Yes.

GLEESON: What was your decision?

GRAVANO: My decision was to ask John to kill him, that he couldn't live with the earlier decision that I had given him.

GLEESON: That Louie Milito couldn't live with the decision?

GRAVANO: Right.

GLEESON: Did you have a discussion with John Gotti about that?

GRAVANO: Yes.

GLEESON: Can you tell us what the substance of the discussion was?

GRAVANO: Just what I said, that he couldn't live with it, that at that point I asked permission to kill him. I told him he was talking about us, the administration, the move we made by putting Big Louie as a captain, and he was talking behind Big Louie's back, it came back to Big Louie, it came back to me. He was talking behind my back, trying to scheme. . . .

GLEESON: What was John Gotti's response?

GRAVANO: He thought I was right. He gave me permission to take him out. He said the only thing is, is he wanted me to use Genie [Gotti] and his crew.

GLEESON: Genie, his [John Gotti's] brother?

GRAVANO: Yes.

GLEESON: At that time what was Genie's position?

GRAVANO: He was a captain.

GLEESON: After that conversation—do you recall, by the way, where you were when you discussed that with John Gotti?

GRAVANO: Down in New York.

GLEESON: Do you recall specifically where you were?

GRAVANO: We were walking in the street.

GLEESON: Did you have a conversation after that with Gene Gotti?

GRAVANO: Yes, I did.

GLEESON: Do you recall where?

GRAVANO: In New York.

GLEESON: Inside or outside?

GRAVANO: Outside on the street.

GLEESON: Was anyone else present when you discussed it with Gene Gotti?

GRAVANO: No.

GLEESON: Can you tell us what that discussion was about?

GRAVANO: We discussed what we would do. He told me that I would be responsible to get him in and the place. He would be responsible for the shooter and getting rid of the body.

GLEESON: You say your responsibility was to get him in?

GRAVANO: Yes.

GLEESON: What do you mean by that?

GRAVANO: Bring him into a location so they could kill him.

GLEESON: Sorry?

GRAVANO: Bring him into a location so they could kill him.

GLEESON: Did he tell you what arrangements he was going to make for the shooters and disposing of the body?

GRAVANO: No.

GLEESON: Did you make arrangements to get Louie Milito in?

GRAVANO: Yes.

GLEESON: Did you come up with a plan?

GRAVANO: Yes.

GLEESON: What was the plan?

GRAVANO: I got in touch with Big Lou in his club. He sent for Louie Milito and told him that we were going to kill Johnny Gammarano, that was basically our plan.

GLEESON: That was the way you were going to get Louie Milito to come in?

GRAVANO: Yes.

GLEESON: Was there a particular reason you chose that plan?

GRAVANO: John was always talking, bad-mouthing Johnny Gammarano, talking about him, and Louie believed it right away, that he was going to be killed.

GLEESON: Louie Milito?

GRAVANO: Yes.

GLEESON: Believed who was going to be killed?

GRAVANO: Johnny Gammarano was going to be killed.

GLEESON: As part of your plan, did you have a place in mind to commit the murder?

GRAVANO: We were supposed to meet at Big Lou's club to discuss killing Johnny Gammarano, and when we were going to go to that club to meet we were going to kill him right then and there.

GLEESON: Kill who?

GRAVANO: Louie Milito.

GLEESON: Where is Big Lou's club?

GRAVANO: Seventeenth Avenue and 77th, in Brooklyn.

A DATE WITH DEATH

GLEESON: Did Big Lou reach out for Louie Milito to get him to come to the club?

GRAVANO: Yes, he did. He made an appointment on a Tuesday night. We all met on a Tuesday night in the club. Louie Milito came down. Big Lou was behind the counter. Me, Genie, a guy named Arnold, was sitting playing cards. Johnny Carneglia was sitting on the couch.

Lou came in. Said hello. He was walking back over to the counter. Johnny Carneglia went in the other room. Had a gun with a silencer on it. Came out. Shot him one time behind the head. When he fell down, he put the gun under his chin, pulled the trigger again.

Arnold went, got a car, pulled up in front of the club. We put the body in the trunk. Johnny Carneglia and Arnold pulled away with the body. Eddie and Huck were at two different intersections watching the street, the avenue, me and Genie went on the street with Big Lou and we waited for them to come back.

GLEESON: Okay. Back up a little bit. You say when Louie Milito came to the club, Big Lou was behind the counter?

GRAVANO: Yes.

GLEESON: Is the club on street level?

GRAVANO: Yes.

GLEESON: That's the level that you were at when this happened?

GRAVANO: Yes.

GLEESON: Before Milito came to the club, were the people who had—people from Genie's crew who were going to be the shooters, were they already there?

GRAVANO: Yes.

GLEESON: When did you find out who Genie had selected?

GRAVANO: Then. When we met in Big Lou's club.

GLEESON: And did Genie come with them?

GRAVANO: Yes.

GLEESON: Who were they?

GRAVANO: Arnold Squitieri, Genie, Johnny Carneglia, myself, and Big Lou.

GLEESON: And you mentioned two other people, Huck and Eddie. Were they already there?

GRAVANO: Yes.

GLEESON: And where were they when the murder took place?

GRAVANO: They were on two separate blocks, a block, a block and a half away from the club on both sides.

GLEESON: Eddie is your brother-in-law?

GRAVANO: Yes.

GLEESON: Huck is Thomas Carbonaro you testified about this morning?

GRAVANO: Yes.

GLEESON: What was their job on either block?

GRAVANO: Just to watch the traffic and see, make sure that there was no police cars or know anything like that.

GLEESON: Who brought the gun?

GRAVANO: They did.

GLEESON: You mentioned that Squitieri—Arnold Squitieri—and John Carneglia drove away with the body?

GRAVANO: Yes.

GLEESON: Were you still at Big Lou's club at that point?

GRAVANO: Yes, I was.

GLEESON: Inside or outside?

GRAVANO: I was inside for a while and then I went outside.

GLEESON: Who was with you?

GRAVANO: Genie was with me. And Big Lou was with me.

GLEESON: Did there come a point when Squitieri and Carneglia returned?

GRAVANO: Yes.

GLEESON: What happened at that point?

GRAVANO: Everybody left. Me, Big Lou, Eddie, and Huck went to Tali's on Eighteenth Avenue and all the other people left.

GLEESON: You mentioned earlier that you did it on—you made an appointment for a Tuesday night?

GRAVANO: Yes.

GLEESON: Was that done at random or was that done for a particular reason?

GRAVANO: We did it on purpose because we knew that there was surveillance by Tali's watching us every Tuesday night, so when we walked in about eight, eight-thirty, we looked normal and we would have the government as our witness.

GLEESON: Is that what you did?

GRAVANO: Yes.

GLEESON: When Squitieri and Carneglia came back, I take it they no longer had the body. Correct?

GRAVANO: No. They didn't have the body, no.

GLEESON: Did you ask them where they took it?

GRAVANO: No.

GLEESON: Did they tell you?

GRAVANO: No.

[. . . .]

CROCODILE ETIQUETTE

GLEESON: Did you talk to Louie Milito's wife and daughter after he was murdered?

GRAVANO: Yes, I did.

GLEESON: Can you describe the circumstances that led to your speaking to them?

GRAVANO: I was a close friend of the family for a long time and there was about fifteen, twenty thousand dollars' worth of construction work that had to be finished in his house that wasn't done. I brought my companies in to finish it. I gave his wife some money. I spoke with his daughter, that I would inquire as far as her father was concerned, whatever their needs or problems were I would take care of. If anybody was to bother them, I would help, and I would look into it the best as I could.

DIBONO TAKES A FALL

GLEESON: Did you know a Louie DiBono?

GRAVANO: Yes.

GLEESON: When did you first meet him?

GRAVANO: Early '80s.

GLEESON: What was it that led you to meet Louie DiBono?

GRAVANO: Construction interests.

GLEESON: Who was he?

GRAVANO: Who was he?

GLEESON: Yes. Was he a businessman?

GRAVANO: He was a businessman.

GLEESON: Did he have a position in the Gambino Family?

GRAVANO: He was a made member of the Gambino Family.

GLEESON: Whose crew was he in?

GRAVANO: Patsy Conte.

GLEESON: In the early '80s, did you have any business relationship with him?

GRAVANO: Yes.

GLEESON: Did you have construction interests at that point?

GRAVANO: Yes, I did.

GLEESON: I believe you testified you had a drywall company, correct?

GRAVANO: Yes.

GLEESON: Could you tell us what the nature of your business relationship was with Louie DiBono in the early '80s?

GRAVANO: He did large drywall jobs in the city, union jobs. I would come in and lump them. I was a nonunion company. I would come in and do the actual physical work.

[. . . .]

GLEESON: Did the business relationship go well?

GRAVANO: No.

GLEESON: What happened?

GRAVANO: Louie DiBono was like a swindler type of guy and he tried to hold up payments and beat us, connive, whatever he—corner every angle.

GLEESON: Did you think he was robbing you?

GRAVANO: Yes, I did.

GLEESON: Did you have a confrontation with him?

GRAVANO: Yes, I did.

GLEESON: This is back in the early '80s, correct?

GRAVANO: Yes.

GLEESON: Where did the confrontation take place?

GRAVANO: In his office, in Long Island.

GLEESON: Was anyone else present?

GRAVANO: There was a bunch of people present. His secretary, a few workers, my brother-in-law Eddie. Five, six people.

GLEESON: Can you tell us what the confrontation, what happened at the confrontation?

GRAVANO: We argued about the monies. Finally I assured him that if he robbed us, he wouldn't enjoy the money. I would wind up killing him.

GLEESON: Did you say that in front of anybody?

GRAVANO: I said it in front of a few people.

GLEESON: You mentioned a rule yesterday, a rule that—against raising your hand against another member of the Family. Do you recall that testimony?

GRAVANO: Yes.

GLEESON: Was this threat to Louie DiBono a violation of the rule?

GRAVANO: Similar.

GLEESON: Similar?

GRAVANO: Yes.

GLEESON: Did anything happen as a result of the threat?

GRAVANO: He went to his captain, which was Patsy Conte. They went to the administration, and they put up a book.

GLEESON: When you say "put up a book," what do you mean?

GRAVANO: They put up a beef that I threatened him and they were asking to have me killed.

GLEESON: Did anything happen as a result of that request they made?

GRAVANO: Frankie DeCicco reached out for me and told me that they were scheduling an appointment in Staten Island in a house—in a diner—and advised me that when I went to the meeting, that if they asked me if I had threatened him, that I should lie and say no.

GLEESON: That was advice given to you by Frankie DeCicco?

GRAVANO: Yes.

GLEESON: Was an appointment set up?

GRAVANO: Yes.

GLEESON: How did you find out about it?

GRAVANO: Frankie DeCicco told me about the appointment.

GLEESON: Did he tell you where to go?

GRAVANO: He told me to go in the diner in Staten Island, Country Diner.

GLEESON: Did you go there?

GRAVANO: Yes.

GLEESON: Alone or with other people?

GRAVANO: I was told to bring my brother-in-law Eddie along with me.

GLEESON: And when you got to the diner, what happened?

GRAVANO: Tommy Bilotti pulled up with a—with a Lincoln, with tinted windows. Told me and Eddie to get in the car, that the meeting was at the house, some house in the basement.

GLEESON: Did you get in the car?

GRAVANO: Yes, I did.

GLEESON: Did you go to a house?

GRAVANO: Yes.

GLEESON: Where was the house?

GRAVANO: Someplace in Staten Island.

GLEESON: Do you know whose house it was?

GRAVANO: No.

GLEESON: When you got there, was anyone else there?

GRAVANO: When we got in, there was the entire administration. There was Paul Castellano, there was Neil, there was

Joe Gallo, there was Patsy Conte, there was Louie DiBono, there was my captain, Toddo, there. There was Frankie DeCicco, Tommy Bilotti, and I believe Di B might have been there.

GLEESON: What happened when you got there?

GRAVANO: Paul spoke a little while and then they made Louie DiBono explain what went on, what I had said, that I made the threat. And they told about the entire situation.

GLEESON: You mentioned that before the meeting Frankie DeCicco had advised you to deny making the threat?

GRAVANO: Yes.

GLEESON: Did you follow his advice?

GRAVANO: No.

GLEESON: What happened?

GRAVANO: I agreed with—that I did threaten him, and I had told them that I never done that with a friend of ours, that this guy was a liar, a cheat, and he was robbing us. I explained how and why I made this threat, and I had asked for permission to kill him right—right at the table there, right in front of him.

GLEESON: What happened when you asked for permission to kill him?

GRAVANO: Paul got a little excited, Neil stopped him, jumped in, said that by me making the admission, that I couldn't—should be killed right on the spot but gave more than reason that Louie was a liar and swindler and he should have been killed years ago.

GLEESON: Who was saying this?

GRAVANO: Neil. He just took over the conversation.

GLEESON: Did Neil take your side in the conversation?

GRAVANO: It seemed like it, yeah.

GLEESON: What was the result?

GRAVANO: They made us shake hands, they made us forget about it, and they made me promise that I would never hurt him.

GLEESON: Did you make that promise?

GRAVANO: Yes.

GLEESON: At that point, that's back in the early '80s?

GRAVANO: Back in the early '80s.

GLEESON: Do you recall how long before the murder of Castellano and Bilotti that took place?

GRAVANO: Quite a while.

GLEESON: At that point, did you stop doing business with Louie DiBono?

GRAVANO: That was another thing. We were to stop doing business with one another.

GLEESON: That was part of the resolution?

GRAVANO: Yes.

GLEESON: Did you stay in the drywall business?

GRAVANO: Yes.

GLEESON: Did you ever go into business with Louie DiBono again?

GRAVANO: When John was the boss and Paul was gone and John was in jail, "Joe Piney" told me that it would be nice if we started something for the boss, especially with Louie, that he was a big contractor. I told him about the problem. He was a little bit aware of it.

GLEESON: I'm sorry? You told "Joe Piney" about what?

GRAVANO: About the problem. I didn't think we would run into the problem again because of different circumstances, the different situation, so I had agreed that as long as "Joe Piney" spoke with him and I spoke with him, that we would put my business interests in the drywall business with his.

We had a meeting with him. We talked to him. I told him the past was the past. We put our interests together. I told him he would run it from his office. He would run the books, the records, the business. I would literally get out of business.

I would give him Joe Madonia, who is a top supervisor in the drywall business. I would give him my entire labor force. He could pay them direct. I would just be on paper as a figurehead. I wouldn't run the business. He could run the business with his payroll department, his—all his own people, his lawyer, his accountant, and just so that we had a percentage of the business, where we would be able to make the boss something.

GLEESON: Did Louie DiBono agree?

GRAVANO: Yes, he did.

GLEESON: When you discussed this with "Joe Piney," did you discuss what piece of the business, if any, would go to the boss?

GRAVANO: Yes. We discussed forty-five percent for me, forty-five percent for Louie DiBono, ten percent for John. A thousand a week for me as far as salary, being I was giving up the company. A thousand a week for Louie DiBono, being he was giving up a company. And that was basically the first agreement.

GLEESON: Did there come a point—by the way, when that was first discussed, where was John Gotti?

GRAVANO: He was in jail.

GLEESON: Did anybody send word to him about this?

GRAVANO: "Joe Piney" could have. I don't know.

GLEESON: You don't know?

GRAVANO: I don't know for sure. I didn't.

GLEESON: You say that was the first agreement. Did it subsequently change?

GRAVANO: He told me, being I was gonna have John Gotti's percentage under my name, I would have fifty-five percent of the company and he would have forty percent. His lawyers advised him it should be fifty-fifty. So, the deal had changed. After a series of meetings I had with him, it was fifty percent for Louie DiBono, fifty percent for myself. My fifty percent, I would pay taxes and would be partners with John fifty-fifty on whatever I took out, and we would raise our salary from a thousand a week to fifteen hundred a week, after taxes take two hundred and fifty each, give to Johnny five hundred a week, and I would wind up with about eight hundred clear, Louie DiBono would end up with eight hundred clear, and John five hundred clear, but me and Louie DiBono were actually chipping it in.

GLEESON: Did that eventually happen, that arrangement you just described?

GRAVANO: Yes.

GLEESON: At that point, did you continue—did you go ahead with this relationship with Louie DiBono?

GRAVANO: Yes.

GLEESON: Did you become, on paper, part owner of any company as a result of that?

GRAVANO: I became part owner of Mario and DiBono Drywall, one hundred fifty percent and Mario and DiBono Fireproofing, I owned fifty percent.

GLEESON: Did any problems develop with that relationship after it was created?

GRAVANO: Yes.

GLEESON: Over how long a period of time?

GRAVANO: It took a little bit of a while, but I don't know how many months, but so many months we wind up with a problem with that.

GLEESON: What were the problems?

GRAVANO: . . . Some of the jobs I gave were getting in touch with me complaining that the jobs weren't being manned, the taxes weren't being paid, the suppliers weren't being paid. The unions got in touch with me, and they weren't being paid. They were the pension and welfare, and I tried to make appointments with Louie DiBono in his office to find out what was going on, and he wouldn't show up at the appointments or make any of the appointments, for some reason.

GLEESON: Did you discuss these problems with John Gotti as they were happening?

GRAVANO: As they got serious, I started discussing them with John.

GLEESON: Was there a particular reason you discussed them with him?

GRAVANO: Two reasons. One, he was my partner and, secondly, he was my boss.

GLEESON: Did you accuse Louie DiBono of anything?

GRAVANO: I accused him of what I accused him of in the early '80s. He robbed us, he started swindling again, and we lost control of him.

GLEESON: When you say you lost control of him, can you describe to the jury how you lost control of him?

GRAVANO: He went completely nuts, this guy. He was staying away for long periods of time, he wasn't coming in. We understood he started taking drugs. He was staying with some girl in Atlantic City or something.

GLEESON: You say he wasn't coming in, coming in where?

GRAVANO: To his business, to us, to anything.

GLEESON: Did there come a point when you proposed a solution to the problem?

GRAVANO: Yes. I wanted to break up my partnership with Louie.

GLEESON: Did you tell that to John?

GRAVANO: Yes.

GLEESON: Did you ever suggest killing Louie?

GRAVANO: Very early, as soon as we had the problem, and I was frustrated. I suggested that I would like to kill him.

GLEESON: What was John's response to that?

GRAVANO: No, to take it easy, relax, and just check out what was going on.

GLEESON: Did you take any steps to end your relationship with Louie DiBono?

GRAVANO: Yes. I had a lot of phone calls, I met with his wife. We ultimately met when his lawyers, had a meeting with my lawyers, and we had a written agreement that we broke up our partnerships, the taxes were paid. I was concerned with the taxes because my name was all over the companies and I could be responsible for them. I made sure the taxes were paid, the unions were paid because I gave my word that they wouldn't get hurt. Some of the suppliers got paid, and a contractor whose job was abandoned, I told him that I would go in and finish the job.

GLEESON: Did you have any difficulty, Mr. Gravano, in terminating your relationship, your business relationship, with Louie DiBono?

GRAVANO: Yes.

GLEESON: What difficulties did you have?

GRAVANO: He wasn't showing up.

GLEESON: Were there particular people you were in contact with in an effort to get him to show up?

GRAVANO: Yes. We were contacting Patsy Conte and Paul Graziano.

GLEESON: Why those two people?

GRAVANO: Patsy Conte was his captain and Paul Graziano was the acting captain, and they were close with him.

GLEESON: Did you, at any point, reach the conclusion that Louie DiBono was afraid to meet with you?

GRAVANO: Yes.

GLEESON: Did you provide any assurances to anybody to get him to meet with you?

GRAVANO: I provided assurances to them that we would meet in the lawyer's office, or wherever he wanted, with as many of his people, I would meet him alone with my lawyer, and I provided him with whatever assurances he wanted.

GLEESON: Did that eventually take place, that meeting?

GRAVANO: Yes.

GLEESON: How long a period of time did it take you, between the time you decided you were going to terminate the relationship and you met in the lawyer's office to sign the documents?

GRAVANO: Say that again?

GLEESON: How long did it take you to finally get him to come in and sign the documents to end your relationship?

GRAVANO: About five, six, seven months. A long time.

GLEESON: During that period, did you discuss these problems with John Gotti?

GRAVANO: Yes.

GLEESON: Was a decision made as to what would happen with Louie DiBono after you terminated your relationship with him?

GRAVANO: John just said I was to break up my partnership with him, and after it was legally broken up, the taxes and everything was paid, I was to stay away from Louie and John would handle him himself.

[. . . .]

GLEESON: On November 16, 1989, you signed papers that ended your business relationship with Louie DiBono, correct?

GRAVANO: Yes.

GLEESON: At that point, were there any outstanding liabilities, as far as you were concerned, for those companies?

GRAVANO: There was one, the tax, state tax.

GLEESON: I am sorry?

GRAVANO: The state tax.

GLEESON: And what kind of liability was that?

GRAVANO: It was about one hundred twenty-nine thousand dollars owed in state taxes.

GLEESON: Do you know which of the companies that you owed the state tax?

GRAVANO: Mario and DiBono Drywall.

GLEESON: You testified that John Gotti was going to take over Louie DiBono, handling Louie DiBono?

GRAVANO: Yes.

GLEESON: Did that happen?

GRAVANO: Yes.

GLEESON: Did you have conversations with him regarding Louie DiBono after that happened?

GRAVANO: Yes.

GLEESON: One conversation or more than one?

GRAVANO: More than one.

INSULT TO INJURY

GLEESON: Did he make any complaints to you?

GRAVANO: He was dealing with Louie and Louie was doing the same thing, making appointments with him, not showing. John would tell Patsy Conte to meet with him, the meeting was set up, and he wouldn't show again.

GLEESON: Did John tell you this?

GRAVANO: Yes.

GLEESON: Did there come a point when he told you whether he had a solution to the problem?

GRAVANO: I believe he became frustrated and eventually said that he was gonna kill him.

GLEESON: Do you believe that or do you remember that happening?

GRAVANO: I remember that happening.

GLEESON: Do you recall when, for the first time, he told you that that would happen?

GRAVANO: Not exactly the dates.

GLEESON: Did he tell you anything about who was going to do it?

GRAVANO: He was gonna give it to Patsy Conte and that crew.

GLEESON: Patsy Conte was the captain of Louie DiBono's crew?

GRAVANO: Yes.

GLEESON: When you say "give to it to them," what do you mean?

GRAVANO: He was going to order Patsy Conte to kill him.

GLEESON: Did he tell you that?

GRAVANO: Yes.

GLEESON: Did you find out, at any point, that some of the complaints about Louie DiBono made to you by John Gotti were tape-recorded?

GRAVANO: Yes.

GLEESON: Did you have occasion, Mr. Gravano, to listen to recordings made at the Ravenite Social Club in conversations including you and John Gotti?

GRAVANO: Yes.

GLEESON: And while you were listening to them, did you have occasion to look at some transcripts?

GRAVANO: Yes.

GLEESON: Let me show you a book of transcripts. The tapes, Mr. Gravano, of those transcripts have already been played to the jury, but I would like to ask you a few questions, if I might.

[. . . .]

GLEESON: Let me direct your attention to a conversation from January 24, 1990, in the apartment [above the Ravenite Social Club]. This is a conversation, the tape of which this jury has already heard. Just take a moment to look at the page, please.

GRAVANO: *(The witness complies.)*

GLEESON: Now, do you recall listening to this conversation?

GRAVANO: Yes.

GLEESON: Do you remember it?

GRAVANO: Yes.

[. . . .]

GLEESON: [Gotti says:] "And he's gotta get whacked! Because he's getting—for the same reason that 'Jelly Belly's' getting it.

You wanna challenge the administration? Well, you will meet the challenge. And you're going."

Who did you understand him to be referring to when he said "Jelly Belly"?

GRAVANO: At that point of the conversation, he's talking about Louie DiBono.

GLEESON: Is that a name that was used more than once for Louie DiBono?

GRAVANO: Yes.

GLEESON: Is that his nickname?

GRAVANO: No. Once we talk about killing him, we gave him a nickname of "Jelly Belly."

GLEESON: When he said "you want to challenge the administration, you'll meet the challenge," what did you understand him to mean by that?

GRAVANO: Louie DiBono was defying the boss's orders. He's defying the administration.

GLEESON: How was Louie DiBono defying the administration?

GRAVANO: He's refusing to come in, he's refusing to listen, and he's doing whatever he wants. The other example would be a guy doing drugs behind his back, defying him.

GLEESON: Did there come a point when you discussed with John Gotti whether other people were gonna be used to kill Louie DiBono?

GRAVANO: As it went on, he got more and more frustrated. I asked him if he wanted me to take care of it. He said no, he would put Bobby Borriello, Charlie Carneglia, and a guy named Tony on it. He would add to the people who were on it already.

GLEESON: You offered to do it yourself?

GRAVANO: Yes.

GLEESON: You were willing to kill him?

GRAVANO: Yes.

GLEESON: You mentioned Bobby Borriello, Charlie—

GRAVANO: Carneglia.

GLEESON: And the kid Tony?

GRAVANO: Yes.

GLEESON: Were they made members of the Family?

GRAVANO: Bobby was.

GLEESON: Whose crew is he in?

GRAVANO: He was with Pete Gotti.

GLEESON: Did you continue to discuss, with John Gotti, the efforts of those people to try and kill Louie DiBono?

GRAVANO: Say that again?

GLEESON: Did you discuss with him, after he told you those people would be doing it rather than you, did you discuss it with him?

GRAVANO: No.

GLEESON: At any point, did you obtain any information about Louie DiBono that was helpful in trying to kill him?

GRAVANO: Toward the end, Joe Madonia came to me with a card, that Louie DiBono was working downtown New York for a big company, and asked me if Louie might be able to get him some drywall work, and he gave me the card, the name of the company he was working for.

[. . . .]

GLEESON: Did anyone else give you any information about Louie DiBono?

GRAVANO: Johnny Gammarano told me where he was working, as well.

[. . . .]

GLEESON: Do you recall where it was Louie DiBono was working?

GRAVANO: In the World Trade Center.

GLEESON: Did you pass along the information [on DiBono] you got from Johnny Gammarano to anyone?

GRAVANO: It was the same exact information as the card.

GLEESON: Did you pass it along?

GRAVANO: Yes.

GLEESON: To whom?

GRAVANO: To John.

A TIME TO DIE

GLEESON: Did there come a point when you learned that Louie DiBono was murdered?

GRAVANO: A couple of weeks after I passed that information.

GLEESON: Who did you learn it from?

GRAVANO: I learned it from—John told me that he was gone.

GLEESON: Did he tell you anything else other than he was gone?

GRAVANO: I don't think so.

GLEESON: Was it in the newspaper?

GRAVANO: No.

GLEESON: Was there ever a point when it was in the newspaper?

GRAVANO: A couple of days later when he was found.

GLEESON: What do you mean, "a couple of days later"?

GRAVANO: A couple of days after he was killed, he was found.

GLEESON: In between, did you talk to anybody about his being killed?

GRAVANO: I talked to Bobby Borriello once.

GLEESON: What did you say to him?

GRAVANO: It didn't come out on television or in the paper and I asked him what happened. Was he sure that happened?

GLEESON: What did he say?

GRAVANO: He assured me the guy was dead. He was in the garage in the World Trade Center. Why it wasn't in the paper or on the news, he didn't know why. Then it came right out.

GLEESON: I am sorry?

GRAVANO: And then it came out then. They found him, and it came out.

GLEESON: A couple of days later?

GRAVANO: Yes.

GLEESON: Were you a member of the administration when the decision was made to kill Louie DiBono?

GRAVANO: Yes.

GLEESON: Did you discuss it with John Gotti?

GRAVANO: Yes.

GLEESON: Did you agree with the decision?

GRAVANO: Yes.

GLEESON: You offered to do it yourself?

GRAVANO: Yes.

GLEESON: Were you personally involved in the murder?

GRAVANO: No.

GLEESON: Did you provide information to John Gotti with the intent that it be carried out?

GRAVANO: Yes.

[. . . .]

GLEESON: By the way, Mr. Gravano, did Louie DiBono ever come into the club after John Gotti was complaining about the fact that he wouldn't come in?

GRAVANO: Yes.

GLEESON: Do you recall when that was?

GRAVANO: Not exactly.

GLEESON: Have you had occasion to listen to a club conversation from March 28, 1990?

GRAVANO: Yes.

GLEESON: Did you recognize that conversation?

GRAVANO: Yes.

GLEESON: Was that the day that Louie DiBono came in?

GRAVANO: Yes.

GLEESON: Was he expected?

GRAVANO: No.

GLEESON: Could you describe to the jury what happened that day?

GRAVANO: I don't know exactly who it was. I believe Patsy Conte or Paulie Graziano came into the club and said Louie DiBono was outside. After refusing to come to a lot of the meetings, he was outside and that he was gonna come in just about unannounced. I guess he thought he caught us off guard and he was pretty safe.

GLEESON: Did he catch you off guard?

GRAVANO: Yes and no.

GLEESON: What do you mean by that?

GRAVANO: He caught us off guard in that we didn't know he was coming, but not that we couldn't react to it.

As a matter of fact, at one point in the conversation with John, the FBI is outside watching the club and I tell John, in a low tone, that if he sends for somebody with a gun with a silencer, we'll turn up the music. He could leave, tell Louie DiBono to be back in a half hour, and I will kill Louie DiBono right in the club. We'll close the club, come back two, three in the morning, and take him out.

GLEESON: When he came in, you offered to kill him in the club?

GRAVANO: Yeah.

GLEESON: You listened to the conversation on tape, correct?

GRAVANO: Yes.

GLEESON: Is your offer on the tape?

GRAVANO: Not really. You can't hear it. It's in a whisper.

GLEESON: Is the reaction of the people in the club on the tape?

GRAVANO: Yes.

GLEESON: What was the reaction?

GRAVANO: They laughed a little bit and just passed over the idea.

GLEESON: Were you serious about it?

GRAVANO: Yes.

GLEESON: Did DiBono come into the club that night?

GRAVANO: Yes.

GLEESON: Did he have a conversation with you in the club?

GRAVANO: I don't remember if he talked with me.

GLEESON: Do you remember whether he talked with anybody?

GRAVANO: I believe he talked with John.

GLEESON: Were you present when he spoke to John?

GRAVANO: I might have been.

GLEESON: Do you remember, one way or another?

GRAVANO: I am not sure.

GLEESON: Why didn't you kill him that night?

GRAVANO: We just passed that idea up.

[. . . .]

CONSTRUCTION AND GARBAGE

GLEESON: You testified that you controlled the Gambino Family's interest in construction. Is that correct?

GRAVANO: Yes.

GLEESON: Were there any other people in the Family with interest in construction?

GRAVANO: Yes.

GLEESON: Who?

GRAVANO: There was quite a few people interested in construction. Outside of me and my crew?

GLEESON: Yes.

GRAVANO: There was Joe Watts had interest in construction, the Westies, Bosco, the boss of the Westies, had interest in construction. Quite a few people.

GLEESON: Were your interests larger than all the others?

GRAVANO: Yes.

GLEESON: Were you the principal person involved in the construction industry in the Gambino Family?

GRAVANO: Yes.

GLEESON: Did you share your earnings with anybody?

GRAVANO: Yes.

GLEESON: With whom?

GRAVANO: With the boss.

GLEESON: Generally speaking, what percentage of what you earned through the Gambino Family interest in construction was shared with the boss?

GRAVANO: What I was handling for the Family, the unions and deals, I kept twenty percent and I sent eighty percent up to the boss.

GLEESON: Did you send it up in check or cash?

GRAVANO: Cash.

GLEESON: How much money did you turn in on average, Mr. Gravano?

GRAVANO: Average one hundred thousand dollars a month, about a million two a year.

GLEESON: Who did you turn it in to?

GRAVANO: To John through Pete.

GLEESON: Was—did you bring it down to the Ravenite Social Club?

GRAVANO: No.

GLEESON: Did you have a regular practice how you turned in the money you turned in?

GRAVANO: Yes.

GLEESON: What was the practice?

GRAVANO: When the money accumulated to a big number, I would talk to John, his brother Pete would come to my house Sunday early in the morning, and I would give it to him in some sort of bag or box or whatever.

GLEESON: Other than the money that you turned in from construction, did you collect any other money to be given to John Gotti?

GRAVANO: Yes.

GLEESON: What money?

GRAVANO: On his birthday or Christmas when the captains chipped in to give him a gift, I collected that money generally. I turned that in as well.

GLEESON: Was there, generally speaking, a size of a birthday gift to be given by each captain?

GRAVANO: Approximately three thousand dollars each.

GLEESON: How about Christmas gift?

GRAVANO: Same thing.

GLEESON: Did people turn in more for a birthday or Christmas gift?

GRAVANO: That was their own business.

GLEESON: Did they give that to you?

GRAVANO: No.

GLEESON: Did they turn it in to you?

GRAVANO: No.

GLEESON: Did you learn whether people turned in more?

GRAVANO: No, that was their personal business with the boss.

GLEESON: Did you ever turn in more than that as a gift?

GRAVANO: Yes.

GLEESON: Birthday or Christmas gift?

GRAVANO: Yes.

GLEESON: When you became part of the administration did you become familiar with other industries that the Gambino Family controlled?

GRAVANO: Yes.

GLEESON: You mentioned a number of times Jimmy Brown?

GRAVANO: Yes.

GLEESON: What was his responsibility?

GRAVANO: Controlled the garbage industry for us.

GLEESON: Did he also run a—

GRAVANO: Yes.

GLEESON: When you say "controlled the garbage industry," what do you mean?

GRAVANO: Private garbage industry. He is the head of the association and he controls the union, [Local] 813, Bernie Edelstein answers directly to Jimmy Brown so he controls the garbage industry for his Family.

GLEESON: Local 813 is what union?

GRAVANO: Garbage.

GLEESON: That is a union responsibility for the garbage?

GRAVANO: Yes. The drivers, I would imagine.

GLEESON: Are you familiar with the details of how Jimmy Brown controlled the garbage haulers?

GRAVANO: No.

GLEESON: Are there any boroughs where the Gambino Family controls the garbage?

GRAVANO: Yes. Manhattan, Queens, and we are partners out in Long Island.

GLEESON: How is the Manhattan—how is that industry controlled in Manhattan?

GRAVANO: Through Jimmy Brown, through the association.

GLEESON: The association of garbage haulers?

GRAVANO: Yes.

GLEESON: How was it controlled in Queens?

GRAVANO: His cousin is in charge of the association there.

GLEESON: What is his cousin's name?

GRAVANO: Right now it is not at the tip of my tongue.

GLEESON: Was his cousin in the Gambino Family?

GRAVANO: He is an associate.

GLEESON: You mentioned your partners in Long Island, is that correct?

GRAVANO: Yes.

GLEESON: Who is the Gambino Family partners with?

GRAVANO: Lucchese Family.

GLEESON: Who controls that?

GRAVANO: Sally Avelino, a captain, controls the industry out there, and we are partners in it and they send us our end usually through Jimmy Brown.

GLEESON: When you say they send you your end, what is an end?

GRAVANO: Whatever money is taken out of that industry is divied up fifty percent for us, fifty percent for our administration.

GLEESON: Did you ever have any involvement in the money by that partnership?

GRAVANO: No.

GLEESON: Do you know how much Jimmy Brown turns in to the boss?

GRAVANO: No.

DEALING DEATH

GLEESON: In 1989 Jimmy Brown came to the administration regarding a murder?

GRAVANO: Yes.

GLEESON: How did that come about?

GRAVANO: Came into John and said a made member, Tommy Sparrow, was—went to the grand jury and was going back. He was advised by his attorney to tell the truth and cooperate and that is exactly what he was going to do.

GLEESON: Whose crew was Tommy Sparrow in?

GRAVANO: Made member in Jimmy Brown's.

GLEESON: Sparrow his nickname or real name?

GRAVANO: I don't know. That is how I know him.

GLEESON: Did you know him well?

GRAVANO: No.

GLEESON: Did Jimmy Brown report this to John Gotti?

GRAVANO: Yes.

GLEESON: As a result of that, what happened?

GRAVANO: John Gotti told me about it. Told me that he had given them a contract to kill him.

GLEESON: He had given a contract to—

GRAVANO: Jimmy Brown. A contract to kill Tommy Sparrow. And he believed Louis Fats and Danny Marino were on it. He wasn't sure how fast it would get done. He told me to get on it and make sure it was done before he went in to the grand jury.

GLEESON: Before Tommy Sparrow went back to the grand jury?

GRAVANO: Yes.

GLEESON: Did you get on it?

GRAVANO: I got involved immediately.

GLEESON: What did you do once you got involved?

GRAVANO: I got ahold of Louie Fats, Danny Marino told me that "Philly Dogs" would be on it. He wasn't coming in. They were talking with him, and I got in touch with Joe Watts to get a place ready.

GLEESON: Place ready for what?

GRAVANO: To bury him. I told—we made an appointment one night. I told Louie Fats to make an appointment with Tommy in a last-ditch effort, Jimmy wanted to talk to him and he could talk, just wanted an opportunity for Jimmy to talk with him and everything would be okay. He wasn't sure if he would come out of his café to meet.

GLEESON: Who wasn't sure?

GRAVANO: Louie Fats. I told him if he doesn't come out we will go back and we will kill him right in the café. When I got things set up, I came back to a place, a warehouse, glass factory warehouse, in Brooklyn where it was done. I went back—I got out of the car with Danny Marino, "Philly" was waiting.

GLEESON: Where were you when—

GRAVANO: Brooklyn.

GLEESON: Whose glass factory?

GRAVANO: "Philly Dogs' " son.

GLEESON: You drove there, did you drive with anybody?

GRAVANO: Danny Marino.

GLEESON: He is a captain on the chart, Government Exhibit 84 [showing the structure of the Gambino Family]?

GRAVANO: Yes.

GLEESON: When you got there with Danny Marino what happened?

GRAVANO: We got out of the car, Lou Fats called me over to the side to talk to me. He told me Tommy came with them, he already did it, he was dead and inside the factory.

GLEESON: Louie Fats told you he shot Tommy?

GRAVANO: Yes. He asked me to help to put the body in a van. I did. I walked back. I told Danny Marino to get in the car. When we got in the car I said it is already done, follow the van out to Staten Island. We went out to Staten Island and parked the van in the back of the diner. We gave the keys to Joe Watts who was there, and Fat Dom, they took the body. The other guys took me home.

And that was the end of it.

GLEESON: Two of the people you mentioned in your description of this were "Philly Dogs," and Louie Fats, who were they?

GRAVANO: Louie Fats was acting captain under Jimmy.

GLEESON: Jimmy Brown?

GRAVANO: Yes. And "Philly Dogs" is a made member in that crew.

GLEESON: Did Joe Watts and Fat Dom take the body away?

GRAVANO: Yes.

GLEESON: Did they ever tell you where it went?

GRAVANO: No.

GLEESON: Were you part of the administration when this murder was ordered?

GRAVANO: Yes.

GLEESON: Did you agree with John Gotti's directions?

GRAVANO: Yes.

GLEESON: Did you participate in it?

GRAVANO: Yes.

[. . . .]

THE FELLOWSHIP OF FRIENDS

GLEESON: Before you were arrested on this case, on December 11, 1990, how frequently did you speak to John Gotti?

GRAVANO: Four, five times a week.

GLEESON: Did you speak to him in person or over the phone?

GRAVANO: In person.

GLEESON: Where?

GRAVANO: Mostly down New York.

GLEESON: When you say "down New York," do you mean the Ravenite Social Club?

GRAVANO: Yes.

GLEESON: Approximately what time of day would you see him down at the Ravenite Social Club?

GRAVANO: At night.

GLEESON: Approximately what time?

GRAVANO: Between six o'clock and eight o'clock.

GLEESON: Did you ever have to send a message to him or contact him earlier in the day?

GRAVANO: Yes.

GLEESON: When did he start his day?

GRAVANO: About twelve, one o'clock.

GLEESON: Where did he start it?

GRAVANO: In Queens.

GLEESON: When you say Queens, what do you mean by that?

GRAVANO: 101st Avenue, Bergin Hunt & Fish Club.

GLEESON: From time to time did you ever have to send a message to him earlier in the day than the hours that you would spend at the Ravenite?

GRAVANO: Yes.

GLEESON: How did you do it?

GRAVANO: I would have Big Lou get in touch with his brother Pete.

GLEESON: Big Lou is the captain who took over your old crew?

GRAVANO: Yes.

GLEESON: Were you concerned while you were the underboss of the Gambino Family about electronic surveillance?

GRAVANO: Yes.

GLEESON: Why were you concerned?

GRAVANO: That none of our conversations would get picked up.

GLEESON: Did you take steps to prevent them from getting picked up?

GRAVANO: Yes.

GLEESON: What steps did you take?

GRAVANO: We took walks in the street. We whispered. We went up to the apartment [above the Ravenite Social Club]. We felt the apartment was safe because an eighty-year-old woman owned the apartment.

GLEESON: Did you feel it was safe to talk up there without being intercepted?

GRAVANO: Yes.

GLEESON: Did you ever discuss the possibility that that apartment was bugged?

GRAVANO: Yes.

GLEESON: When?

GRAVANO: When Jimmy Brown went to a grand jury and he was asked questions about an apartment, if he was ever in an apartment.

GLEESON: Did you continue to use the apartment after you learned that Jimmy Brown had gone in to the grand jury and been asked about it?

GRAVANO: Maybe once or twice.

GLEESON: Whose apartment was it?

GRAVANO: It was a guy who had died, he was a made member in our Family, and that was his wife's apartment.

GLEESON: Mr. Gravano, did you ever consider having all of your conversations outdoors?

GRAVANO: We had most of them outdoors. It was impossible to have them all outdoors.

GLEESON: Why?

GRAVANO: Sometimes the weather didn't permit it. Sometimes we were tired.

GLEESON: When you were arrested in this case, there was an indictment, correct?

GRAVANO: Yes.

GLEESON: That indictment later got superseded?

GRAVANO: Yes.

THE ART OF MURDER

GLEESON: How many murders were you charged with?

GRAVANO: Three.

GLEESON: When you decided to cooperate, you told the government about sixteen others, correct?

GRAVANO: Yes.

GLEESON: Was your involvement the same in each of the murders?

GRAVANO: No.

GLEESON: Did the type of involvement you had vary?

GRAVANO: Yes.

GLEESON: Can you describe the different roles you had?

GRAVANO: Sometimes I was a shooter. Sometimes I was a backup guy. Sometimes I set the guy up. Sometimes I just talked about it.

GLEESON: When you set the guy up, would you arrange for other people to murder him?

GRAVANO: Yes.

GLEESON: Did you have the ability to make those arrangements?

GRAVANO: Yes.

GLEESON: Did you make arrangements to dispose of bodies?

GRAVANO: Yes.

GLEESON: Did you, for example, did you have the ability to get body bags?

GRAVANO: Yes.

GLEESON: How many times were you actually the shooter?

GRAVANO: Once.

GLEESON: Did it matter to you, Mr. Gravano, whether you were the shooter or not?

GRAVANO: No.

GLEESON: Why not?

GRAVANO: Because when you go on a piece of work it doesn't matter what position you're in. You're all out there. You're all liable to get charged the same. It doesn't make any difference though.

GLEESON: Did you ever commit any murders alone?

GRAVANO: No.

GLEESON: Did you commit any murders other than with other members or associates of the crime family that you happened to be with when they were committed?

GRAVANO: No.

GLEESON: Did the superseding charge you pled guilty to list all of the murders?

GRAVANO: Yes, it did.

GLEESON: Let me show you what's been marked for identification as Government Exhibit 905 and particularly page six.

(Handed to the witness.)

First, is that document the superseding charge to which you pled guilty?

GRAVANO: Yes.

GLEESON: And does it list the murders to which you pled guilty?

GRAVANO: Yes.

GLEESON: You testified on Monday that the first murder you committed was Joe Colucci, correct?

GRAVANO: Yes.

GLEESON: Who were you with when that murder was committed?

GRAVANO: The Colombo Family.

GLEESON: Did you commit it with other associates of Shorty Spero's crew in the Colombo Family?

GRAVANO: Yes.

GLEESON: That's at the bottom of the list, correct?

GRAVANO: Yes.

GLEESON: With the date 1970, correct?

GRAVANO: Yes.

GLEESON: Between 1977 and 1982, there are seven murders on that list. Is that right, Mr. Gravano?

GRAVANO: Yes.

GLEESON: Did the defendants in this case have any involvement at all in any of those seven murders?

GRAVANO: No.

GLEESON: Are the names of the people, the victims of those murders, set forth on the list?

GRAVANO: Excuse me?

GLEESON: Are the names of the victims of those seven murders set forth on the list?

GRAVANO: Yes.

GLEESON: One of them is an unidentified male, in 1977, correct?

GRAVANO: Yes.

GLEESON: Did all seven of them involve other members and associates of the Gambino Family?

GRAVANO: Yes.

GLEESON: One of those names is your brother-in-law, correct?

GRAVANO: Yes.

GLEESON: Nick Scibetta, correct?

GRAVANO: Yes.

GLEESON: After 1982, the next one up the list is January 7, 1986, Nicky Mormando. By what name did you know him?

GRAVANO: "Nicky Cowboy."

GLEESON: "Nicky Cowboy"?

GRAVANO: Yes.

GLEESON: Did that murder take place before or after the murders of Paul Castellano and Tommy Bilotti?

GRAVANO: It took place after.

GLEESON: Approximately three weeks after, correct?

GRAVANO: Yes.

GLEESON: Who was "Nicky Cowboy"?

GRAVANO: He was a guy with the Gambino Family, with my crew.

GLEESON: He was in your crew?

GRAVANO: In Brooklyn.

GLEESON: Why was he murdered?

GRAVANO: He was starting his own crew and wound up with a very serious drug problem.

GLEESON: Who was he starting his own crew with?

GRAVANO: Michael DeBatt, other people he was talking with who had drug problems.

GLEESON: Did the problem with "Nicky Cowboy" develop over a period of time?

GRAVANO: Yes, it did.

GLEESON: Was it in existence before Paul Castellano and Tommy Bilotti were murdered?

GRAVANO: Yes.

GLEESON: Did you discuss the problem with anyone?

GRAVANO: I discussed it with Frankie DeCicco.

GLEESON: Was the murder planned before the murders of Tommy and Paul?

GRAVANO: Yes.

GLEESON: And who was it committed by?

GRAVANO: Me and my crew.

GLEESON: And the defendants had no involvement at all in that, correct, Mr. Gravano?

GRAVANO: Correct.

GLEESON: Now, the top ten names on the list span the period from December 16, 1985, Paul Castellano and Thomas Bilotti, to October of 1990, Louie DiBono. Correct?

GRAVANO: Yes.

GLEESON: Of those, how many involved John Gotti?

GRAVANO: All of them.

[. . . .]

CROSS-EXAMINATION: ALBERT J. KRIEGER, COUNSEL FOR JOHN GOTTI

KRIEGER: Mr. Gravano, I want you to go back in your own mind to the life of crime that you have described for this jury over the last couple of days. You indicated in response to questions put by Mr. Gleeson that amongst other things you had committed numerous armed robberies. Do you recall saying that?

GRAVANO: Yes.

KRIEGER: You said that you did that before you went into the military in the '60s. You said that you did it after you came out. Remember?

GRAVANO: Yes.

KRIEGER: Now, it would be, would it not, an almost impossible chore to count up the number of armed robberies that you perpetrated, right?

GRAVANO: I don't know if I did that many that I couldn't count it up. But I didn't keep a record or—of anything like that.

KRIEGER: And certainly a substantial number of them are lost in the recesses of your memory is what you're telling us?

GRAVANO: It's possible.

KRIEGER: Now, we can plug in a bunch of other crimes, such as burglary, which you mentioned, probably assaults, a few other things, as well, correct?

GRAVANO: Probably.

KRIEGER: Now, when you decided that you were going to make this deal with the government, those old crimes that you had committed were really not your major concern, were they?

GRAVANO: Sure, they were.

KRIEGER: Well, then you're telling us, sir, that when you made your deal, that you were looking for some kind of benefit for those past crimes, correct?

GRAVANO: I—I knew at that time that I would have to tell my entire lifetime what crimes I was involved in, what I did, and I would have to tell the government the truth, and I thought of all of it.

KRIEGER: Well, outside of the disclosure of your life of crime, according to your arrangement, you weren't concerned, were you, that you could be prosecuted for a robbery you committed in 1970, for example, correct? You're in 1991. You are not worried about being prosecuted for a crime twenty-one years old, are you?

GRAVANO: I guess not.

KRIEGER: You had enough familiarity with prosecutions to know that there was such a thing as a statute of limitations, right?

GRAVANO: Yes.

KRIEGER: And it is true, is it not, that you felt that the statute of limitations had run to bar the prosecution of some of these robberies, the burglaries, some of the shylocking, et cetera, correct?

GRAVANO: Could you say that again? I didn't understand that.

KRIEGER: I said, sir, you knew enough that you understood that the statute of limitations would bar, would not permit prosecution, or you could use the statute as a defense, to prosecution for some of these robberies, burglaries, shylocking, that had occurred many years ago, right?

GRAVANO: I'm still not a hundred percent sure of that. But I would imagine there is a statute of limitations. I don't know where it falls. I'm not a lawyer. I'm aware that there is a statute of limitations, but where it falls, what cases, what crimes, I am not a hundred percent clear or sure of it.

KRIEGER: To put it a different way, sir, when you entered into your deal, you were looking to get rid of all of your problems that had arisen as a result of your life of crime, correct?

GRAVANO: I was looking to turn my life around and part of it was telling the truth [about] my entire life-style, where I came from. Whether it was in—covered by statute of limitations or covered by the deal wasn't all that important to me.

KRIEGER: Mr. Gravano, what you were looking for, were you not, was not to spend all of your remaining days on this earth in jail, correct?

GRAVANO: I would imagine part of the reason is that.

KRIEGER: Oh, the reason, sir? I suggest to you, the reason, yes or no?

GRAVANO: Part of the reason.

KRIEGER: Part of the reason?

GRAVANO: Yes.

KRIEGER: And another reason was you wanted to turn yourself around and be a model citizen, correct?

GRAVANO: No. Not exactly.

KRIEGER: Not even remotely, correct?

GRAVANO: Not exactly.

KRIEGER: You are not looking forward, are you, to getting out of jail and advertising that you would like to be guardian of orphan children?

GRAVANO: No.

KRIEGER: Or a role model for the youth in this city? The answer to that is no, also, isn't it?

GRAVANO: No, that's not the answer. That's not the answer.

KRIEGER: The answer is, you want to be a role model?

GRAVANO: Maybe that some other kids don't get their lives destroyed like I did.

KRIEGER: You destroyed your own life?

GRAVANO: That's what you say.

KRIEGER: Well, somebody, I'm sure, came up to you in 1968 when you got out of the Army—it was '68, wasn't it?

GRAVANO: Sixty-six.

KRIEGER: Sixty-six, when you got out of the Army, and said to you, Sammy, there is only one road open for you. That's go out with a gun and rob people. That never happened, did it?

GRAVANO: When you grow in a neighborhood like I grew in, and you grew with the people I grew with, it was an environment. I was a kid.

KRIEGER: Go ahead.

GRAVANO: When I was a kid I was involved in gangs, dropped out of school in the eighth grade. It was an environment. It was not something—I just grew with it. It didn't seem wrong, the whole life-style didn't seem wrong.

KRIEGER: In effect, the devil made me do it?

GRAVANO: The devil didn't make me do it. I did it on my own.

KRIEGER: Okay.

GRAVANO: But the life-style did.

KRIEGER: I guess that what you are saying is that you want—you want the world to think of Sammy Gravano as a poor victim of environment and circumstances, correct?

GRAVANO: No. I don't want the world to think anything.

KRIEGER: You would prefer that the world didn't think anything of you? Right?

GRAVANO: I don't understand that question.

GLEESON: Objection to the relevance.

JUDGE GLASSER: Sustained.

KRIEGER: I will withdraw the question, sir. In the society which you say you grew up and which shaped your life, a person who is playing the role that you are playing at this point would be called a certain name, isn't that so?

GRAVANO: Probably.

KRIEGER: And that name is?

GRAVANO: An informer.

KRIEGER: Some other word?

GRAVANO: Rat.

KRIEGER: Now, sir, what you don't want the world to think of you as is that Sammy Gravano will be remembered as a rat?

GLEESON: Objection.

JUDGE GLASSER: Sustained.

KRIEGER: Mr. Gravano, when you were arrested on or about December 11, 1990, you hoped, did you not, that you would be released on bail?

GRAVANO: Yes.

KRIEGER: And as a matter of fact, sir, you have heard since December 11, 1990, tape recordings of discussions that you had with others concerning the probabilities of your being released on bail, correct?

GRAVANO: Yes.

KRIEGER: Then, sir, when you were detained without bail, it came, relatively speaking, of course, as a kind of shock to you, correct?

GRAVANO: No.

KRIEGER: It was just one of those things that happened and I'll sleep it off, that's what you're saying?

GRAVANO: It is just one of those things I knew growing up in the street, in the life—like you say, there's certain laws I did know. When I saw the case of this magnitude, it would be fairly obvious that I wouldn't be let out.

KRIEGER: Fairly obvious you would be?

GRAVANO: Not let out.

KRIEGER: Okay. Then you are saying, sir, you did not expect to be released on bail?

GRAVANO: I hoped to be released on bail. But seeing the charges and the tapes and everything that was brought up in front of the judge, I kind of thought that the chances were slim.

KRIEGER: All right. Come December 11, 1990, you are in jail, right?

GRAVANO: Yes.

KRIEGER: And it is true, is it not, that you have been in jail since?

GRAVANO: Yes.

[. . . .]

KRIEGER: Now, sir, you told us yesterday that before 1985, all of the crimes that you had committed had no connection whatsoever to John Gotti, right?

GRAVANO: Right.

KRIEGER: Now, after 1985—well, it was 1985 and after, wasn't it, when you first started to have some contact, real contact? I am not talking about passing contact, you started to have some contact with Mr. Gotti. Is that correct?

GRAVANO: I had the contact before '85.

KRIEGER: Maybe I am using the wrong word. You testified yesterday, and correct me if my recollection is incorrect, that you met Mr. Gotti in 1977 or 1978. Do you remember?

GRAVANO: Yes.

KRIEGER: And that you started to see him on a relatively regular basis sometime after 1985. Is that correct?

GRAVANO: I don't believe that is what I said.

KRIEGER: You say it now?

GRAVANO: I say I met John in '77, and we both became made members of the Gambino Family. I saw John periodically at wakes and weddings and business dealings that our Family had, but I had no personal business dealings with John or no partnership or relationship in that way before '85.

KRIEGER: In 1985 or thereabouts your relationship with him changed?

GRAVANO: Yes.

KRIEGER: In 1985 or thereafter, sometime after 1985, where you started to see him, I think your testimony was, and again feel free to correct me, four or five times a week?

GRAVANO: After '85?

KRIEGER: Yes.

GRAVANO: Yes.

KRIEGER: Now, in that period of time you got to know him, didn't you?

GRAVANO: Yes.

KRIEGER: Right?

GRAVANO: After '85?

KRIEGER: Yes.

GRAVANO: I got to know him better.

KRIEGER: You got to know him better. You got to know his temperament better, right?

GRAVANO: Yes.

KRIEGER: You got to know his habits better, right?

GRAVANO: Yes.

KRIEGER: You got to know his principles better, right?

GRAVANO: Yes.

KRIEGER: And you got to know some very strong philosophical stands that he took or takes, correct?

GRAVANO: Yes.

KRIEGER: One of them is, is it not—let me just touch on something before I ask you this question concerning that topic. You killed somebody, didn't you, because that person was involved with drugs, right?

GRAVANO: Yes.

KRIEGER: "Cowboy" ["Nicky Cowboy," nickname of Nicky Mormando]?

GRAVANO: Yes.

KRIEGER: And as a matter of fact, you also, within about ten months after killing "Cowboy," killed [Michael] DeBatt for very much the same thing, right?

GRAVANO: Yes.

KRIEGER: The drug situation, you've got a stand against drugs, haven't you?

GRAVANO: Yes.

KRIEGER: And you have a principle that you are against drugs, right?

GRAVANO: Yes.

KRIEGER: Now, you know, sir, as an absolutely unquestioned fact that John Gotti is dead set against drugs, right?

GRAVANO: Yes.

KRIEGER: You knew that in 1985, correct?

GRAVANO: Yes.

KRIEGER: You knew it in '86, '87, '88, '89, and '90?

GRAVANO: Yes.

KRIEGER: You knew it when you were in [jail] together waiting for this case to go to trial?

GRAVANO: Yes.

KRIEGER: Right?

GRAVANO: Yes.

[. . . .]

KRIEGER: Now, sir, there were numerous, were there not, numerous days, evenings, times—better word, times—numerous times you would be in the Ravenite [Social Club] itself and have a conversation with somebody, right?

GRAVANO: Yes.

KRIEGER: And there were numerous times, not as numerous as going to the club, but there were numerous times when you would have a conversation with somebody in the hallway, right?

GRAVANO: Not that many times, but sometimes.

KRIEGER: It happened, didn't it?

GRAVANO: Not often.

KRIEGER: However many times, it happened. Is that correct?

GRAVANO: Yes.

KRIEGER: When you—there were some private conversations that you had in the Ravenite Club with whoever you were speaking?

GRAVANO: I guess so.

KRIEGER: But if you wanted real privacy what you used to do was step out of the club. Is that correct?

GRAVANO: Yes.

KRIEGER: And you would step out of the club and do different things depending upon different circumstances including the weather, right?

GRAVANO: Yes.

KRIEGER: If it was a nice pleasant afternoon you might do what you have called a walk talk. Is that correct?

GRAVANO: Yes.

KRIEGER: And we have already covered the situation where you might step out in the hallway, right?

GRAVANO: Yes.

KRIEGER: And there came a time, did there not, when you used that apartment upstairs as a place of privacy. Is that correct?

GRAVANO: Yes.

KRIEGER: And when you went up to the apartment and used the apartment, Mr. Gravano, it was, was it not, with the intention to have a truly private conversation, correct?

GRAVANO: Yes.

KRIEGER: And in the conversation that you would have in the apartment, well, you kind of let it all hang out, right?

GRAVANO: I guess so.

KRIEGER: At times when you were up in the apartment you would be there with Mr. Gotti. Is that correct?

GRAVANO: Yes.

KRIEGER: And as you indicated to us a few moments ago you became quite knowledgeable as to Mr. Gotti's temperament. Is that correct?

GRAVANO: You could say that.

KRIEGER: In the years after 1985—well, you knew that Mr. Gotti had a hot temper, right?

GRAVANO: Yes.

KRIEGER: And when his temper was flaring he would speak in rather extreme terms? You understand what I am saying, sir?

GRAVANO: No.

KRIEGER: You don't?

GRAVANO: No.

KRIEGER: Well, you remember yesterday you were saying that sometimes he uses phrases just, it's really just an expression, correct?

GRAVANO: I remember saying that.

KRIEGER: And you know that he would use expressions such as on one day he might say—I think you heard this—might say, "I will cut his head off," "I will sever his head." You heard him say things like that, didn't you?

GRAVANO: Yes.

KRIEGER: And you also heard him the very next day say about that person whose head was going to be severed, "I guess he's a nice guy, doesn't make trouble," and talk about him with the same tones I am talking at the moment, correct?

GRAVANO: Yes.

KRIEGER: Typical John Gotti, exploded one minute, calm down the next, right?

GRAVANO: Yes.

KRIEGER: As a matter of fact, just to use another example, a fellow, Mr. Moscatiello, you know who he is?

GRAVANO: Yes.

KRIEGER: Periodically when John Gotti would get mad, threatened even to blow up his house, right?

GRAVANO: *(No response)*

KRIEGER: You heard that?

GRAVANO: I heard it.

KRIEGER: You knew as a fact as you sit here it happened more than once, not blowing up the house, hearing threats, you know he said it time and again, right?

GRAVANO: I know he said it once.

KRIEGER: House didn't get blown up?

GRAVANO: No.

KRIEGER: Mr. Moscatiello's family and everybody is alive and well?

GRAVANO: Yes.

KRIEGER: Just the same as the fellow whose head was going to be severed, right?

GRAVANO: He did what he was supposed to do.

KRIEGER: Just the same as the fellow whose head was going to be severed, he is alive and well today?

GRAVANO: Yes.

KRIEGER: Right?

GRAVANO: Yes.

KRIEGER: Now, sir, in your relationship with Mr. Gotti, you found, did you not, that in a conversation with you, explaining something that had happened or reporting a conversation which he had heard about, he would play different roles, almost play the parts of the people he was telling you about, correct?

GRAVANO: You lost me with that one.

KRIEGER: Okay. I realize I well could have with that question. You had conversations, did you not, with Mr. Gotti where he would tell you that he spoke with so-and-so who told him that such-and-such had happened, right?

GRAVANO: Yes.

KRIEGER: And that "John Jones" had said this to "Richard Wright," okay, making up names, he would repeat a conversation?

GRAVANO: Yes.

KRIEGER: When repeating the conversation, suddenly John Gotti would play the part of "John Jones" saying, "I said to him," correct normal speech patterns, right?

GRAVANO: That he would play the other guy's role?

KRIEGER: Yes.

GRAVANO: I am lost.

[. . . .]

KRIEGER: Come October of 1990, in or about the time that you're making up your mind to make a deal, there were certain thoughts in your head about what could happen to you, correct?

GRAVANO: Yes.

KRIEGER: First of all, you knew that under the charges contained in this indictment, and the indictment under which you were prosecuted, you could very well wind up with life terms without benefit of parole on more than one count, correct?

GRAVANO: Yes.

KRIEGER: And in the federal system, when you're sentenced to a life term without benefit of parole, you come out of jail in a box, correct?

GRAVANO: I guess so.

KRIEGER: Every single day of your life is spent in jail, right?

GRAVANO: Yes.

KRIEGER: You also knew, did you not, that you would probably—you believed yourself to be a candidate for confinement at Marion, Illinois, right?

GRAVANO: We were told that in [the Metropolitan Correctional Center] that that would be a likelihood.

KRIEGER: That would be what?

GRAVANO: A likelihood.

KRIEGER: And you knew Marion, Illinois, to be the toughest prison in the federal system, right?

GRAVANO: Yes.

KRIEGER: And you also knew that at Marion, Illinois, you are locked down. That is, in your cage twenty-three hours a day, right?

GRAVANO: Yes.

KRIEGER: And you also knew that you're lucky at Marion if you get a shower once a week, correct?

GRAVANO: I believe it's two times a week.

KRIEGER: That makes it great. Besides the fact that you, as anyone else, doesn't want to spend his or her life in jail, besides that, you felt, sir, you felt, Mr. Gravano, that the prospect of that happening to you was so great that you started to look for a way to cut your losses, right?

GRAVANO: No.

KRIEGER: I am sorry, I didn't hear you?

GRAVANO: No.

KRIEGER: You did not look for a way, in October of 1991, to cut your losses? Yes or no?

GRAVANO: That's not what you just asked me.

KRIEGER: I thought that's what I asked you, but phrased it exactly the reverse fashion. I will withdraw the last two questions and put it to you again.

In October of 1991, taking into consideration what we just discussed about Marion, taking into consideration the severity of the charges against you, taking into consideration your mind-set that you would probably be convicted, you decided to look for a way to cut your losses, yes or no?

GRAVANO: No.

KRIEGER: Okay. You decided to make a deal with the government because it's the civic thing to do?

GRAVANO: No.

KRIEGER: You decided to make a deal with the government because you were looking for something that would benefit Sammy Gravano, correct?

GRAVANO: No.

KRIEGER: You were looking—well, you were looking to—were you looking to do the right thing?

GRAVANO: Not exactly.

KRIEGER: Sir, you told us on direct that you took an oath, according to you, joined some organization or association and one of the—and portions of the oath that you took was that you would not violate that oath, right?

GRAVANO: Yes.

KRIEGER: And one of the reasons for your taking the oath, if not the only reason, back in the '70s, or when it was that you took that oath, was because it was good for you, right?

GRAVANO: I don't recall I said that.

KRIEGER: I didn't ask you whether you said that. I am asking you, sir, when you took that oath, you took it because it was good for you?

GRAVANO: No.

KRIEGER: It was of no benefit or advantage to you to take that oath?

GRAVANO: You probably wouldn't understand. It's a way of life with me in the street and that's why I took the oath.

KRIEGER: Which elevated your status, right?

GRAVANO: It made me accepted by my peers.

KRIEGER: All right. That's good for you, correct?

GRAVANO: It depends on how you look at it.

KRIEGER: Well, not from where you are right now, apparently, but in the years after 1977, up to December 11, 1990—well, you profited from that oath, right?

GRAVANO: No.

KRIEGER: Okay. As a result of the life that you led, sir, you made money?

GRAVANO: Yes.

KRIEGER: Within the life-style—as you just reminded me—within the life-style you gained status?

GRAVANO: Yes.

KRIEGER: I think the term is you gained "respect," correct?

GRAVANO: I guess so.

KRIEGER: And, sir, there were both, within your life-style, social benefits and material benefits, right?

GRAVANO: Yes.

KRIEGER: You went from being a guy who was running around and sticking guns in people and grabbing money, to a man who was—well, very active in the construction industry, correct?

GRAVANO: Yes.

KRIEGER: You went from a person who may have been struggling to put ends together, to a man who was reporting an income in excess of a half-million dollars a year, correct?

GRAVANO: Yes.

KRIEGER: You went from a man who may have lived humbly in the '60s, an environment of which you spoke, to a home in Staten Island and probably had in excess of a million dollars put into it, correct?

GRAVANO: That, you're not correct on. That, you're not correct on.

KRIEGER: Less than a million dollars?

GRAVANO: A lot less.

KRIEGER: A lot less. You lived humbly and simply?

GRAVANO: I guess.

KRIEGER: You guess?

GRAVANO: Yeah.

KRIEGER: Tell us. You should know your own life-style, sir. You should know whether you're living well or you're not living well.

GRAVANO: I'm living well.

KRIEGER: Pardon?

GRAVANO: I said, I'm living well.

KRIEGER: Now?

GRAVANO: Not right this minute.

KRIEGER: You made a deal. The deal that you made, sir, is the document that you signed and that the government moved into evidence yesterday—Government's Exhibit 904. Do you remember?

GRAVANO: Yes.

[. . . .]

KRIEGER: You felt, did you not, sir, that you had something to offer to the government, correct?

GRAVANO: Yes, I guess so.

KRIEGER: And what you had to offer to the prosecution was, was it not, the fact that you were going to plead guilty to killing Louie DiBono? Right?

GRAVANO: I don't understand the question.

KRIEGER: Well, you were charged in an indictment with which you are familiar that included as the most serious counts, murder charges, right?

GRAVANO: Yes.

KRIEGER: Three of those murder charges were, as you understood it, laid right at your doorstep, correct?

GRAVANO: I was charged with them.

KRIEGER: Pardon?

GRAVANO: I was charged with them.

KRIEGER: Well, the relationship with the people who were killed was one of their being your business associates, right?

GRAVANO: Yes, I guess so.

KRIEGER: No "I guess so." Yes or no?

GRAVANO: It was charged that they were my business associates?

KRIEGER: Oh, I'm talking about the fact that Louie Milito was an old friend of yours, correct?

GRAVANO: He was an old friend or a business associate. You asked—

KRIEGER: He was both?

GRAVANO: He wasn't a business associate at that time.

KRIEGER: Louie Milito was not a business associate of yours? Is that what you're saying?

GRAVANO: He was.

KRIEGER: All right. Then the—Louie Milito, the victim in the Louie Milito count, was an old friend and business associate of yours, correct?

GRAVANO: Yes.

KRIEGER: Now, Louie DiBono, he, too, was a person that you had known for some number of years, correct?

GRAVANO: Yes.

KRIEGER: With whom you had a business relationship?

GRAVANO: Yes.

KRIEGER: And Mr. DiBernardo was another individual whom you had known for some years, correct?

GRAVANO: Yes.

KRIEGER: And you had worked together with Mr. DiBernardo, right?

GRAVANO: Yes.

KRIEGER: Now, those three individuals were the victims in three of the four murder counts, right?

GRAVANO: Yes.

KRIEGER: The other murder counts came out of the Castellano situation, right?

GRAVANO: Yes.

KRIEGER: Castellano and Bilotti, we can treat them as one, correct, for the purposes of these questions? You have no problem with that?

GRAVANO: No problem.

KRIEGER: On each one of the murder counts you were exposed to a penalty of life imprisonment without benefit of parole, correct?

GRAVANO: I believe so.

KRIEGER: Now, in exchange for your pleading guilty, for your coming to the prosecution and saying, "I committed these murders," they were going to be so grateful and so overjoyed and so ecstatic with your plea, they'd say, "We will deal your whole thing out for twenty years," right?

GRAVANO: I don't believe so.

KRIEGER: Of course not. Isn't that correct? They wouldn't do that, would they? You did not expect by merely coming to the prosecution, sir, and saying, I'm willing to plead guilty to these three murders, that you would get an arrangement for a reduced maximum exposure of twenty years, correct?

GRAVANO: I would have to admit my entire past, not just these three murders.

KRIEGER: So your answer is, you would not get the benefit of the twenty-year sentence by merely coming in and saying, "I'm guilty as charged?" That's right, isn't it?

GRAVANO: I guess so.

KRIEGER: Sir, not a guess. Yes or no?

GRAVANO: I am not one hundred percent sure.

KRIEGER: You're telling us now then, Mr. Gravano, that it is your belief that if you were to have contacted Mr. Maloney, Mr. Gleeson, Ms. Ward, Mr. Cotter [the prosecution team], and said, "Sir, Ms. Ward, I want to plead guilty, set my maximum exposure to twenty years," they would have said, "Oh, sure, Mr. Gravano." You're not saying that, are you?

GRAVANO: No.

KRIEGER: You're not saying, are you, Mr. Gravano, that you could have called any one of these prosecutors, contacted them, and said, "I will not only plead guilty, I will plead guilty to some murders you may not even know about, give me twenty years"? That's no deal either, is it?

GRAVANO: I didn't get that question.

KRIEGER: You called one of the prosecutors, said, "I'm willing to plead guilty to the indictment as charged, and I will also plead guilty to some murders of which you know nothing. In exchange for that, set my max to twenty years." You wouldn't expect them to do that either, would you?

GRAVANO: I don't know. No, I don't think so.

KRIEGER: Now, without going through all the variations on plugging in all of the crimes you have committed and asking you the same questions that I have just put to you, it is true,

Mr. Gravano, is it not, that the key to your deal, the key to your deal, is your being a witness, right?

GRAVANO: No.

KRIEGER: The key to the deal is your saying to the prosecutors, "I have been a bad boy. I want to bare my chest to you and tell you all the bad things I have done, and in exchange for that give me a slap on the wrist. Give me a kiss on the cheek, reduce my lifetime exposure to a maximum of twenty years." That's what you're saying?

GRAVANO: No. But I could answer the question, if you want me to answer.

KRIEGER: You had something else to offer, right? Yes or no?

GRAVANO: I had made a deal with the government.

KRIEGER: Try yes or no first, please. You had something else to offer, yes, no?

GRAVANO: I didn't go in with an offer.

KRIEGER: Pardon?

GRAVANO: I didn't go in with an offer.

KRIEGER: You had something else to give to the prosecution, correct?

GRAVANO: My life-style.

KRIEGER: Your testimony?

GRAVANO: Yes.

KRIEGER: Your being a witness?

GRAVANO: Yes.

KRIEGER: Right?

GRAVANO: Yes.

KRIEGER: Your testifying against John Gotti?

GRAVANO: Yes.

KRIEGER: Your testifying against John Gotti on this Castellano case?

GRAVANO: Yes.

KRIEGER: And as a result, and as a result, Mr. Gravano, prosecutors agreed to file an information to which you would plead guilty, pursuant to an arrangement where instead of life without parole, you would face a maximum sentence of twenty years, correct?

GRAVANO: Yes.

KRIEGER: Now, further, the arrangement, naturally, required you to come into a court and plead guilty, correct?

GRAVANO: Yes.

KRIEGER: And when you came into court to plead guilty, as our law requires, the court advised you of the exposure that you would have as a result of the plea of guilty? What I'm saying in simpler words, the court told you what the range of sentence could be?

GRAVANO: Yes.

KRIEGER: And in your case, under your arrangement, in your plea, the sentence could be anything from twenty years in jail, subject to good time reduction, all the way down to probation, and walk right out of the courtroom, correct?

GRAVANO: Possibility.

KRIEGER: Now, the possibility of whether you get probation or six months or one year or two years or five years or any sentence, the grade, the amount of the sentence is affected, is it not, by something within your plea agreement, correct? Right?

GRAVANO: I don't follow that again.

KRIEGER: Well, there is—you read the plea agreement carefully, didn't you?

GRAVANO: Yes.

KRIEGER: And you read the plea agreement which had been reached after negotiation between your lawyer and the prosecution, correct?

GRAVANO: Yes.

KRIEGER: And in accordance with a lawyer who—with whom you were satisfied had your best interests at heart, correct?

GRAVANO: Yes.

KRIEGER: Now, the lawyer explained the plea agreement to you?

GRAVANO: Yes.

KRIEGER: And the plea agreement provided that the prosecution agreed that if the prosecution determines, not the judge, but if the prosecution determines that you have cooperated fully, and provided substantial assistance to law enforcement, then they would file a certain paper with the court, correct?

GRAVANO: Sentencing?

KRIEGER: For sentencing, yes.

GRAVANO: No.

KRIEGER: All right. Let me show you what has been marked Government Exhibit 904 in evidence. This is a photocopy and I ask you if on the last page, page five, your signature appears?

GRAVANO: Yes.

KRIEGER: And your signature appears under the legend which says, "I have read this plea agreement and discussed it with my attorney. I hereby acknowledge that it fully sets forth my agreement with the office of the United States Attorney for the Eastern District of New York. I state that there have been no additional promises or representations made to me by any officials of the United States government in connection with this matter.

"Dated November 13, 1991.

"Signed Salvatore Gravano."

GRAVANO: Yes.

KRIEGER: You put your name down there after you read that paragraph, didn't you?

GRAVANO: Yes.

KRIEGER: Now, when you said you read it, you meant it?

GRAVANO: Yes.

KRIEGER: When you read it, you understood it, didn't you?

GRAVANO: Yes.

KRIEGER: Okay. Let's look at paragraph seven.

"If the office determines that Salvatore Gravano"—the office, by the way, is the United States Attorney's office, is it not?

GRAVANO: Yes.

KRIEGER: The prosecution.

"If the office determines that Salvatore Gravano has cooperated fully, provided substantial assistance to law enforcement, and otherwise complied with the terms of this agreement, the office will file a motion with the sentencing court pursuant to sentencing guideline Section 5K1.1, setting forth the nature and extent of his cooperation with the office, including its investigative and prosecutive value, truthfulness, completeness, and accuracy."

That's what that sentence says, correct?

GRAVANO: Yes.

KRIEGER: Okay. Now, after my having read this sentence to you from Government's Exhibit 904 in evidence, is your recollection now refreshed that the prosecution has agreed to file a certain paper in regard to your sentencing?

GRAVANO: Doesn't say anything about my sentencing or the time. It just says that it would file a motion notifying the judge on what I have done.

KRIEGER: After you have been sentenced?

GRAVANO: Before I am sentenced.

KRIEGER: So it pertains to your sentencing, doesn't it?

GRAVANO: It pertains to how the judge is going to sentence me, I would imagine.

KRIEGER: Well, that would pertain to your sentencing, correct?

GRAVANO: Yes.

KRIEGER: It's something coming from the prosecution to the sentencing judge that is, is it not, to be informational to the sentencing court, correct?

GRAVANO: Yes.

KRIEGER: And it is your understanding that if the prosecution sends in a motion pursuant to Section 5K1.1 of the sentencing guidelines, that praises you, you hope to get a lesser sentence than you would otherwise, am I not correct, sir?

GRAVANO: Yes.

[. . . .]

KRIEGER: Let's look at the next sentence.

GRAVANO: All right.

KRIEGER: "In this connection, it is understood that the office's determination of whether Salvatore Gravano has provided complete cooperation and substantial assistance, and the office's assessment of the value, truthfulness, completeness, and accuracy of the cooperation shall be binding upon him."

You understand what that means, don't you?

GRAVANO: Yes.

KRIEGER: They make a decision, you've got to live with it, right?

GRAVANO: They make a decision on my truthfulness and I got to live with it, yes.

[. . . .]

KRIEGER: All right. Sir, you have been called as a witness, have you not, in order to help the government in its prosecution in this case, right?

GRAVANO: Yes.

KRIEGER: And in order to help the government in its prosecution of this case, you see yourself, do you not, as a witness that will be of assistance to the government in obtaining the conviction of John Gotti?

GRAVANO: No.

KRIEGER: You see yourself as a witness called by the government in the government's efforts to obtain an acquittal of John Gotti?

GRAVANO: No.

KRIEGER: All right. You see yourself, then, as a person who just has no interest whatsoever in what the outcome of this case will be, right?

GRAVANO: That I have no interest?

KRIEGER: That you have no interest. You don't care what happens? Let the jury come in guilty—excuse me, sir—let the jury come in guilty, let the jury come in not guilty. Means nothing to you. That's what you are telling the court and the jury, correct?

GRAVANO: In a way. They're the jury. And I'm not a juror.

[. . . .]

KRIEGER: Isn't it a fact that what you said to the government at the get-go, from the beginning, was "Yes, I will tell you about murders. Yes, I will tell you about criminal activity involving shylocking, labor racketeering, I will tell you about all those things." That is what you said, right?

GRAVANO: That is what I was involved in, that is what I would confess to.

KRIEGER: That is what you were confessing to?

GRAVANO: Yes.

KRIEGER: By saying that, you consider, do you not, you disclosed all of the facts of all the criminal acts of murders, the nineteen murders you had committed and all the labor racketeering and all the extortion and all the shylocking. Isn't that so?

GRAVANO: To the best of my ability, yes.

KRIEGER: Then as time went on, they would come back to—well, is there another murder that can you tell us about, and you would talk about that murder. Isn't that the way the debriefing went?

GRAVANO: Not exactly.

KRIEGER: Close enough?

GRAVANO: Not really, the debriefing goes on, but not that we find nineteen and look for more.

KRIEGER: I am talking about covering all the general disclosures on your part about your criminal life, right?

GRAVANO: They were looking to be debriefed on the ceremony, on my life-style, and what went on in the past, constantly debriefing.

KRIEGER: Asking you for more and more information in regard to your criminal activity, correct?

GRAVANO: I believe that they are very interested in the understanding of my life and style.

KRIEGER: I am asking you about details of your criminal activities.

GRAVANO: Yes.

KRIEGER: And if it comes to pass you remember a crime you forgot, you tell them about it?

GRAVANO: Yes.

KRIEGER: When you remember a crime that you had forgotten you tell them about it, you expect not to be prosecuted for the disclosure of that criminal act regardless of when you disclosed it, correct?

GRAVANO: I would imagine if I left out a detail in good faith that there is a possibility nothing would happen from it.

KRIEGER: Probability, I suggest.

GRAVANO: Probability, good word.

KRIEGER: Go even further. If you thought you were going to be prosecuted for it you would make a deal to make sure you wouldn't be prosecuted for it?

GRAVANO: No.

KRIEGER: Whatever happens happens, if they want to send me away it is all right too, that is your attitude?

GRAVANO: I think that's what you said before as far as a motion going to the judge, my sentencing judge, it would be evaluated, if I forget something they would take this into consideration and when I had the sentencing, whatever it would be, it would be.

KRIEGER: It is, is it not, to your best interest to have included within your disclosure as much of your criminal life as you could possibly recall so that there is an end to prosecution of Sammy Gravano, right?

GRAVANO: Yes. The more honest and truthful I am, I guess the less chance—

KRIEGER: The better the deal to you?

GRAVANO: The less chance—the more of a chance I have of starting a new life without having a problem, what you just said.

KRIEGER: It's awful to start a new life and the government learns that you had killed DeBatt or that you had killed "Cowboy" or that you had killed your brother-in-law, that would certainly affect your future, wouldn't it?

GRAVANO: Probably break the deal, I would come back in the system and probably affect my future pretty good.

KRIEGER: Probably?

GRAVANO: Definitely, a better word.

KRIEGER: When Mr. Gleeson was asking you questions concerning whether the government knew of these various murders, you were responding that you told them and you pled guilty in order to get them behind you, right?

GRAVANO: Not really.

KRIEGER: I guess then the only reason that you told about your brother-in-law, told about all of these various murders, was a kind of sense of public interest or public curiosity, right?

GRAVANO: No. Why I did it again was back to the agreement with the government. I was supposed to be debriefed, tell the truth, not withhold anything. It wouldn't be in my best interest to hide something from the government at this point. Once I went into the arrangement to tell the truth, what would be my purpose to hide something? It would only come back to haunt me.

KRIEGER: Right. That is to your interest to disclose anything that could come to your door, anything that could be hung on you because you wash your past clean with this plea, is that correct?

GRAVANO: Yes. It wouldn't pay me to lie.

KRIEGER: Now, sir, of course the government did not have to be told by you about the Castellano murder, DiBernardo, Milito, or DiBono murders because they were included in the indictment, is that correct?

GRAVANO: Yes.

KRIEGER: And the government had a distinct interest in obtaining from you your version of events in regard to those murders, right?

GRAVANO: Yes.

KRIEGER: And you basically told them, did you not, pretty much the same thing that you told us here in this courtroom about Mr. DiBernardo, Mr. Milito, and Mr. DiBono, is that correct?

GRAVANO: Yes.

[. . . .]

KRIEGER: Let me go back, if I might, to December 16, 1985. When we ended Monday morning I had been asking you some questions concerning white trench coats, fur hats. Do you recall?

GRAVANO: Yes.

KRIEGER: Let me go back, if I might, to the events of that evening. You and a group of others meet in this park, the location of which you don't recall, but it being some fifteen, twenty minutes, correct, from 46th Street and Third Avenue, downtown near the water?

GRAVANO: Yes.

KRIEGER: Now, you had gotten to this park, you told us, having driven from Staten Island with Joe Watts, correct?

GRAVANO: Yes.

KRIEGER: And you drove from Staten Island with Joe Watts right from the place where you had been, I think the term you used was "bunking in," correct?

GRAVANO: Yes, I believe so.

KRIEGER: And you came, did you not, with Joe Watts's car?

GRAVANO: I don't remember the vehicle.

KRIEGER: All right. In any event, after meeting for these few moments at the park, it was, was it not, the first time that most of the people who were there learned that there was a real, honest-to-God plot to kill Paul Castellano that was going to be carried out right then and there, right?

GRAVANO: They knew of the plot before. They knew the name then. If—if they didn't know it before, but they knew this then officially. They knew about a plot. They knew that we were going to go kill somebody.

KRIEGER: They knew that you were going to kill somebody from the conversation held the night before in your office?

GRAVANO: Yes.

KRIEGER: That's what you testified to, do you recall?

GRAVANO: Yes.

KRIEGER: That you met with this group of people and all the same people who were at your office with the exception of Frank DeCicco met in the park?

GRAVANO: Yes.

KRIEGER: That's your testimony now?

GRAVANO: Yes.

KRIEGER: All right. Now, of the people, those such as—well, let me put up my list of names and go through it again, if I might.

[. . . .]

Let me put a black check mark to indicate that he's there in the park.

John Gotti?

GRAVANO: Yes.

[. . . .]

KRIEGER: Frank DeCicco, well, we know he's up in the restaurant, right?

GRAVANO: Yes.

KRIEGER: Salvatore Gravano, yes, black check mark.

Angelo Ruggiero?

GRAVANO: Yes.

KRIEGER: Black check mark.

John Carneglia?

GRAVANO: Yes.

KRIEGER: Black check mark.
Iggy Alogna?

GRAVANO: Yes.

KRIEGER: Black check mark.
Anthony Rampino?

GRAVANO: Yes.

KRIEGER: Same thing.
Eddie Lino?

GRAVANO: Yes.

KRIEGER: Sally Scala?

GRAVANO: Yes.

KRIEGER: And Vincent Artuso?

GRAVANO: Yes.

KRIEGER: Now, let's go back. Vincent Artuso did not know when he came to the park that he was engaged in a plot or a participant in a plot to kill Paul Castellano?

GRAVANO: I believe that's correct.

KRIEGER: Sally Scala, same thing?

GRAVANO: I believe that's correct.

KRIEGER: Eddie Lino?

GRAVANO: Yes.

KRIEGER: Anthony Rampino?

GRAVANO: Yes.

KRIEGER: Iggy Alogna?

GRAVANO: Yes.

KRIEGER: Johnny Carneglia?

GRAVANO: Yes.

KRIEGER: You told us Angelo Ruggiero had plotted with you from almost a year before?

GRAVANO: He knew.

[. . . .]

KRIEGER: It must have occurred to you, sir, it must have occurred to you that when you speak with these people in the park, that maybe one of them would say, "Hey, wait a minute, I don't mind going out on a plan to kill 'John Jones,' but I have objections to going out to kill Paul Castellano," must have occurred to you, didn't it?

GRAVANO: These are the loyal people to us, and it didn't occur to me that that would happen. I don't think that it occurred to anybody else that that would happen. These are our people.

KRIEGER: These are what you characterize as your people. They're going to do whatever you say, without any independent thought?

GRAVANO: That group is basically John's people, my people—

KRIEGER: Whomever's they may be. You're saying these people would go and do whatever they were told, right?

GRAVANO: Yes.

KRIEGER: Then they certainly could have been told, could they not, of what everything was all about the night before, a week before, a month before, eight months before, couldn't they, and be trusted just the same, right?

GRAVANO: In reality, probably.

KRIEGER: Okay. Now, according to you, these six people, as well as all the other people say, "Well, let's go out and do this 'piece of work,' " and everybody goes about to his particular assignment, right?

GRAVANO: I guess so.

KRIEGER: According to your testimony Monday morning, the night before where people, who was going to be the shooters, general location, et cetera, all had been planned out, right?

GRAVANO: A good part of it.

KRIEGER: Well, you've testified, did you not, that the meeting in the park was to avoid having people just wandering onto 46th Street in some kind of haphazard fashion, I'm paraphrasing what you said?

GRAVANO: Yes.

KRIEGER: But that was the sense of it, was it not?

GRAVANO: Yes.

KRIEGER: And that as you've testified, come the arrival on 46th Street of some of these people, there were going to be four people who were going to put themselves right in front of 210 East 46th Street, Sparks Steak House, correct?

GRAVANO: In that near vicinity, yes.

KRIEGER: And they did not have to be told, did they, according to you, that when Paul Castellano and Thomas Bilotti drive up, shoot them, right? Those four? They didn't have to be told that, they knew that's what they were supposed to do that night at that place, right?

GRAVANO: Yes.

KRIEGER: Now, those four people were, were they not, and I'll put an "O" alongside the name, Vincent Artuso?

GRAVANO: Yes.

KRIEGER: Eddie Lino?

GRAVANO: Yes.

KRIEGER: John Carneglia?

GRAVANO: Yes.

KRIEGER: Number four?

GRAVANO: Fat Sally.

KRIEGER: By the way, Fat Sally was fat, wasn't he?

GRAVANO: At one time in his life. Not at this particular point he wasn't too fat.

KRIEGER: Pardon?

GRAVANO: At one point in his life he was heavy, not at this point.

KRIEGER: He wasn't skinny then, was he?

GRAVANO: He wasn't really fat. The name stuck with him.

KRIEGER: Now, Iggy Alogna, Angelo Ruggiero and Anthony Rampino, you, Joe Watts, and John Gotti are unaccounted for at this moment, right? We haven't put them anyplace?

GRAVANO: Yes.

KRIEGER: We put those four in front of Sparks, so they're out of the way?

GRAVANO: In the vicinity of Sparks, sure.

KRIEGER: Now, let's leave out of this mix for a moment you and John Gotti, okay?

GRAVANO: Okay.

KRIEGER: Joe Watts, Angelo Ruggiero, Iggy Alogna, three names, three men, right?

GRAVANO: Yes.

KRIEGER: Those three are not across the street from Sparks, are they?

GRAVANO: They're up the block toward Second Avenue.

KRIEGER: When you say up the block, they're up toward Second Avenue, correct?

GRAVANO: Yes.

KRIEGER: Now, you knew what 46th Street looked like at that time, didn't you?

GRAVANO: Yes.

KRIEGER: And you knew how it looked when you were making the plan, correct?

GRAVANO: Basically.

KRIEGER: You knew, for instance, that 46th Street—you're sufficiently familiar with New York, 46th Street in particular, that at least from Lexington Avenue, which is the next block west from Third Avenue, that from Lexington Avenue, at least to Second Avenue, because that's the relevant area here, that 46th Street is a three-lane street, correct?

GRAVANO: Including the parking spots?

KRIEGER: Yes, sir.

GRAVANO: Yes.

KRIEGER: There's a lane on the right, a lane on the middle, and a lane on the left, right?

GRAVANO: Yes.

KRIEGER: You also knew, did you not, that parking was prohibited during the rush hour anyplace on 46th Street between Lex and Second Avenue, right?

GRAVANO: I didn't know the parking regulations, no.

KRIEGER: Pardon?

GRAVANO: I didn't know the parking regulations, no. I don't know what they are.

KRIEGER: Well, when you were planning don't you think that it would have been a good idea to figure out where cars park, whether you can park on the right, whether you can park on the left, whether you can't park at all, considering where you're going to be? You had to have a spot, according to your plan?

GRAVANO: We don't have to have a spot. We're sitting in the car.

KRIEGER: When you're sitting in the car, you mean traffic just flows around you, after all, Salvatore Gravano is in there in his car, and Mr. Gotti is sitting in the car, the waters are going to part, no car is going to—police are going to let you sit there, everybody is going to let you sit there wherever you want, that's what you're telling us?

GRAVANO: I'm not saying that. It was a spot there, we parked there. If there wasn't a spot there we would have moved onto another location, another spot. That's what I'm talking about.

KRIEGER: My question to you is would it not have been a good idea, Mr. Gravano, to know what the parking regulations are in that area and what the flow of traffic is like in that area, yes or no?

GRAVANO: I find it very difficult to answer. I didn't know what the parking spots were like or what the restrictions were. It may have been a good idea, but it's not something that we thought of or I thought of.

KRIEGER: If we look at this drawing, which is supposed to be a fair and accurate representation of what 46th Street was like on December 16, 1985, we find certain physical things as, for instance, lampposts located where they're supposed to be, we find traffic lights, we see references to sidewalks. You understand that, don't you?

GRAVANO: Yes.

KRIEGER: Now, we know that there's new building construction within roughly two hundred feet of Sparks, right? See, it says it, new building construction?

GRAVANO: Did I know that at the time or by looking at the chart?

KRIEGER: Well, don't you think that if you're going to engage in a plan to kill Paul Castellano and Thomas Bilotti in the middle of the rush hour on 46th Street, and the people who are going to execute them are going to escape down to Second Avenue, that they should know whether the street is blocked or not? Doesn't that make simple fundamental sense?

GRAVANO: The street wasn't blocked and we knew that, but I didn't notice the new construction, no matter I wasn't interested in the new construction.

KRIEGER: You're saying that the street wasn't blocked?

GRAVANO: No.

KRIEGER: You're saying that this representation putting the new construction in such a place that it takes away one of the three lanes is not correct?

GRAVANO: I wasn't interested in the parking spot at that particular point.

KRIEGER: Sir, isn't that where the traffic flows?

GRAVANO: Traffic flows in the middle of the street.

KRIEGER: You in your lifetime in New York have never been delayed in traffic because of construction, that's what you're telling us, huh?

GRAVANO: I didn't say that.

KRIEGER: You never have been delayed in going crosstown Manhattan and finding the three lanes are restricted to two? You've never had that happen to you?

GRAVANO: I've had that happen.

KRIEGER: Pardon?

GRAVANO: I've had that happen.

KRIEGER: And you've also had it happen that New Yorkers being New Yorkers, would park alongside of the construction just as quickly as they'll park alongside of the sidewalk, correct?

GRAVANO: I don't know what they would do.

KRIEGER: You don't know what they would do?

GRAVANO: No.

KRIEGER: You've never seen it happen?

GRAVANO: I've seen it happen.

KRIEGER: Okay. It's something that you should take into consideration, is it not, because if they do, then you're pinched to one lane, right?

GRAVANO: But that didn't happen. It went pretty smooth.

KRIEGER: I'm not asking you that. I'm saying that in your understanding of what was there, what was there, you should, should you not, have taken into consideration that you'd be down possibly to one lane, right? You didn't?

GRAVANO: The street was flowing. I didn't take these things into consideration. I didn't take the construction into consideration.

KRIEGER: Okay. Then you're also saying, are you not, that you did not go up to 46th Street on the fifteenth, on the fourteenth, or even the morning of the sixteenth, to check it out?

GRAVANO: No.

KRIEGER: Now, Mr. Watts, Mr. Alogna, Mr. Ruggiero were someplace on 46th Street down toward Second Avenue. That's your testimony, correct?

GRAVANO: Mr. Watts, who?

KRIEGER: Iggy Alogna?

GRAVANO: Yes.

KRIEGER: And Mr. Ruggiero?

GRAVANO: Yes.

KRIEGER: And you can't tell us whether they were standing on one of the corners of Second Avenue and 46th Street or whether they were standing in the middle of the construction or whether they, too, had decided to stand in front of Sparks Steak House because you didn't see them, right?

GRAVANO: Well, they were up the block.

KRIEGER: Yes or no, you didn't see them?

GRAVANO: No, they weren't in front of Sparks. They were up further.

KRIEGER: You didn't see them?

GRAVANO: No.

KRIEGER: You can tell us that you didn't see them in front of Sparks because you tell us that you can see Sparks?

GRAVANO: Yes.

KRIEGER: So if you didn't see them in front of Sparks, you feel comfortable in saying they weren't in front of Sparks?

GRAVANO: They were up the block.

KRIEGER: Right. But you can't tell us that they were in front of the fruit market on the southwest corner of Second and 46th, you can't tell us they were in front of the apartment building at 241 East 46th, you really don't know from your own senses of observation where they were, right?

GRAVANO: Not by seeing them, no.

KRIEGER: Mr. Rampino was, according to your testimony, if I recall it correctly, someplace across the street from Sparks, correct?

GRAVANO: On the opposite side.

KRIEGER: Now, according to your testimony, you came up to this area with Mr. Gotti?

GRAVANO: Yes.

KRIEGER: You drove from this park, wherever it may have been, up there with Mr. Gotti in a car?

GRAVANO: Yes.

KRIEGER: And when I say you drove, I'm misstating it, am I not, because your testimony is that Mr. Gotti drove?

GRAVANO: Yes.

KRIEGER: Now, you came up as you've testified, to the northwest corner of Third Avenue and 46th Street, correct?

GRAVANO: Yes.

[. . . .]

KRIEGER: And when you got to this corner, as you sit here now, you recall the downtown side of 46th Street having cars parked on it?

GRAVANO: This side?

KRIEGER: Downtown side?

GRAVANO: Yes.

KRIEGER: Far right-hand side?

GRAVANO: Yes.

KRIEGER: Right. That leaves us two lanes, doesn't it?

GRAVANO: Yes.

KRIEGER: You park in the far left-hand lane?

GRAVANO: Yes.

KRIEGER: And by park, I mean stop the car?

GRAVANO: Yes.

KRIEGER: Now, you could not, could you, find a space to stop the car, according to your testimony, of sufficient size to keep the car from sticking out either into the sidewalk or into the traffic coming up on Third Avenue, right?

GRAVANO: Well, we're not into the traffic, but we're sticking a little bit too far into the crosswalk.

KRIEGER: So naturally, considering what has brought you up to 46th Street and Third Avenue, considering the fact that you have a gun in your pocket, considering the fact that you have a walkie-talkie, the last person that you want to have a conversation with is a police officer because your car is sticking into the crosswalk, correct?

GRAVANO: Yes.

KRIEGER: Now, as a result of that, you then drive around the block, right?

GRAVANO: Yes, we give a spin around.

KRIEGER: And because you've driven around the block, something has changed on this block so that you are able now to stop the car near the corner and the car will not intrude into the crosswalk, correct?

GRAVANO: Yes.

KRIEGER: Something had to change, otherwise you just would have backed up?

GRAVANO: The car that was behind us moved away.

KRIEGER: All right. Now, with the car that's behind you and with the cars that are parked on the right-hand side, there's only one lane of traffic moving down 46th Street to the east, am I not correct?

GRAVANO: Yes.

[. . . .]

KRIEGER: And it has been, has it not, your experience, that when any crosstown street in midtown Manhattan gets restricted down to one lane, there is at least slowly moving traffic, right? It's been your experience, isn't it?

GRAVANO: It's been my experience that's all that moves down any of those streets, it's a one lane, there's two parking spots on each side and there's the lane that flows. That's my experience in the city. All the streets are like that.

KRIEGER: Sir, my question to you is, that in your experience, that when a crosstown street, midtown Manhattan, rush hour, is restricted to one lane, traffic moves very slowly? That's my question.

GRAVANO: Sometimes it moves slow.

KRIEGER: It's your testimony then, sir, that you noticed nothing unusual 46th Street–Third Avenue with traffic being restricted or choked down to one lane, that's what you're saying, roughly five-thirty, December sixteenth, nine days before Christmas, shopping night?

GRAVANO: There's a lot of traffic, there's a lot of people. There's always the one lane.

KRIEGER: Okay. And it isn't any one lane where you can go thirty miles an hour from corner to corner?

GRAVANO: There's no cars I guess you can go that fast.

KRIEGER: During the rush hour?

GRAVANO: Sometimes the traffic moves.

KRIEGER: Sir, you described yourself as a backup shooter, right?

GRAVANO: Yes.

KRIEGER: Now, a backup shooter would be, as the words indicate, either a person to back up the four shooters that you've described, maybe to go running up the block and shoot some more bullets into the two men who were killed, or to help protect—well, that wasn't your role, was it?

GRAVANO: Both.

KRIEGER: You mean that if you, sitting back here on this corner, saw Mr. Bilotti out in the street because you didn't see Mr. Castellano, did you?

GRAVANO: No.

KRIEGER: You see Mr. Bilotti out on the street and he's wriggling, it's your job to jump out of the car, pull your gun, run approximately two-thirds the length of a football field, go up to this body in the street and shoot it? That's your role?

GRAVANO: No.

KRIEGER: Maybe it is, I don't know. That's your role?

GRAVANO: That's not a role of a backup shooter, if he got away and came toward me, he would have ran into me.

KRIEGER: Now—

GRAVANO: That's my role.

[. . . .]

KRIEGER: When you get to this corner, after making the circuit around the block, putting yourself into position to adopt, to assume your role as backup shooter, at that moment, lo and behold, who comes alongside but Paul Castellano and Thomas Bilotti, correct?

GRAVANO: Yes.

KRIEGER: They got to wait for the light to change, correct?

GRAVANO: Yes.

KRIEGER: However long that takes, that takes?

GRAVANO: Not too long.

KRIEGER: They promptly drive across the street, and because you say there's no traffic, they immediately go to Sparks and pull up in front of Sparks, right?

GRAVANO: I didn't say there was no traffic, but that's—yes. Sure, that's what they did.

KRIEGER: You notice, do you not, cars parked in front of Athlete's Foot—I'll even be more precise, a van or two parked in front of Athlete's Foot?

GRAVANO: Not really.

KRIEGER: You don't remember that?

GRAVANO: No.

KRIEGER: Bilotti parks the car, does he not, under the lamppost that is indicated right here to the west of Sparks Steak House, do you remember?

GRAVANO: He parks right in front of Sparks.

KRIEGER: You're saying he parks right in front of Sparks, which will push him past the lamppost?

GRAVANO: Approximately right in front. I don't know where the lamppost is.

KRIEGER: Give or take a few feet he's right in front of Sparks?

GRAVANO: Yes.

KRIEGER: All right. You have no recollection of cars being parked west?

GRAVANO: There was—

KRIEGER: Behind?

GRAVANO: I believe there was some cars parked there, but I don't know if there was a van. I'm not sure.

KRIEGER: All right. There were cars parked?

GRAVANO: I believe so, yeah.

KRIEGER: And you saw some vehicles parked here on the north side of the street, didn't you?

GRAVANO: I believe so.

KRIEGER: Now, relying upon your recollection, we know from your testimony there's only one lane of traffic going down 46th Street, correct?

GRAVANO: I believe so.

KRIEGER: All right. Now, you, of course, can't see what's happening on the sidewalk, right? I'm talking about the south sidewalk, your vision is [blocked] by parked cars?

GRAVANO: I have a decent vision of them standing above, when they're standing near above the cars, I can't see the lower half of their body.

KRIEGER: I'm not asking you about people. I'm saying that your vision is blocked as to what's taking place on the sidewalk, that's all that I'm saying?

GRAVANO: That's all.

KRIEGER: You can see everything that's taking place on the sidewalk?

GRAVANO: No. I can't see the lower half of their bodies.

KRIEGER: Their, you mean the shooters?

GRAVANO: Anybody's.

KRIEGER: You can see people walking around, heads and shoulders above the cars that are parked there, correct?

GRAVANO: Yes.

[. . . .]

KRIEGER: Now, I think you indicated on your direct examination this car had tinted windows, right?

GRAVANO: Yes.

KRIEGER: And if my recollection serves me, you were able to see into, coincidentally, another Lincoln Continental in which Bilotti and Castellano were because of their happenstance of turning on the domelight, or that didn't occur?

GRAVANO: Yes, it occurred. We saw that very clearly because of that, but we knew the car anyway.

KRIEGER: On December 16, 1985, John Gotti was a person well known to law enforcement, right?

GRAVANO: I would assume so.

KRIEGER: You knew that as a fact, didn't you?

GRAVANO: In 1985? He was known, yes.

KRIEGER: It occurred to you, did it not, that a wandering police officer or a citizen, anybody, going past 46th Street and Third Avenue, and one would venture to say depending on the length of time you were there, may have been tens of hundreds or hundreds of people walking past the intersection, right?

GRAVANO: Yes.

KRIEGER: That anyone of them, being a law enforcement officer or police officer, looking in at—the front window was not tinted dark, was it?

GRAVANO: No.

KRIEGER: Looking in the front window seeing the driver John Gotti and then reading about Castellano and Bilotti being killed, might be at least an investigative clue, correct?

GRAVANO: I don't follow the question.

KRIEGER: Sir, John Gotti, as you've indicated was well known to law enforcement?

GRAVANO: Yes.

KRIEGER: As of December 16, 1985, right?

GRAVANO: Yes.

KRIEGER: He was also a person, was he not, who had received some media notice before December 16, 1985, correct?

GRAVANO: Not much, I don't think.

KRIEGER: Enough, he had been in the newspapers, had he not?

GRAVANO: Not much.

KRIEGER: You testified a few moments ago that Mr. Gotti was known to law enforcement at that time, right?

GRAVANO: Yes.

KRIEGER: If Mr. Gotti was seen, identified, reliably, as being on the scene of the homicide of Mr. Castellano and Mr. Bilotti, it had to bring, it would have to bring, in your opinion, an enormous amount of heat to Mr. Gotti and those with whom he associates, correct?

GLEESON: Objection.

JUDGE GLASSER: Sustained.

KRIEGER: In your opinion, sir, if you were observed by law enforcement at this scene, together with Mr. Gotti, you would feel yourself, would you not, as a subject of the investigation by law enforcement into the death of Mr. Castellano and Mr. Bilotti?

GLEESON: Objection.

JUDGE GLASSER: Sustained.

KRIEGER: Is it state of mind?

JUDGE GLASSER: Speculative, irrelevant.

KRIEGER: Let me approach this from the south pole instead of the north pole. You did not want to be recognized as being on the scene, is that correct?

GRAVANO: Yes.

KRIEGER: I take it no one of any of the other individuals would want to have been recognized as being on the scene?

GRAVANO: No.

KRIEGER: Now, you had detailed for us a number of reasons why what you saw occur from this corner took place, remember?

GRAVANO: Yes.

KRIEGER: You said in response to a question put by Mr. Gleeson, that he, Castellano, was selling out "the Family" for his own basic reasons, this man Piccolo had been killed by another Family, that he had other Families handling matters which should have been handled by his own, and there was a continuing problem with Angelo's tapes, right?

GRAVANO: Yes.

[. . . .]

KRIEGER: You knew that the tapes were going to be evidence in the case?

GRAVANO: Yes.

KRIEGER: You knew that he had obtained copies of the tapes?

GRAVANO: Angelo did?

KRIEGER: Yes.

GRAVANO: Yes.

KRIEGER: And you also knew, did you not, that perhaps a year or more before December 16, 1985, Paul Castellano had been indicted, right?

GRAVANO: Yes.

KRIEGER: And you also knew that Paul Castellano had been indicted and that there were tapes involved in Paul Castellano's case, correct?

GRAVANO: Yes.

KRIEGER: And at least ten months before Paul Castellano's death, you knew that the tapes that were generated at Paul Castellano's house came about at least in part as a result of the tapes from Angelo Ruggiero's house, correct?

GRAVANO: Yes. I believe so.

KRIEGER: You also knew in February of 1985 that Paul Castellano was trying to get hold of Angelo Ruggiero's tapes, right?

GRAVANO: Yes.

KRIEGER: And whatever steps had been taken in regards to his legal proceedings to get those tapes you are not necessarily familiar with, are you?

GRAVANO: No.

KRIEGER: You learned, however, did you not, there came a time during the year 1985 when Mr. Castellano's lawyer obtained a copy of the Ruggiero tapes?

GRAVANO: Yes.

KRIEGER: Now, in February of 1985, when you go to talk to Angelo Ruggiero, the problem about the tapes, you characterize it as a problem, the problem about the tapes existed, correct?

GRAVANO: Existed.

KRIEGER: It existed?

GRAVANO: Yes.

KRIEGER: And it also existed, did it not, that Angelo Ruggiero had adopted a position that he was not going to turn the tapes over to Paul Castellano in February 1985, correct?

GRAVANO: Yes.

KRIEGER: This tape situation was a situation that you believed to have some importance, correct?

GRAVANO: Yes.

KRIEGER: And you for one felt it would be perhaps an embarrassment, perhaps lead to troubles or difficulties, if Paul Castellano got hold of those tapes, right?

GRAVANO: I just viewed them as a problem. I wasn't on the tapes, Angelo was. It was a problem for him, not me.

KRIEGER: You sympathized with Angelo's decision?

GRAVANO: Yes.

KRIEGER: You understood his position, right?

GRAVANO: I understood the problem, yes.

KRIEGER: Of course, when you spoke to Angelo, that's the first time, and you told him to—you wanted to know where John

Gotti stood and where Frank DeCicco stood, well, you learned did you not, that John Gotti's attitude, if he expressed one in February 1985, was to turn over the tapes, right?

GRAVANO: I don't believe so.

KRIEGER: All right. Since February of 1985, you have heard, have you not, John Gotti on tape saying to Neil Dellacroce and to Angelo Ruggiero, turn over the tapes?

GRAVANO: I heard John Gotti say that. I don't know if it is that conversation.

KRIEGER: You heard John Gotti say that, you don't remember to whom he said it?

GRAVANO: I remember Neil wanted them.

[. . . .]

KRIEGER: It is a fact, is it not, that John Gotti's statement telling Angelo to turn over the tapes to Paul Castellano is contradictory to your testimony containing an expressed reason for participating in the killing of Paul Castellano because John Gotti didn't want the tapes turned over?

GLEESON: Objection.

JUDGE GLASSER: If you can answer that, I will permit it.

GRAVANO: Could you ask that again, please?

KRIEGER: You want me to ask it again?

GRAVANO: Yes.

KRIEGER: Okay. Maybe if I break it down. You gave four reasons as to why in your opinion there was a plan to kill Paul Castellano, correct?

GRAVANO: Yes.

KRIEGER: One of the reasons that you gave was the ongoing problem with Angelo's tapes, correct?

GRAVANO: Yes.

KRIEGER: You have also testified, have you not, that it was that John had stated, John Gotti had stated to Angelo Ruggiero, to turn over the tapes to Paul Castellano? Correct?

GRAVANO: I believe so, yes.

KRIEGER: Now, sir, it is inconsistent, is it not, that John would participate in a plan to kill Paul Castellano for the reason of keeping the tapes from Paul Castellano under those circumstances. Isn't that so?

GRAVANO: No. He knows what is on the tapes at that point. It is not the exclusive reason.

KRIEGER: Sir, the tapes—

GRAVANO: It was on the tapes, not turning them over.

KRIEGER: The tapes are unimportant to John Gotti, are they not?

GRAVANO: Are of importance?

KRIEGER: Unimportant?

GRAVANO: I don't know if unimportant. They are important. What is on the tape is important and gotten to the point they can't stop but give the boss the tapes at this point.

KRIEGER: Sir, you don't know what is on the tapes?

GRAVANO: Just what I heard.

KRIEGER: Have you ever listened to the tapes?

GRAVANO: No.

KRIEGER: Never read the transcript?

GRAVANO: No.

KRIEGER: You don't know whether John Gotti was saying to Angelo Ruggiero on or about February 15, 1985, turn over the tapes, do you?

GRAVANO: No.

KRIEGER: You don't know whether John Gotti was saying to Angelo Ruggiero on December 15, 1985, to Angelo Ruggiero, turn over the tapes. You don't know that either?

GRAVANO: No.

KRIEGER: If I were to ask you the same question directed to every day between February 16, 1985, and December 16, 1985, your answer would be the same, wouldn't it?

GRAVANO: If he spoke to him every day and said this?

KRIEGER: That you don't know when and where and under what circumstances from your own observation John Gotti spoke with Angelo Ruggiero concerning the tapes, correct?

GRAVANO: Correct, he could have had a lot of conversations.

KRIEGER: Let me go back to December 16, 1985. I think I stopped questioning you about the events of that evening when you and John Gotti are stopped at the northwest corner of 46th Street and Third Avenue in his Lincoln and you are looking eastward on 46th Street, correct?

GRAVANO: Yes.

KRIEGER: Now, you told us that you had a clear vision—unobstructed view, I should say, where Mr. Bilotti pulled the car in which he and Mr. Castellano were when they parked at or near Sparks Steak House, correct?

GRAVANO: Yes.

KRIEGER: You also told us you were able to see from shoulders up the people on the street, that is on the south side of 46th Street?

GRAVANO: Yes.

KRIEGER: Now, you were not able to see exactly where Mr. Rampino was, were you?

GRAVANO: I saw him across the street.

KRIEGER: You saw him across the street at the same time you are watching the south side of the street?

GRAVANO: No.

KRIEGER: You saw him at some time before across the street?

GRAVANO: When, before the shooting, when the shooting started I was watching the shooting.

KRIEGER: When Mr. Castellano and Mr. Bilotti drive past you, your attention focuses on that car, correct?

GRAVANO: Yes.

KRIEGER: You see the car park, correct?

GRAVANO: When I first saw it?

KRIEGER: You see the car park?

GRAVANO: Yes.

KRIEGER: And immediately thereafter you see the four gentlemen with white trench coats and fur hats, two to a side, go to the car?

GRAVANO: Tommy Bilotti gets out first before that happened.

KRIEGER: Tommy Bilotti gets out completely?

GRAVANO: Yes, he is getting out of the car.

KRIEGER: He is getting out of the car?

GRAVANO: Yes.

KRIEGER: And bingo, it happened?

GRAVANO: He is out of the car by that time.

KRIEGER: By that time it happened?

GRAVANO: Yes.

KRIEGER: And it is true, is it not, from your observation on that evening that—well, the minute or so that I have been asking you questions about it here and now, is a longer period of time than the incident took?

GRAVANO: Yes.

KRIEGER: It was literally an event that could be measured in seconds, correct?

GRAVANO: Probably.

KRIEGER: And as quickly as it happened, that is as quickly as the shooters got out of the neighborhood, right?

GRAVANO: Yes.

KRIEGER: Now, the shooters who were together over here, indicating an area in front of Sparks Steak House, left and moved east, right?

GRAVANO: Yes.

KRIEGER: Your attention was not focused upon them, was it?

GRAVANO: My attention was focused on them.

KRIEGER: Was not?

GRAVANO: Was.

KRIEGER: You watched to see that they started to leave, correct?

GRAVANO: Yes.

KRIEGER: And then they were out of your sight?

GRAVANO: Yes.

KRIEGER: Out of your sight someplace along the south side of 46th Street, correct?

GRAVANO: Yes.

KRIEGER: And certainly didn't go parading down the middle of the street, did they?

GRAVANO: No.

KRIEGER: You didn't see Mr. Rampino anymore, and you didn't see the other three gentlemen, Mr. Watts, Mr. Alogna, Mr. Ruggiero?

GRAVANO: Correct.

KRIEGER: Of course, you have no recollection as to whether the light was red or green for east-west traffic on Third Avenue, right?

GRAVANO: No.

KRIEGER: Of course, you do recall that there was a lot of excitement on the street right after all the shooting? It doesn't take place and people just yawn and go on about their business, right?

GRAVANO: *(No response)*

KRIEGER: If you recall?

GRAVANO: Happens quick, people are in shock, and there is not too much confusion right away. They don't react.

KRIEGER: But there was confusion?

GRAVANO: I imagine so.

KRIEGER: You saw confusion?

GRAVANO: A little.

KRIEGER: You saw people run from the place, from the immediate scene, right?

GRAVANO: I didn't really pay attention to the people around.

KRIEGER: You didn't observe?

GRAVANO: I was observing, but I was doing what I was supposed to do.

KRIEGER: What you were supposed to do was sit in the car and observe, correct?

GRAVANO: Be a backup shooter.

KRIEGER: Being a backup shooter you see a body lying in the street, you see the shooters leaving, you have no further role to play, do you?

GRAVANO: No, our function is to leave.

KRIEGER: Everything is completed, you are not going to run down the block and take Mr. Bilotti's pulse?

GRAVANO: No.

KRIEGER: Or Mr. Castellano's?

GRAVANO: No.

KRIEGER: As a matter of fact, the smartest and wisest thing is to get out of the neighborhood, right?

GRAVANO: Sure.

KRIEGER: But you didn't do that?

GRAVANO: We did that.

KRIEGER: What you did do, sir, was, whether the light changed right then and there, you had to wait for a full cycle or not, in Mr. Gotti's car, you and Mr. Gotti drove, I think the word is slowly, that is how you described it, didn't you?

GRAVANO: Yes.

KRIEGER: Drove slowly across Third Avenue over to where the homicide had taken place and you looked out the window—had to roll it down?

GRAVANO: No.

KRIEGER: You looked out the window and said: "By gosh, Tommy Bilotti is dead?"

GRAVANO: Without the "by gosh."

KRIEGER: Without the "by gosh?"

GRAVANO: Yes.

KRIEGER: Then you went on?

GRAVANO: Yes.

KRIEGER: Now, of course, of course, let's think, if we can, of all the things that could have happened between you looking out at Mr. Bilotti and pronouncing him dead, and your getting out of the block?

GRAVANO: Things that could have went wrong?

KRIEGER: Yes.

GRAVANO: All right.

KRIEGER: When you started to drive across the street you did not know as a fact, sir, as to whether the block was empty, did you?

GRAVANO: Not completely, no.

KRIEGER: You did not know, sir, whether someone who was parked could have pulled out and blocked your way, did you?

GRAVANO: Possibility.

KRIEGER: You did not know, sir, that perhaps coming down Second Avenue there would have been first a civilian car that could have blocked the intersection, correct?

GRAVANO: I guess there is a possibility of that too.

KRIEGER: Blocking an intersection is not something which never happens in the city of New York, is it?

GRAVANO: No.

KRIEGER: Such a thing is gridlock. Is that correct?

GRAVANO: Yes.

KRIEGER: You did not know whether someone was here, because now we are starting to tick off minutes, time you leave the corner and drive down the block it is no longer a split second, correct?

GRAVANO: No, it is seconds and what we are doing is following the shooters out. We didn't know what they did.

KRIEGER: You can't see them?

GRAVANO: Correct, we follow them out.

KRIEGER: That is not what you described for us?

GLEESON: Objection to the conversation.

JUDGE GLASSER: Sustained.

KRIEGER: What you have testified to, if I understand your testimony, is that you drove slowly down the block and you looked out at Mr. Bilotti's body. That is what you testified?

GRAVANO: As I passed I looked down.

KRIEGER: You also testified what I described to you in response to Mr. Gleeson's questions concerning what did you do, correct?

GRAVANO: Yes.

KRIEGER: You did not testify in response to any question, did you, put to you by Mr. Gleeson, that you were going down the block following the shooters. You didn't say that, did you?

GRAVANO: I don't know if he asked me that.

KRIEGER: Your recollection, you didn't say it?

GRAVANO: I don't believe so.

KRIEGER: Now, sir, we've got to take out whether seconds or minutes, an unknown because we don't know whether you had to wait for the light or not, right?

GRAVANO: I don't believe we caught the light. I believe we made the light.

KRIEGER: An assumption?

GRAVANO: Yes.

KRIEGER: Actual recollection, you don't know?

GRAVANO: I don't remember.

KRIEGER: Okay. You go across the street, you drive slowly, down to roughly I think I described it as two-thirds of a football field, looked out, and you see Mr. Bilotti, you don't see the shooters, you don't see Mr. Rampino, and then you decide to leave the area, continue on to leave the area?

GRAVANO: Continue on. Leaving the area the minute we are leaving the spot.

KRIEGER: Okay. Now, I think I was at the point where you don't know whether somebody called 911, right?

GRAVANO: No.

KRIEGER: You don't know whether there is going to be a response by police well within seconds or within minutes, do you?

GRAVANO: *(No response)*

KRIEGER: Yes or no?

GRAVANO: 911 usually takes about three minutes.

KRIEGER: You plug that in, it is going to take three minutes?

GRAVANO: Yes.

KRIEGER: Even if there is a cop who happens to be coming down Second Avenue in his cruiser, prowl car, and over by 46th and 47th on Second Avenue and swing right in the block because there is a report of a double homicide, could happen?

GRAVANO: I would think that would take longer. If [that] happened we are in big trouble.

KRIEGER: Any one of these happened, Sammy Gravano and John Gotti are caught on the block with Paul Castellano's body and Tommy Bilotti's body, if any of those things happen, right?

GRAVANO: There is a possibility, yes.

KRIEGER: I guess you could abandon John's car and go running down the street and let the police wonder how come John Gotti's car was on 46th Street between Second and Third Avenue within feet of where the bodies of Castellano and Bilotti are found?

GRAVANO: When I said that, I don't make reference to his personal car. He came with it. Whether a stolen car or his car or somebody else's car, it is his car because he came with it. I got into his car. That is what I made reference to.

[. . . .]

KRIEGER: There is a meeting, is there not, according to your testimony, with Mr. Joseph Gallo shortly after December 16, 1985?

GRAVANO: Yes.

KRIEGER: And it is—it is your testimony, isn't it, that Mr. Gallo said that you must never admit it, correct?

GRAVANO: Yes.

KRIEGER: Now, he is saying that to a group of people who according to your testimony all know of it, right?

GRAVANO: Yes.

KRIEGER: All were participants in the plan, correct?

GRAVANO: Yes.

KRIEGER: Means you have to further pass it on to all of the others who had knowledge of the plan, correct?

GRAVANO: These people didn't have actual knowledge of the plan, they assumed.

KRIEGER: We are talking about people, Joe Watts, we are talking about people such as Angelo Ruggiero, we are talking about Iggy Alogna, and Rampino, Eddie Lino, Scala, we are talking about a whole bunch of people, there were ten people on December 16, 1985, as far as your testimony is concerned, correct?

GRAVANO: Yes.

KRIEGER: There weren't ten people meeting with Joe Gallo?

GRAVANO: No.

KRIEGER: There has to be word given to the other people, correct?

GRAVANO: I don't know if they need the word. They assumed, they know what they did.

KRIEGER: My gosh, you certainly don't need the word, do you?

GRAVANO: No, I don't really—

KRIEGER: Joe Gallo is going through an exercise elevating form over substance or doing something that is real, he is warning you, one or the other, making a fool of himself or not?

GRAVANO: He is talking about rules in the commission. A higher level than these people are involved in—

KRIEGER: He didn't talk to you?

GRAVANO: He is talking about the commission. The rules and regulations as far as killing the boss, the commission, as far as making a new boss, as far as the responsibility of owning up to this situation. He's talking about that.

In substance—

KRIEGER: Go ahead?

GRAVANO: These people, most of them were not even made, they don't have to be told not to admit to this even though they are told. I don't think they need any conversation that this shouldn't be discussed, that we just whacked out the boss.

KRIEGER: You are saying they were told?

GRAVANO: Might have been.

KRIEGER: They were told, correct?

GRAVANO: You are talking about two different meetings, when Joe Gallo told us as far as making a new boss, get permission, and recommendations to get a commission seat. He was telling us the rules and regulations, go along with the other Families who are going to ask about it.

[. . . .]

KRIEGER: Now, you and Mr. Gotti, according to your testimony, didn't have to keep secrets from one another about what happened on December 16, 1985, right?

GRAVANO: No.

KRIEGER: According to your version of events he knew what you did, you knew what he did, right?

GRAVANO: Obviously.

KRIEGER: And it would be the height of silliness for you to say to John Gotti, "I don't know who killed Paul Castellano," as it would be for John Gotti to say to you, "I don't know who killed Paul Castellano," unless it were true. Right?

GRAVANO: No.

KRIEGER: Now, sir, when you were in MCC [Metropolitan Correctional Center]—by the way, by the way, just one other thing, I want to touch one base before I get you to MCC. When you were in MCC, you became familiar with at least some of the tapes, correct?

GRAVANO: Yes.

KRIEGER: And there were discussions as between yourself and Mr. Gotti concerning what was on some of the tapes. Correct?

GRAVANO: Yes.

KRIEGER: And it is a fact, is it not, that you were aware that Mr. Gotti—Mr. Gotti was aware of the November 30 tape in which, as we've all heard here in the court, he states at a number of times that he does not know who killed Paul Castellano? You were aware of that in the MCC, were you not?

GRAVANO: I'm aware of that before, at MCC, after.

KRIEGER: Okay. Now, you also were aware, were you not—well, you had conversations with Mr. Gotti, didn't you, that the government may well adopt a position that they could rely upon the portions of the tape that they considered incriminating, but on the portions of the tape that were not incriminating, that tended to show innocence, that, oh, well, that was for advertising, or that was not with a person whom he could rely on or with whom he would exchange this kind of information, that was the conversation, was it not? Correct? You knew that that was what Mr. Gotti told you?

GRAVANO: He might have, yes.

KRIEGER: When you had conversations concerning Mr. [Mike] Coiro's conversation with you and with Mr. Gotti on November 30, correct?

GRAVANO: Yes.

KRIEGER: And in that conversation with Mr. Coiro and with you, Mr. Gotti says, does he not, for the first time that evening, "I don't know who killed Paul." In substance, right?

GRAVANO: When he's talking to Coiro?

KRIEGER: Yes.

GRAVANO: Yes.

KRIEGER: And it was discussed, was it not, as between you and Mr. Gotti, that what the government's position was going to be, well, of course Mr. Gotti would deny it, because Mike Coiro is not one of the members of this Family that you've described?

GRAVANO: He's a lawyer.

KRIEGER: Correct?

GRAVANO: He's a lawyer, Mike Coiro.

KRIEGER: So Mr. Gotti is not going to admit it to Mr. Coiro, correct?

GRAVANO: We're not going to admit it to anybody.

KRIEGER: All right. Then on further examination of the tapes of that day we come to a conversation in which Mr. Coiro is not present, where he's talking to you, where you're talking about Nino Gaggi, you're talking about Paul Castellano, and well, the focus of the conversation, the focus of the conversation comes about because of television programs a couple of days before, correct?

GRAVANO: Yes.

KRIEGER: And the television programs a couple of days before, well, they try to picture what they understand, what the media understands happened, right?

GRAVANO: Yes.

KRIEGER: And they also predict, do they not, that there will be an indictment shortly after November 30, 1989, charging Mr. Gotti and others with participation in the, in bringing about the death of Mr. Castellano and Mr. Bilotti, right?

GRAVANO: I don't know if they quote the dates, but—

KRIEGER: Not an exact date, but they say pretty soon?

GRAVANO: Yeah. It could be, yeah.

KRIEGER: Now, that's a matter of concern to you, right?

GRAVANO: Yes.

KRIEGER: It's a matter of concern to Mr. Gotti, correct?

GRAVANO: Yes.

KRIEGER: Under any circumstances neither one of you wants to be prosecuted, correct?

GRAVANO: Yes.

KRIEGER: Now, in the course of the conversation that you're having on November 30, and I'm not talking about the Coiro conversation I'm talking about the conversation—

GRAVANO: After.

KRIEGER: —which is marked as beginning at about 8:15?

GRAVANO: Yes.

KRIEGER: In that conversation, well, many things are discussed, are they not?

GRAVANO: A few things are discussed.

KRIEGER: The situation concerning what happened with Mr. Castellano is just one of a number of topics, correct?

GRAVANO: A few of them were discussed, I believe.

KRIEGER: All right. Now, the statement, the statement by Mr. Gotti that he does not know who killed Paul Castellano is agreed to by you, correct?

GRAVANO: You didn't complete the statement, but—you didn't complete the statement.

KRIEGER: I didn't?

GRAVANO: He also says in that statement I believe that the cops there, and I agree with that.

KRIEGER: He says, does he not, and I'm paraphrasing it, that for all he knows, the cops may have killed him, he says I know, I don't know who killed him, and you agree, correct?

GRAVANO: Something to that effect.

KRIEGER: This conversation, Mr. Gravano, is one—is in one of the two locations that you considered most private. Correct?

GRAVANO: We're having that conversation with Frankie, I believe.

KRIEGER: That conversation is in a place where you, one of the two places that you considered most private. Correct?

GRAVANO: Yes, we feel it's private.

KRIEGER: And you certainly don't believe that it's being overheard. Correct?

GRAVANO: No, we don't believe it's overheard. We hope not.

KRIEGER: And you're not saying that in the hope that the FBI is hearing, is listening to it, or the organized crime task force is listening to it, and in effect you're advertising innocence, correct? That's not what's going on, is it?

GRAVANO: When we developed that conversation, we talked like that just about all the time, no matter where we are, we're just getting into the habit of talking like that.

KRIEGER: When you talk about that all the time, so that's why we only hear it only once or twice in probably thousands of hours of tapes, correct?

GRAVANO: Could be.

KRIEGER: So obviously you don't talk about it all the time, correct?

GRAVANO: Castellano murder?

KRIEGER: Correct.

GRAVANO: No, we don't talk about it.

KRIEGER: Now, Mr. Gotti had told you, had he not, not once, not twice, maybe ten times, from 1989 right through, that— let's break it up to when you get indicted. Before you get indicted, Mr. Gotti had said to you numerous times, had he not, that "We will beat this case," referring to the Castellano case. Correct?

GRAVANO: He made reference to that, yeah.

Afterword

JOHN MILLER

IT WAS MONDAY, March 2, 1992, when Salvatore (Sammy the Bull) Gravano first sang for his supper, and the government wasn't taking any chances with the highest-ranking, most significant mobster ever to rat on his gang in U.S. history.

Security that day was even tighter than usual. A crowd of deputy U.S. marshals was packed into the rows of spectators. A line of muscle-bound FBI agents—the special Hostage Rescue Team sent up to New York from the FBI academy in Quantico, Virginia—sat along a bench just inside the well of the courtroom. Sporting unfashionable crew cuts, they were the Bureau's shooters, commandos in gray suits, the meanest dudes the Bureau had. Directly behind them sat eleven of John Gotti's closest pals and supporters. They didn't seem pleased to have their view of the proceedings blocked by the wall of G-men in front of them. The feds, for their part, didn't seem to mind at all.

The tension was palpable. Gravano's appearance was the break the government needed and the defense had feared. For Gravano was the last man John Gotti had expected to betray

him. He loved Sammy. And Sammy, he felt sure, loved h
Never before had Gravano refused an order. In the past, when Gotti had barked, Sammy bit. He was a tough guy's tough guy. That he might turn rabid and attack his master was a possibility Gotti apparently had never reckoned on.

Why Gotti never saw it coming remains a mystery. After all, Gravano's entire history suggested that when backed into a corner, he always took the most drastic way out. That usually meant whacking whoever he regarded as standing in his way. His reputation as one of the more feared enforcers in the Mafia was well deserved. He was a guy who never seemed to lose even a nanosecond's worth of sleep no matter whom he killed—whether the victim happened to be his wife's brother or a business partner or his best friend. Once it became clear that Gravano had decided to rat on Gotti, the Gambino clan sought to dismiss his bloody deeds as the work of a man who didn't really have the balls to pull the trigger himself. As one of Gotti's friends put it: "Sammy was a drugstore cowboy. He had a fancy hat, he wore nice shiny boots, but he didn't know how to ride a horse. He didn't kill nobody. He'd get two kids to kill them. Then a few weeks later, he'd get someone to kill the two kids." But this was a distinction without much difference. Certainly it mattered not at all to the nineteen dead men whose murders Gravano would confess to.

Gravano with a gun was a dangerous man, no doubt about it. But Gravano's mouth would prove just as lethal. The government had taken steps to ensure that Gravano wouldn't crack once he took the stand. The moment he had decided to switch sides, his care and feeding became a top priority for the FBI. He was removed from New York's Metropolitan Correctional Center, where Gotti and his codefendant Frank Locascio were held, and flown secretly to Quantico. The Bureau went to great lengths to keep Gravano happy. Even his passion for boxing was indulged. A host of young agents volunteered to get into the ring with Sammy, never doubting that they would easily beat this rank amateur. They were wrong. It quickly became a matter of pride. The Bureau flew in a big Indian agent from Illinois who had a reputation with his hands. He slammed Gravano with a body punch that caused Sammy to growl and double over, holding his sides. For a moment, his government minders were scared. What if things got out of hand? What if Gravano were injured so badly that his testimony was delayed? "Jesus," one agent laughed, "what if he got fucking amnesia?" They slacked off on the sparring after that.

The government couldn't afford to lose this case. Gotti had already beaten them three times before. The FBI's image was at stake. If Gravano was going to help them tie the bow, they would find a way to make sure the knot would be pulled tight. Gravano would help them get Gotti in exchange for a maximum twenty years in the pen, and in the process the Gambino Family would be gutted. Gravano was a gusher, and his decision to tell them everything he knew was black gold. His memory would prove nearly photographic. No detail from his violent past was too small or too gory to have been forgotten. Best of all, Sammy told them everything about the Paul Castellano hit—how it was planned, who the designated shooters were, how it went down.

Still, the government couldn't be entirely sure that Gravano wouldn't buckle under pressure. He was, they realized, all alone. His wife, Debra, and his son and daughter had vowed never to have anything to do with him again. As far as they were concerned, he was history. They had refused to accompany him into the Federal Witness Protection Program. He would be left to twist in the wind with his newfound friends.

* * *

"Our next witness is Salvatore Gravano," said John Gleeson, the assistant U.S. attorney.

"Okay," said Judge I. Leo Glasser.

The courtroom on the fourth floor of the Brooklyn Federal Courthouse was utterly silent. Nobody moved. Even Gotti, whose constant gestures of contempt had driven the prosecutors nuts, sat still. Only the smirk that was perpetually stuck on his mug seemed to twitch. It took an agonizing four full minutes from the time Gleeson called Gravano as a witness until the door behind the witness stand opened. Suddenly Sammy entered, surrounded by agents in front and behind him. No one spoke or coughed or even seemed to breathe. I remembered the first time I ever saw this man they called The Bull.

As the principal investigative reporter for WNBC-TV, I had been assigned to keep track of John Gotti as he rose to the top of what was regarded as America's largest Cosa Nostra Family. No one had ever gotten an interview with Gotti, and in late October 1987, I was determined to be the first, even if I had to "ambush" him with his henchmen as he took one of his frequent "walk talks" outside the Ravenite Social Club, his hangout in Little Italy. My camera crews took up their positions. I knew from past experience that the men who always accompanied Gotti would try to cover the lenses of any nosy cameras that managed to come too close. On this particular night, though, I had come prepared with more cameras and lights than Gotti's men had hands.

As Gotti and two men neared the middle of the block, I struck. He tried to escape. The two men accompanying him, one tall and the other short, tried their best, cursing and shoving my crew. But one of the three cameras we had was always in Gotti's face as I peppered him with questions I knew he was never going to answer like "Are you the head of the Gambino crime family?"

"Easy, Sammy," he said to the short one.

"Frank!" he called to the taller man as he wagged an index finger. Gotti was a man who, above all things, was obsessed with appearances. He professed bewilderment: "I always treat you like a gentleman, John. This is no good." But it was good enough to make the evening news, and that was good enough for me.

Later, I showed the videotape to the late John Gurnee, perhaps the New York City detective with the most intimate knowledge of Gotti and his men. "Who are these other two guys with John?" I asked. "The tall guy is Frankie Locascio, an old-time wiseguy," he said. "The little guy is Sammy the Bull. He's the guy to watch. A rising star."

Now, five years later, Gravano was a star all right—the government's, and now I and everyone else would get a chance to watch Sammy give the performance of his life. Like everyone else, I wondered how he would do on the stand. Would he freeze up? Or back out? Would he hold up on cross-examination?

Gleeson, who had been taunted by Gotti as a "meek little mouse," stood at the lectern at the far end of the jury box. Gravano, his hair greased back, and decked out in a gray double-breasted suit, took his seat in the witness box at the other end. The tall, thin Ivy League prosecutor with the horn-rimmed glasses couldn't have provided a starker contrast. The questioning began. Sammy's answers, delivered in a calm and icy monotone, would prove so compelling in their brutal candor and detail as to strip Gotti and Locascio's lawyers of any convincing defense.

The defense team was stunned, deprived of any viable strategy capable of undoing the damage that was daily being inflicted on their clients. Albert Krieger, Gotti's lawyer, was said to be a fearsome cross-examiner. A man with a rich baritone and a shaved head, he looked like a cross between Kojak and Daddy Warbucks. Anthony Cardinale, Locascio's attorney, had grown up in Brooklyn and had become partners with F. Lee Bailey before striking out on his own. During the cross-examination, Gravano refused to be rattled. Nothing seemed to work. Not the courtly manner of Krieger, who was at pains to offend neither the judge nor the jury. Not the brasher tactics of Cardinale, who became increasingly exasperated with the judge's refusal to allow seven of the eight witnesses the defense wanted to call, including an audio expert to question the content and meaning of the tape transcripts that had been so meticulously prepared by the FBI.

Cardinale went ballistic. If the government was permitted to put a witness on the stand to testify as to the accuracy of the FBI's transcripts, why couldn't the defense put on a witness to give its interpretation? "I can't understand it," said Cardinale, "and I'm sorry if I'm losing my temper. I have had enough . . . I can't believe what's going on here. I can't believe it, as a practicing lawyer for fifteen years in cases as complex as this—"

Judge Glasser cut Cardinale off: "I'm holding you, sir, in summary contempt, and I'll prepare a certificate to that effect in accordance with 42(a) of the Federal Rules of Criminal Procedure. I'll deal with the penalty imposed, Mr. Cardinale—"

Cardinale interrupted the judge in mid-sentence: "Do it right now, judge, really."

At the defense table, Krieger turned pale. Gotti, however, looked elated. When the yelling was over and Cardinale had returned to the defense table, Gotti reached over to shake his hand. Krieger, for his part, sought to placate the judge by blaming Cardinale's outburst on pressure and stress. Gotti would give Krieger hell for it later.

The differences in style between the defense attorneys were obvious to even the most casual of observers. Where Krieger was careful and conservative, Cardinale was cocky and aggressive. Both men, however, seemed baffled by the government's case. Only John Gotti seemed to know where he was going. And all he seemed to want was a good fight—with the judge, the prosecutor, and, most of all, with his ex–best friend, Sammy the Bull.

Gotti wasn't the only one who wanted to confront Gravano. During Sammy's second day on the stand, a woman screaming in Italian tried to burst through the courtroom doors. United States Marshal Charles Healey had his security officers pull the distraught woman into his office. Healey, a retired homicide detective with a soft bedside manner, gave her a tissue and asked her to explain herself. Her name, she said, was Anna Carini, and she was the mother of two sons who had gone to see Sammy Gravano one warm night in 1986. That was the last time she had seen them alive.

I remembered the Carini brothers quite vividly. I was there when the cops pulled their bullet-ridden bodies out of two cars that had been parked together. They both wore fancy warm-up suits. One had a weight lifter's belt around his waist. That they had been dealing drugs, robbing banks, and doing small-time hits for a local hood was an open neighborhood secret. Apparently only their mother didn't know. She did know one thing, however: somehow, Sammy Gravano was to blame.

The following day a woman named Rose Massa broke free from the long line of would-be spectators who waited sometimes all day and in vain to get into the trial. As she approached me, I could see she was nervous and upset. She quickly introduced herself and got to the point. Her brother was Michael DeBatt. He had been killed in the summer of 1987, in Tali's, the club Gravano owned in Brooklyn. Sammy had come to the funeral. Indeed, there was hardly a funeral of any of his victims that he missed. Rose Massa had been Gravano's secretary at the construction company he headed. She told me she wanted to see Sammy on the stand, but the marshals had refused to let her up. I spoke to Healey, and he agreed to make room for her provided she promised not to make a scene. She took a seat in the back of the courtroom, and left at the lunch break, telling me, with a shake of her head, "In our neighborhood, Sammy's middle name was 'Do the Right Thing,' and now look at him."

Each day Gravano was on the stand a young man in a turtleneck sat in the second row. He stared at Gravano day after day. Joey D'Angelo was just nineteen. Years before, Joey's father, Stymie, had been killed in a stick-up in Tali's. He told me Gravano thought of him as an adopted son. D'Angelo was a tough kid, saying he had met Gravano "at the funeral parlor after my father died." Ever since, he had worshiped the man. Joey learned from Gravano that the key to being a man was to do the right thing and keep your mouth shut. I asked him what he saw in Gravano's eyes when he caught his glance on the witness stand. "I saw shame," he replied.

After Gravano had been on the stand for five days straight, Judge Glasser suspended the trial for a day so that a member of the jury could attend a family funeral. The jury was anonymous and sequestered. Marshals guarded the twelve jurors and four alternates around the clock. Forty hotel rooms at the rate of $106 a night were rented. Limousines with dark tinted windows took them to and from hotels. Their names were kept secret from both the defense and prosecution. Not even the judge was permitted to know their names. The list was locked in the court clerk's safe, and only a court order could break it out.

Concern for the jury's safety was to be expected. Despite the fact that the jury in Gotti's last trial had been anonymous, it was not sequestered. One of the jurors, it turned out, was friendly with one of Gotti's friends. Prosecutors said the man made a deal to sell his vote for $60,000, and on February 24, 1992, smack in the middle of Gotti's new trial, the man was arrested and charged with obstruction of justice. He pleaded not guilty. The government was determined that this time things would be different. This time they were.

After Sammy's testimony, the trial was, for all practical purposes, over. As far as the government was concerned, Gravano had done his finest piece of work, and it began to look as if Gotti was finally finished. The defense took a last, desperate shot at Gravano and the government in their closing statements. For two days, Krieger and Cardinale railed against the prosecutors, accusing them of putting on a show trial and cutting a deal with a ruthless killer who would do anything to save his own skin.

The jury didn't buy it. On April 2, after deliberating for only a day and a half, the panel of seven women and five men put an end to the reign of the most feared gangster in decades. John Gotti showed no emotion as the forewoman pronounced him guilty of all fourteen counts, ranging from murder to racketeering to tax evasion, with which he had been charged. (Although Frank Locascio was acquitted of one minor charge of illegal gambling, he too went down for the count.) Ever the boss, ever the fighter, Gotti patted his lawyers on the back and promised his demoralized supporters that he'd win on appeal. "We'll be all right," Gotti said as the marshals led him from the courtroom and back to the Manhattan jail cell to contemplate the several life terms and the few hundred years behind bars that he now faced.

The government was jubilant. "The Teflon is gone," said the

head of the FBI's New York office. "The Don is covered with Velcro."

Outside her parents' home in Howard Beach, Queens, Gotti's daughter Victoria was defiant, telling reporters that the whole trial was a sham. "My father," she said, her voice proud and strong, "is the last of the Mohicans."

Who's Who

The following cast of characters is provided to enable the reader to identify many of the names that appear in the Gotti tapes. Some names could not be identified with certainty and are thus omitted. Much of the biographical information was drawn from the testimony of FBI Special Agent Lewis D. Schiliro, a prosecution witness in the 1992 Gotti trial. Schiliro was the coordinating supervisor, beginning in 1989, overseeing the investigation of organized crime in New York. It is important to remember that not every person who is referred to on the Gotti tapes is affiliated with organized crime or is in any other way associated with crime or criminals. One should not assume any guilt by reference or association.

■ ■ ■

ALBIE TRIMMING A New York garment center company that produces zippers and linings for women's garments.

PIETRO ANGELO Deceased member of the Gambino family.

ANGELO *See* Angelo Ruggiero.

ARC PLUMBING Arc Plumbing and Heating Corporation, a New York firm employing John Gotti as a salesman.

JOE ARCURI Giuseppe Arcuri, a long-time *capo* in the Gambino Family.

BENNY Benny "Eggs" Mangano, underboss in the Genovese Family.

BOSCO Bosco Radonjich, boss of the Westies, an Irish gang notorious for its brutality. Also affiliated with Marine Construction Company. Currently a fugitive, and thought to be in Yugoslavia.

BRACCIOLE Nickname of Louie Ricco, a *capo* in the Gambino Family.

JOE BREWSTER Also known as Joe Delmonico. He is a business agent for Local 23 of the bricklayers' union in New York, and is a soldier in the Gambino Family.

JIMMY BROWN Nickname of James Failla, a *capo* in the Gambino Family, ex-chauffeur to Carlo Gambino. Said to control New York's garbage industry.

BRUCE Bruce Cutler, flamboyant defense attorney who successfully represented John Gotti in previous trials.

JOE BUTCH Nickname of Joseph Corrao, a Gambino Family *capo*.

"BUTTERASS" *See* Georgie DiCicco.

MIKE CARBONE Secretary-treasurer of Teamsters Local 282 in New York. According to FBI testimony at the 1992 Gotti trial, the local is controlled by the Gambino Family.

CARMINE Carmine Sciandra, owner of Top Tomato, a produce retailer operating throughout New York City.

CARNEGLIA John Carneglia (also known as "Carneg"), a Gambino Family soldier, is currently serving fifty years in prison for heroin trafficking.

PETE CASTELLANO Cousin of Paul Castellano.

THE CHIN Nickname of Vincent Gigante, boss of the Genovese Family.

COFFEY Joe Coffey, head of New York City's Organized Crime Homicide Task Force.

JIMMY COONAN Former head of the Westies, a notoriously brutal Irish gang in Manhattan. Currently serving a life sentence for murder.

CORKY Corky Vastola, a member of the DeCavalcante Family, according to Salvatore Gravano's testimony at the 1992 Gotti trial.

JOE CROTTY A member of the Westies, an Irish gang in Manhattan. Brother-in-law of Jimmy Coonan.

SAL D'ACQUISTO Deceased Gambino Family member.

JOHNNY D'AMATO Underboss of the DeCavalcante Family in New Jersey, according to FBI testimony at the 1992 Gotti trial.

DANNY *See* Danny Marino.

FRANKIE DAP Nickname of Frank D'Apolito, a *capo* in the Gambino Family.

FRANKIE DECICCO Gambino Family *capo* who became underboss after betraying Paul Castellano in 1985. He died in a car bombing on April 13, 1986.

GEORGIE DECICCO Also known as "Butterass," he is a *capo* in the Gambino Family, and uncle of Frankie DeCicco.

DI B Nickname of Robert DiBernardo, Gambino Family member, in charge of pornography industry. Murdered by Salvatore Gravano on orders of John Gotti on June 5, 1986.

LOUIE DIBONO A soldier in the Gambino Family, he was murdered at the behest of Salvatore Gravano on orders of John Gotti on October 4, 1990.

ERNIE BOY Nickname of Oreste Abbamonte, a longtime Mafia drug trafficker.

FAT ANGELO *See* Angelo Ruggiero.

FAT DOM Fat Dom Burgese, a candidate for induction into the Gambino Family. Sponsored by Jack (Jackie Nose) D'Amico.

FATSO *See* Angelo Ruggiero.

FAT TONY Nickname of Tony Proto (also called "Tony from New Jersey"), a candidate for induction into the Gambino Family. Died in 1990. Sponsored by Mike Mandaglio, a *capo* in the Gambino Family.

"FISH" Nickname of Vincent Cafaro, a Gambino Family member who became a government cooperating witness.

JOE FRANCOLINO Soldier in the Gambino Family, and cousin to Eddie Lino.

FRANKIE *See* Frankie DeCicco.

FRANKIE THE BUG Nickname of Frank Sciortino, a soldier in the Colombo Family, according to law enforcement sources.

JOHNNY G. *See* Johnny Gammarano.

JOE GALLO Former Gambino Family *consigliere*, now serving ten years in prison for racketeering.

JOHNNY GAMBINO A Gambino Family *capo*, a relative of Carlo Gambino, and cousin of Tommy Gambino.

TOMMY GAMBINO A *capo* in the Gambino Family, son of Carlo Gambino, and cousin of Johnny Gambino. In February 1992, he and other defendants agreed to pay a $12 million fine in a settlement of state racketeering charges with the Manhattan district attorney.

JOHNNY GAMMARANO A soldier in the Gambino Family (also known as "Johnny G."). Cousin to Danny Marino.

GAS *See* Gaspipe.

GASPIPE Also known as "Gas," Anthony Casso is underboss of the Lucchese Family.

GEM STEEL A New York steel company, Gem Atlas Steel specializes in large buildings. Controlled by the Gambino Family. *See* Louis Milito.

GENIE Gene Gotti, brother of John Gotti, now serving fifty years in prison for heroin trafficking.

GERRY Gerald Shargel, an attorney for Anthony (Tony Lee) Guerreri, a codefendant in John Gotti's 1990 trial.

MRS. GIACALONE Diane Giacalone, assistant U.S. attorney, Eastern District of New York, and chief prosecutor in racketeering case against John Gotti in 1985—a trial in which Gotti was acquitted.

JOE GLITZ Nickname of Joseph Glitzia, a Genovese Family member.

GOOD-LOOKING JACKIE Nickname of John Giordano, a *capo* in the Gambino Family.

PETE GOTTI Brother of John Gotti, he was acquitted in the "Windows" case, which involved bid-rigging of window installation in New York City. *See* Windows.

MIKEY GOUT A member of the Genovese Family, according to law enforcement sources.

JACKIE John Giordano, member of the Gambino Family, and nephew of Joe Piney.

JELLY BELLY Nickname of Louie DiBono, used by John Gotti and Salvatore Gravano. *See* Louie DiBono.

JOHNNY G. *See* Johnny Gammarano.

JOE *See* O'Brien.

JO JO Jo Jo Corozzo, a Gambino Family soldier, according to FBI testimony at the 1992 Gotti trial.

GERRY LANG Nickname of Gennaro Langella, underboss of the Colombo Family.

JIMMY LA ROSSA Attorney who represented Paul Castellano.

BUDDY LEAHY President of Marine Construction Company. Also known as Francis Leahy.

TONY LEE Nickname of Anthony Guerreri, associate of John Gotti's, and his codefendant in Gotti's 1990 trial—a trial that ended in acquittal.

BOB LEVY A close associate of the Gambino Family, according to Salvatore Gravano's testimony at the 1992 Gotti trial.

EDDIE LINO Soldier (later *capo*) in the Gambino Family, and cousin to Joe Francolino. Shot to death in 1990.

FRANKIE LOC *See* Locascio.

LOCAL 23 A bricklayers' union in New York City said to be controlled by the Gambino Family, according to government testimony at the 1992 Gotti trial.

LOCASCIO Frank Locascio, also known as Frankie Loc, a made member of the Mafia at age twenty-three in 1956. Acting underboss (and later *consigliere*) to John Gotti, and convicted with Gotti in April 1992 on charges of murder and racketeering. He was acquitted on one minor count of illegal gambling.

LORENZO Last name unknown, a candidate for induction into the Gambino Family. Sponsored by Johnny Gambino.

LOUIE *See* Louis DiBono.

LOUIE THE COFFEE BOY Louis Vallario, a *capo* in the Gambino Family and, according to John Gotti, a former "coffee boy."

JOE MADONIA Partner of Salvatore Gravano in a drywall company.

MARATHON Marathon Construction Company, a firm controlled by Salvatore Gravano that specializes in cement.

MARINE Marine Construction Company, a large New York cement company controlled by the Gambino Family, according to FBI testimony at the 1992 Gotti trial.

DANNY MARINO A Gambino Family *capo*, and cousin to Johnny Gammarano.

MARIO Last name unknown, a candidate for induction into the Gambino Family. Sponsored by Louie (Bracciole) Ricco, a *capo* in the Family.

JOE MESSINA Joseph Messina, underboss of the Bonanno Family, heroin trafficker and friend of John Gotti's.

MIKE Michael Coiro, an attorney for John Gotti's men, was convicted in 1989 of racketeering and obstruction of justice. Now serving fifteen years in prison.

LOUIS MILITO Also known as Liberio Milito. Controlled Gem Steel, a New York construction company, for the Gambino Family. Murdered at the behest of Salvatore Gravano on orders of John Gotti on March 8, 1988.

NASABEAK Nickname for Paul Castellano, murdered boss of the Gambino Family.

NEIL Aniello Dellacroce, former underboss to Paul Castellano. Died of cancer on December 2, 1985.

NINA Wife of Paul Castellano.

NINO Nino Gaggi, a *capo* in the Gambino Family.

JACKIE NOSE Nickname of Jack D'Amico, a *capo* in the Gambino Family.

O'BRIEN Joe O'Brien, FBI agent in charge of electronic surveillance of Paul Castellano. He is coauthor of *Boss of Bosses: The Fall of the Godfather: The FBI and Paul Castellano.*

PAUL Paul Castellano, brother-in-law and successor to Carlo Gambino as boss of the Gambino Family upon Gambino's death from natural causes in 1976. Castellano was murdered (along with his chauffeur and bodyguard, Tommy Bilotti) in front of Sparks Steak House in Manhattan on December 16, 1985.

PETE Pete Castellano, cousin of Paul Castellano.

JOE PINEY Nickname of Joseph Armone, official *consigliere* of the Gambino Family. Convicted of racketeering, he died in prison in late February 1992. He was buried in Brooklyn on March 2, the day Salvatore Gravano took the stand to testify against his former boss, John Gotti.

POLLOK John Pollok, an attorney for some of John Gotti's men.

"PONCHO" Nickname of a candidate for induction into the Gambino Family. Sponsored by Frankie Dap[olito].

PRISCO Anthony Prisco, a soldier in the Genovese Family, according to law enforcement sources.

TONY PROTO *See* Fat Tony.

LOUIE RICCO Also known as "Bracciole," Ricco is a Gambino Family *capo*.

JOHN RICCOBONO Deceased Gambino Family member.

RICHIE Richie Martino, a candidate for induction into the Gambino Family. Sponsored by Frank Locascio.

JOHN RIGGI Boss of the DeCavalcante Family in New Jersey.

JOHN RIZZO A candidate for induction into the Gambino Family. Sponsored by John (Good-Looking Jack) Giordano.

GASPARE ROMANO Deceased Gambino Family member.

ANGELO RUGGIERO A Gambino Family soldier, promoted to *capo* by John Gotti. Also known as Fat Angelo and Fatso. Died of cancer on December 5, 1989.

LOUIE SACCENTI A candidate for induction into the Gambino Family, sponsored by Salvatore Gravano.

SAL Nickname of Salvatore Ruggiero, brother of Angelo Ruggiero, and major heroin trafficker. Died in airplane crash in 1982.

SALLY Sally Vitale, acting boss of the Bonanno Family, according to FBI testimony at the 1992 Gotti trial.

SAM Salvatore (Sammy the Bull) Gravano, close friend of John Gotti, self-confessed murderer of nineteen men, replaced Joe Gallo as Gambino Family *consigliere* in 1988. Promoted to underboss in 1990. Became an informer and cooperating government witness in John Gotti's 1992 trial on charges of murder and racketeering.

BOBBY SASSO President of Teamsters Local 282 in New York. (On April 15, 1992, Sasso resigned from his post.) The union is responsible for the drivers that bring equipment or supplies into construction sites. According to the FBI, the local is controlled by the Gambino Family.

DONNY SHACKS Nickname of Dominick Montemarano, a *capo* in the Colombo Family, according to Salvatore Gravano's testimony in the 1992 Gotti trial.

BARRY SLOTNICK Defense attorney in New York; represented John Gotti at his 1987 trial.

SPERO Anthony Spero, a member of the administration of the Bonanno Family.

STYMIE'S SON Joseph (Joey) D'Angelo, whose father was killed in a robbery in Tali's, the Brooklyn bar owned by Salvatore Gravano.

TOMMY Tommy Cacciopoli, a candidate for induction into the Gambino Family. Sponsored by Peter Gotti.

TOP TOMATO A New York City produce retailer. *See* Carmine.

TORY Son of Frank Locascio.

SAM TURONE Deceased member of the Gambino Family.

VIC Vic Amuso, a member of the administration of the Lucchese Family, according to FBI testimony at the 1992 Gotti trial.

VINNIE Vincent Artuso, an associate of the Gambino Family.

JOE WATTS According to the FBI, Watts is associated with Marine Construction Company, over which the Gambino Family exercises control.

WINDOWS Term referring to a case involving a bid-rigging scheme between four New York crime families and several unions involved in the installation of windows. *See* Pete Gotti.

ABOUT THE CONTRIBUTORS

RALPH BLUMENTHAL is a reporter for *The New York Times*. In his nearly thirty years with the *Times,* Blumenthal has covered leading stories around the nation and overseas, from the battle against organized crime to the war in Vietnam and Cambodia. He is the author of *Last Days of the Sicilians: At War with the Mafia.*

JOHN MILLER is a reporter for WNBC-TV in New York City. He has covered organized crime in New York for the past ten years, and has reported on John Gotti since 1985. Miller has received numerous awards for his work, including a 1992 Emmy Award for coverage of breaking news.